Teacher Education and the Social Conditions of Schooling

Critical Social Thought

Series editor: Michael W. Apple
Professor of Curriculum and Instruction and Educational Policy
Studies. University of Wisconsin-Madison

Already published

Teacher Education and the Social Conditions of Schooling

DANIEL P. LISTON and
KENNETH M. ZEICHNER

Routledge

New York   London

Published in 1991 by

Routledge
An imprint of Routledge, Chapman and Hall, Inc.
29 West 35 Street
New York, NY 10001

Published in Great Britain by

Routledge
11 New Fetter Lane
London EC4P 4EE

Library of Congress Cataloging in Publication Data

Liston, Daniel Patrick.
    Teacher education and the social conditions of schooling / Daniel
P. Liston, Kenneth M. Zeichner.
       p.   cm.—(Critical social thought)
    Includes bibliographical references and index.
    ISBN 0-415-90071-9.—ISBN 0-415-90233-9 (pbk.)
    1. Elementary school teachers—Training of—United States.
2. Education—Social aspects—United States.   I. Zeichner, Kenneth
M. II. Title. III. Series.
LB1715.L53   1991
370'.71'22—dc20   90-43769

British Library Cataloguing in Publication Data also available.

Contents

Series Editor's Introduction

All too many proposals for the education of teachers are formed in a vacuum. They ignore the political and economic context in which education as a whole takes place. They treat as somehow beside the point the relations of inequality that dominate our society.[1] In the process, these proposals often fail to challenge the prevailing distribution of economic, political, and cultural power.

At the same time, they are less than insightful about the daily conditions of teachers' work. In a period where the conservative restoration has created a situation where schools are blamed for nearly everything that is wrong with society, when there is a profound mistrust of teachers and curricula, it is very hard to be a teacher. Added to this are the effects of the very real economic crisis that affects so many of our cities and rural areas, where many teachers and students work in conditions that would be laughable were they not so tragic.

Indeed, with all of the rhetoric about teaching and professionalism, about enhancing teachers' power and about raising pay and respect, the reality of many teachers' lives bears little resemblance to the rhetoric. Rather than moving in the direction of increased autonomy, in all too many instances the daily lives of teachers in classrooms in many nations are becoming ever more controlled, ever more subject to administrative logics that seek to tighten the reins on the processes of teaching and curriculum. Teacher development, cooperation, and "empowerment" may be the talk, but centralization, standardization, and rationalization may be the strongest tendencies. In Britain and the United States—to take but two examples—reductive accountability and teacher evaluation schemes and increasing centralization have become so commonplace that in a few more years we may have lost from our collective memory the very possibility of difference. Indeed, there are areas in the United

States where it has been mandated that teachers must teach *only* that material which is in the approved textbook. Going beyond the "approved" material risks administrative sanctions.

An odd combination of forces has led to this situation. Economic modernizers, educational efficiency experts, neo-conservatives, segments of the new right, many working and lower middle class parents whose own mobility is dependent on technical and administratively oriented knowledge have formed a tense and contradictory alliance to return us to "the basics," to "appropriate" values and dispositions, to "efficiency and accountability," and to a close connection between schools and an economy in crisis.[2]

While we need to be cautious of being overly economistic in our analysis, it is still the case that educators have witnessed a massive attempt—one that has been more than a little successful—at exporting the crisis in the economy and in authority relations *from* the practices and policies of dominant groups *onto* the schools. If schools and their teachers and curricula, as well as our teacher education institutions, were more tightly controlled, more closely linked to the "western tradition" and to the needs of business and industry, more technically oriented, with more stress on traditional values and workplace norms and dispositions, then the problems of achievement, of unemployment, of international economic competitiveness, of the disintegration of the inner city, and so on would supposedly largely disappear.

In the United States, a multitude of reports told us that because of the inefficiency of our educational system and the poor quality of our teachers and curricula our nation was at risk. In Britain, a similar argument was heard. Teachers were seen as holding on to a curriculum that was "ill-suited to modern technological and industrial needs and as generally fostering an anti-industrial ethos among their students. In all respects, schools and teachers were portrayed as failing the nation". Industry was turned into a "dirty word," a fact that supposedly contributed greatly to the nation's industrial decline.[3]

As I have argued at great length in *Education and Power* and *Teachers and Texts*,[4] there is immense pressure currently not only to redefine the manner in which education is carried out, but what education is actually *for*. This has not remained outside the classroom but is now proceeding rather rapidly to enter into classroom life. It has altered our definitions of what counts as good teaching and what counts as an appropriate education for our future teachers.

The professional and popular literature is filled with material demanding changes—some piecemeal, others more radical—in teacher education. Most, however, whether intentionally or not fit all too easily within these conservative tendencies.[5] What is needed right now is a progressive alternative, one that deals directly with the massive inequalities of power and resources that are so much a part of this society and one that suggests the direction teacher education should follow if it is to make a difference. To do this of course means that we must take a position that is expressly critical of the ways our economic, political, and educational organizations function.

Liston and Zeichner recognize this overtly. As they put it:

> Teacher education plays an important role in relation to the current crisis in our schools and society. Contrary to the popular view that teacher educators should somehow maintain political neutrality, it is our belief that every plan for teacher education takes a position, at least implicitly, on the current institutional form and social context of schooling. Teacher education programs can serve to integrate prospective teachers into the logic of the present social order or they can serve to promote a situation where future teachers can deal critically with that reality in order to improve it.

Grounding themselves explicitly in one of the most vital traditions in education, that of social reconstructionism, Liston and Zeichner elaborate a set of proposals for teacher education that takes this socially critical project as seriously as it deserves. Yet, it is not only teacher education that needs to be seen in relation to the inequalities in the larger society. Teaching itself also needs to be understood in gender, race, and class terms.

Take gender as one example. This is especially important given the history of teaching as primarily "women's paid work." In his finely detailed volume, *Teachers' Work,* R. W. Connell reminds us that "The sexual division of labor is one of the most conspicuous facts about the teaching workforce, operating between sectors of education as well as within schools. Beyond subject specialization, general assumptions about masculine and feminine character and capacities come into play."[6]

Historical sensitivity is crucial here. The fact that teaching was associated with women's paid work, "at a time when virtually every other profession in American life was dominated by men," meant that teachers would constantly have to struggle to gain professional status.[7] Many teachers simply were not trusted. It was assumed in many sections of the United States that only centralized control of curricula, texts, and teaching could ever lead to high quality.

Some of this centralized attitude can be seen in the opinions of Stratton Brooks, the Superintendent of Schools in Boston in the first decade of this century. When asked to what extent teachers should have a say in school policy, his answer was totally unambiguous. "It seems clear to me that the answer is, not at all."[8] Unfortunately, this is an attitude that has not always remained in the past.

Much more needs to be said here, not only about the ways teaching has been constructed around gender dynamics in society but around those of race and class. These questions are not only of historical import. The limited composition of our teachers today says much about our ability to deal adequately with the changing population of the country. And the ways even these teachers are educated—usually without sufficient critical attention being paid to the relations of power inside and outside of education—leaves them less able than they might be in dealing with the conditions they will face everyday.

What of the daily conditions teachers face? What Liston and Zeichner call the social conditions of teachers' work are often characterized by pressures such as deskilling and intensification, growing poverty and community disintegration, rightist attacks on schools, and a bureaucratization of control that sometimes seems to harken back to Stratton Brooks.[9] Even those teachers who work in more economically advantaged areas are facing pressures that threaten to turn their work into merely acting as conduits for the knowledge and values of the powerful. Yet, few teachers willingly accept such a redefinition of their roles, in part *because* of what they face everyday.

Physically, teaching may be one of the "soft" jobs. But in terms of what might be called *emotional* labor, it is one of the most demanding.[10] Unlike the all too frequent stereotypes of uncaring and uninvolved teachers who act mechanically and then simply pick up a paycheck, the reality of most teachers' involvement is strikingly different. Teachers' consistent willingness to care deeply about their students is of great importance to understanding their lives. "It is one of the most important, though least tangible, assets that the education system has. . . . For the majority of teachers . . . this capacity to care is a . . . real presence in their work."[11] Think of being with a group of children for most of the day for an entire year, of trying to teach them by and large to the very best of your ability. This is why "failure" on the part of students to learn can be so personally devastating to teachers.[12]

Unfortunately, in schools where teachers must deal with the immense consequences of poverty and all that this entails, a major factor in many teachers' experiences is just this—the possibility of failure. Since teachers do in fact take personal responsibility for students learning— even when the barriers created by economic conditions and conditions in local communities may make it so very difficult to succeed—the fact that many students do not do well is a very real burden on teachers' resilience, enthusiasm, and self esteem.[13] Yet, even given this, teachers continue to struggle, to work hard in conditions that for many of them are not the best to say the least.

All of these points say something very significant about teacher education. How do we educate teachers in ways that blend together critical awareness with skills and dispositions that enable them both to be successful in their daily realities *and* to be able to reconstruct these realities in more democratic ways? How do we then combine these with an ethic of caring? A first step is to comprehend what actually is happening in classrooms, the complex, fulfilling, and sometimes draining experiences of teachers themselves every day. Any proposal for teacher education that is not grounded in a critical understanding of the social and educational conditions of teachers' lives is almost beside the point. It is this recognition that adds even more power to *Teacher Education and the Social Conditions of Schooling* and its analysis of alternatives in teacher education and of the research and curriculum policy involved in it.

The vision that stands behind the book is clear. What we need is a kind of realism that enables current and future teachers to take a critical view of their situations but that does not collapse into cynicism[14] and does not simply follow the lead of or play into the hands of the conservative restoration that is so powerful today. Once again, the authors' own words are best.

It is our hope that this book which articulates a specific set of proposals for teacher education in the United States, a set of proposals we have identified as social reconstructionist in its lineage, will contribute in some way to focusing attention in teacher education on the need to broaden the current emphasis in the field from one focusing exclusively on excellence and on strengthening intellectual competence in teacher education, to one that also includes a passionate commitment to educational equity and to the elimination of the conditions of poverty in the United States. Teacher education has an important role to play in the movement toward a more just and humane society.

What Liston and Zeichner are calling for has a valued history. It responds to what critical teachers and teacher educators have argued for and done in the past. Teachers as a whole never limited their activities to only being "instructors" of what other people decided they should teach. Many teachers were themselves curriculum planners, community leaders and organizers, and political activists in movements for a more just society. Should we expect the same now? Isn't this what teacher education should be about? *Teacher Education and the Social Conditions of Schooling* gives us reason to be optimistic that the answers will be *yes,* if its thoughtful and provocative analysis and proposals for action are indeed carried out.

Preface

In this book, we offer a set of proposals aimed at the improvement of teacher education programs and the conditions of schooling in the United States. These proposals, which emphasize the reflective analysis of and moral deliberation over the dilemmas of teaching, schooling, and society by prospective teachers and teachers come, in part, out of our own continuing work as practicing teacher educators. One of us is a director of an elementary student teaching program; the other teaches educational foundations courses to prospective elementary school teachers. Some of the conceptual and programmatic reforms that we describe in this book have been and continue to be implemented, studied, and improved upon in the teacher education programs at our respective institutions.

Our proposals also stem from our deep sense of outrage with the many injustices that continue to plague our system of public schooling in the United States despite a rhetoric of equality and justice, and with the social, economic, and political conditions in the society as a whole that contribute toward and help legitimate these inequities. Many recent commentators who have examined our system of public education in the U.S. have convincingly documented the continued existence of a "crisis of inequality" in our schools, which appears to be getting worse, despite all the numerous "innovations" that have been implemented in the last decade (National Coalition of Advocates for Students 1985; Bastian et al. 1985; Carnegie 1988). It is clear that the quality of education that a child receives in our public schools continues to be dependent in no small measure on that child's race and social-class background (Katznelson and Weir 1985). To some extent it has always been true, with few exceptions, that public schools serving children of the affluent have been more lively, imaginative, and interesting places than ones serving children of the poor (Graham 1988). A recent report of the New York State Task

Force on the Education of Children and Youth at Risk (Kolbert 1988) concludes, for example, that its state public school system is now a two-tiered system that is failing to provide even a minimally adequate education to its neediest students. This report concludes that in schools of the first tier, typically located in affluent and stable communities, high expectations are held for students. On the other hand, in schools of the second tier, typically located in the inner areas of our urban centers, low expectations and aspirations are often communicated to students who, for the most part, are not given a full opportunity to succeed. This failure on our part to provide even minimal levels of quality in the education of the segment of our school population that is largely working class, poor, and nonwhite[1] has reached crisis proportions in our inner cities—where it is estimated that in some cases from 50 to 80 percent of students do not finish high school (Bastian et al. 1986).

Both race and social class have a lot to do with whether students will become casualties of school failure. Poor students are three times more likely to become dropouts than students from more economically advantaged homes (Committee on Policy for Racial Justice 1989). Schools with higher concentrations of poor students have significantly higher dropout rates than schools with fewer poor students (Council for Economic Development 1987; Neckerman and Wilson 1988). Pallas, Natriello, and McDill (1989) discuss how race is associated with educational disadvantages:

> Recent results from the National Assessment of Educational Progress (NAEP) have shown that the reading and writing skills of black and Hispanic children are substantially below those of white children, at each of grades 3, 7, and 11 (Beaton, 1986; NAEP, 1985). In addition, Hispanic and black youth are less likely to complete high school than white youth (Ekstrom, Goertz, Pollack, and Rock, 1986). Anecdotal evidence suggests that in some cities, the school dropout rate of black and Hispanic youngsters exceeds 60%. (Aspira 1983)

A recent study in Chicago showed that "of the 25,500 black and Hispanic students enrolled in nonselective inner city high schools, 63% did not graduate. Of the 9,500 who did, only 2,000 read at or above the national average" (Schorr 1988, p. 9). The similarities in these patterns of educational stratification by race and by social class are not surprising given the strong association between race and poverty in the U.S. "If a school has a high proportion of blacks and Hispanics, it is very likely that the school has a high proportion of poor people. There are extremely few low-income white schools in metropolitan America. There are very few black and Hispanic schools without a substantial portion of poor children" (Orfield 1988, p. 52). The Council for Economic Development (1987, p. 9) concluded that although most people who live in poverty in the U.S. are white, blacks and Hispanics are more likely to be poor than whites.

> Over 20 percent of children under 18 currently live in families whose incomes fall below the poverty line, and 25 percent of all children under six are now living in poverty. Although almost two-thirds of all poor children are white, both blacks and Hispanics are much more likely to be poor; 43 percent of black and 40 percent of Hispanic children live in poverty. Black children are nearly three times as likely to live in poverty as white children. . . . (Council for Economic Development, 1987, p. 9)

This failure to provide a minimally adequate education to thousands of poor children has reached such a magnitude that Orfield (1988) has argued that the underlying patterns of stratification by race and social class are so great that they enable a reliable prediction of a school's test scores without any information at all about the educational program in a school or school district. These problems of inequality are not limited to our urban centers with large concentrations of poor and minority families. Even in places as middle class and white as Madison, Wisconsin, for example, this crisis can be seen in the differential levels of achievement of white and African-American students in the public school system (Ptak, 1988). These problems can also be seen outside of urban areas where poverty and inequality hamper many rural students (Ornstein and Levine 1989). In fact, contrary to the stereotype, a disproportionate number of poor families, most of whom are white, live in rural areas. During the last decade, the economic situation in rural areas has worsened dramatically. Since 1978, poverty in rural areas has grown at twice the rate in urban areas (Rosewater 1989; Somersan 1988).

One consequence of these problems has been the abandonment of our public schools by the middle and upper classes, leaving them largely to the poor, working class, and people of color. Boston is a case in point. In this city, where approximately 60 percent of the 600,000 residents are white, the proportions of public school students are approximately

24 percent white, 48 percent African-American, 19 percent Hispanic, and 8 percent Asian-American (Gold 1988). These disproportions reflect the situation in almost every one of the large urban centers across the U.S.[2] Although there are many isolated examples that can be cited where dedicated teachers and individual schools are providing good-quality education to those who are typically not served by the public schools, there is overwhelming evidence that our system of public schooling, as a whole, perpetuates and reinforces social-class and racial stratification by such means as unequal allocation of resources to different schools (Koff 1985),[3] by the structural arrangements through which subject matter is delivered (Oakes 1985), through the expectations and practices of teachers (e.g., Rist 1970, Persell 1977, Shannon 1985), and through the content of curricular materials (Anyon 1979).

In addition to all this evidence of racial and social-class inequities in our public schools, there is also a vast literature that documents the need to focus on gender. Apple et al. (1989), for example, discuss various ways in which our schools as currently constituted reproduce patriarchal relations: (1) in the authority patterns and staffing within schools where the majority of teachers are women and the majority of administrators are men; (2) in the segregation of teaching staff by subject matter where women tend to be concentrated in English, the language arts, and foreign languages and are relatively scarce in mathematics and most sciences; (3) in the absence and distortion of women's perspectives and history in the formal school curriculum; (4) in the differential distribution of knowledge by gender within classrooms that is a result, in part, of differential teacher-student interactions; and (5) in the continued contribution of school counseling to gender inequality. (Also see Kelly and Nihlen 1982, Apple 1986, and Leach 1988.)

These aspects of gender inequity within schools are complemented by the increased feminization of poverty in the society as a whole (Garfinkel and McLanahan 1985). One consequence of the increased association between poverty and female-headed households is that a large number of children are now being raised in poor families headed by women. This is especially the case for African-Americans where it is estimated that just over 50 percent of African-American children live in families headed by single women (Kniesner, McElroy, and Wilcox 1986).

We must be careful here to avoid the implication that we think that this crisis of inequality as manifested in the differential treatment of and educational outcomes for students according to their race, social class, and/or gender originated within the schools and was created by the attitudes and practices of staff and/or school organizational structures. We also strongly reject the view that is still prevalent in educational circles that the causes for educational failure reside in inherent deficiencies in individual children or their parents (Clayton 1989). These problems of educational inequity and failure are linked with a whole host of other "rotten outcomes" outside of the school and beyond the characteristics of individual children and their families (Schorr 1988). The alleged crisis in U.S. schools is, in fact, a reflection of a larger crisis in the society as a whole.

Recent studies clearly indicate the strong associations between poverty and a variety of childhood problems, including educational disadvantages.[4] Other rotten outcomes include a greater likelihood of inadequate housing, malnutrition, recurrent and untreated health problems, child abuse, physical and psychological stress, childhood pregnancies, violent crime during adolescence, and drug abuse (Schorr 1988, Rosewater 1989). Over thirteen million children in the United States now live in conditions of poverty that make them highly vulnerable to these pernicious outcomes (U.S. Children and Their Families 1987).[5] It is very clear from all this that educational interventions alone will not be sufficient to overcome the problems of inequality in our schools. This does not mean, however, that what we do in schools or in teacher education does not matter. On the contrary, one of the central arguments we will make in this book is that whatever one does in teacher education is necessarily related to these problems of poverty, suffering, and hopelessness among our children, whether acknowledged or not.

Teacher education plays an important role in relation to the current crisis in our schools and society. Contrary to the popular view that teacher educators should somehow maintain political neutrality, it is our belief that every plan for teacher education takes a position, at least implicitly, on the current institutional form and social context of schooling (Crittenden 1973). Teacher education programs can serve to integrate prospective teachers into the logic of the present social order or they can serve to promote a situation where future teachers can deal critically with that reality in order to improve it. The dominant position within the U.S. teacher education community throughout most of the twentieth century, with few exceptions, has been to accept the social context of schooling as given, even when efforts have been made to alter the institutional form of schooling and teacher education. Teacher education in the U.S. has always been largely divorced from attempts at societal reconstruction.

> The standard pattern of teacher education taught that the school was to pass *on* the social heritage, it was not to appraise the social order, let alone try to change it. Teachers were to fit into the society. (Rugg 1952, p. 22)

This tendency by the founders of our current system of teacher education to adopt what Rugg (1952) referred to as the "conforming way" has continued in subsequent generations of teacher educators, frequently with the approval of teacher education students who for the most part are supportive of the status quo in schooling and society (Lortie 1975, Ginsburg 1988).[6] Throughout this century—with the exception of relatively few efforts such as the National Teacher Corps (NTC) and Trainers of Teacher Trainers (TTT) programs, and efforts to integrate multicultural perspectives and social-foundations courses into the teacher education curriculum—teacher education in the United States has demonstrated a lack of commitment to ameliorating social and economic inequalities that extend beyond the school. Despite all the attention to effective teaching, and the knowledge bases of teacher education, very little effort has been made within the teacher education community to try to ensure that all children will benefit from the excellence that we are promised, and that the proposed reforms are said to produce. The crisis of inequality in our public schools and the glaring inequities, injustices, and inhumanities in our society are barely even mentioned in the contemporary teacher education literature. We agree with Fine (1987) who argues that this tacit acceptance of social stratification as an overlay on public schooling reinforces such stratification, however well intended educators' interventions are within schools.[7]

It is our hope that this book which articulates a specific set of proposals for teacher education in the United States—a set of proposals we have identified as social reconstructionist in its lineage—will contribute in some way to focusing attention in teacher education on the need to broaden the current emphasis in the field. The emphasis should go beyond focusing exclusively on excellence and on strengthening intellectual competence in teacher education. It should also include a passionate commitment to educational equity and to the elimination of the conditions of poverty in the United States. Unless we can achieve as a people a society where everyone's children can be guaranteed their basic human rights to adequate shelter, food, health care, and the promise of high-quality education and a meaningful job, all our talk about excellence in education will accomplish very little. Teacher education has an important role to play in the movement toward a more just and humane society. It is toward the realization of this more just and humane United States that this book is dedicated.

There are a few limitations in the analyses presented in this book that we wish to make clear from the onset. First, although we view teacher education as a process that continues throughout a teacher's career, the focus in this book is on the preservice portion of that education, prior to initial teacher certification. Furthermore, our ideas are focused on the substance of the preservice teacher education curriculum and not on the particular organizational structures through which that curriculum is delivered. Our proposals are applicable to preservice teacher education programs offered in different types of institutions (e.g., research universities, liberal arts colleges), to programs of different lengths, and to programs offered at both the graduate and undergraduate levels. While we give some attention in the book (especially in chapter 7) to the numerous institutional obstacles that we believe need to be overcome for our goals for teacher education programs to be realized, we do not take sides here with regard to the numerous structural issues (e.g., program length) that frequently dominate the literature. We believe that these organizational issues are less important in the final analysis than the decisions that we make about the purpose and substance of our teacher education programs.

Finally, although we feel strongly that teacher education is a responsibility that needs to be taken more seriously in all areas of our colleges and universities, as well as in at least some of our public schools that assume a special role in teacher preparation,[8] we focus in this book on the educational studies portion of preservice teacher education programs, the foundations courses, methods courses, and clinical experiences that are offered by faculty in schools, departments, and colleges of education. Although this focus on the educational studies component of preservice teacher education programs addresses only part of what needs to be dealt with in the reform of U.S. teacher education,[9] it deals with that part of the preservice teacher education curriculum which is under the control of the education faculty and school-based teacher educators to whom this book is directed. Although we focus directly on educational studies, much of what we will have to say about the kind of moral deliberation that we believe needs to go on within teacher education programs is applicable as well to the academic components of teacher education programs.[10]

Outline of the book

In the first chapter, "Traditions of Reform in U.S. Teacher Education," we describe four traditions of reform in twentieth-century U.S. teacher education: the academic, social efficiency, developmentalist, and social reconstructionist. Each tradition is illustrated with examples from early to mid-century and contemporary teacher education programs. The main purpose in presenting these reform traditions is to situate our own social-reconstructionist proposals for teacher education within a broader range of alternatives.

In the second chapter, "The Aims of Teacher Education," we outline what we believe ought to be the central aims of a teacher education program. We maintain that teacher educators ought to educate future teachers to be capable of giving good reasons for their educational actions. In our view, this aim is accomplished best when prospective teachers understand the various ways in which distinct educational traditions have defined the role of teachers, the activity of teaching, and the social context of schooling.

In chapter 3, "Teachers' Knowledge, Models of Inquiry, and the Social Context of Schooling," we argue that: (1) many current conceptions of teachers' knowledge do not adequately portray teachers' perceptions of the larger social and political context and how these perceptions affect their teaching; (2) the dominant models of inquiry proposed to enable an examination of teachers' practices do not sufficiently mine teachers' assumptions and beliefs about the social context of schooling; and (3) our extant knowledge about and understanding of the social context of schooling have both educational and instrumental value for prospective teachers.

In chapter 4, "Bringing the Social Context of Schooling into Teacher Education," we maintain that the individualistic bias in teacher education can be altered, in part, by the inclusion of curricular content focused on the institutional and social contexts of schooling. We present a set of larger concerns and specific issues that, we think, encourages prospective teachers to think about the institutional and social contexts of schooling. We highlight the importance of an enlarged cultural understanding for prospective teachers with examples of how our framework can be applied to an analysis of the conditions of teachers' work, issues of racial discrimination, and issues of gendered repression.

In chapter 5, "Research for Teaching and Teacher Education," we formulate a set of guidelines for research efforts that are focused on teaching, teacher education, and the social context of schooling. Essentially we call for research that views teachers as engaged in "situational practices," examines both the internal and external dynamics of teachers' "situations," and takes teachers' and teacher educators' concerns into account.

In chapter 6, "Programmatic Implications of a Social-Reconstructionist Approach to Teacher Education," we draw upon our own experiences at the University of Wisconsin-Madison, and Washington University, and on the experiences of several other social-reconstructionist teacher education projects in the U.S. and abroad. We describe a variety of pedagogical strategies and curricular plans that are supportive of our proposals for the conceptual reorientation of U.S. teacher education.

In the seventh and final chapter, "Asserting the Social-Reconstructionist Agenda in Teacher Education," we consider various structural and institutional changes that we believe need to occur if our proposals for teacher education are to be realized. Here we discuss several different actions and arenas, in addition to teacher education practice itself, in which a visible presence of social-reconstructionist perspectives is needed: university politics and state politics, interventions to democratize school practices, and involvement in political action aimed at reforming societal structures and institutions.

Acknowledgments

We would like to thank the following people who have read and responded to portions of this manuscript at different stages in its development: Michael Apple, Lanny Beyer, Greg Birchall, Michael Dale, Kathleen Densmore, Mary Ann Dzuback, Sharon Feiman-Nemser, Jesse Goodman, Morwena Griffiths, Martin Haberman, Dona Kagan, Herb Kliebard, Gloria Ladson-Billings, Susan Noffke, Sorca O'Connor, Dan Pekarsky, Louis Smith, Bob Tabachnick, and Wally Ullrich. We would like to thank Lois Dykstra, Donna Mlsna, and John Pingree for their careful work in the preparation of the manuscript. We would also like to thank Scott Fletcher and Liza Finkel for their work on the indices. Finally, we would like to acknowledge the National Academy of Education and Washington University–St. Louis for providing support for Dan Liston to work on this project.

We wish to thank the editors of the *American Educational Research Journal*, the *Journal of Education for Teaching* and the *Journal of Teacher Education* for permission to reprint material previously published in their journals.

To Michele with love. D.L.
To Andrea with love. K.Z.

1

Traditions of Reform in U.S. Teacher Education

A tradition is an argument extended through time in which certain fundamental agreements are defined and redefined in terms of two kinds of conflict: those with critics and enemies external to the tradition who reject all or at least key parts of those fundamental agreements, and those internal, interpretative debates through which the meaning and rationale of the fundamental agreements come to be expressed and by whose progress a tradition is constituted. . . . To appeal to tradition is to insist that we cannot adequately identify either our own commitments or those of others in the argumentative conflicts of the present except by situating them within these histories which made them what they have now become. (MacIntyre 1988, pp. 12–13)

Current teacher education reforms

Our proposals for the improvement of teacher education in the U.S. come at a time of intense discussion and debate over the future of teacher education in our country. Since the publication of *A Nation at Risk* in 1983, the attention of the public, the corporate sector, and the education community has once again focused on the ways in which teachers are selected, prepared, and supported and assessed at various points in their teaching careers. These reports also come at a time of increased intervention by state educational agencies into the conduct of teacher

*Reprinted with permission from the *Journal of Teacher Education*, Vol. 41, Number 2, pp. 3–20.

education programs and of declining resources (local, state, and federal) for the support of these programs (Cushman 1975, Cronin 1983). In the last decade or so, many reports have been issued that provide an assessment of the current status of teacher education programs and specific proposals for reform. These reports have been offered by individual teacher educators speaking for themselves (e.g., Smith 1980, Gideonse 1982, Kerr 1983; Joyce and Clift 1984, Noddings 1986, Giroux and McLaren 1987); by organizations and deans of schools, departments, and schools of education (e.g., National Commission for Excellence in Teacher Education 1985, the Holmes Group 1986, 1990, Travers and Sacks 1987); by teacher associations (e.g., American Federation of Teachers 1986, National Education Association 1982); organizations of higher-education institutions (Johnston et al. 1989) Travers and Sacks 1987); university-wide task forces (e.g., the University of Wisconsin System 1990); state-education-department–sponsored commissions (e.g., California Commission on the Teaching Profession 1985); federal-government–sponsored commissions and reports (Study Commission 1976); and by foundation-initiated task forces and commissions (e.g., Carnegie Forum on Education and the Economy 1986, 1989). All this activity focused on teacher education reform has occurred at a time when the entire scope of undergraduate education in the U.S. has also been the subject of much critical discussion and debate (e.g., National Institute of Education 1984, Boyer 1987).

The reforms for teacher education that have been proposed in all these various reports and proposals vary greatly. They include changes in the ways in which prospective teachers are recruited and selected, in the content, organization, structure, and control of preservice and inservice education programs, in the institutional conditions of schooling that facilitate and/or inhibit the work of teachers and other staff, and in the structure and organization of the occupation of teaching. One issue upon which many contemporary reports agree is that the improvement of teacher education in the U.S. must be linked with comprehensive efforts to reform the institutional conditions within which teacher education programs exist and the institutional conditions of schooling within which the graduates of teacher education programs must work. The place of teacher education programs in relation to our institutions of higher education and public schools has been a central concern in many of the contemporary reports and is so in ours as well. As we mentioned earlier, however, what has been missing from many of the contemporary reports, is some statement about the societal conditions that must be brought about to enable the kinds of changes that are proposed for schooling and teacher education to be realized. Many of the changes that are now being proposed for teacher education and the institutional conditions of schooling in the United States, for example, will require a substantial investment of new resources in the enterprise.

It is our belief that many of the enduring problems of teacher education that have undermined reforms throughout this century can only be dealt with if certain social and political prerequisites are established that involve the realignment of public resources at the societal level. This is not to say that more resources alone will solve the problems of teacher education. Increased levels of resources must be coupled with changes in the content, organization, and pedagogical and social relations within programs, a point we will elaborate throughout this book. One important part of our argument is that in order for significant improvements to occur in teacher education we must keep in mind both a democratic conception of schooling and a democratic view of society.

It is not our purpose here to catalog and critique all of the numerous proposals for reform contained in contemporary teacher education reports such as those to raise standards for program entry and exit, to increase and decrease course work of various kinds, to lengthen programs, or to remove teacher education from the undergraduate context.[1] It is our goal, however, in this first chapter, to identify and situate the central commitments in our own proposals by locating them within the general discourse of teacher education reform during this century.

One of the most notable characteristics of the contemporary teacher education reports is their lack of historic consciousness. One is hard-pressed to find explicit reference in these documents to any of the major efforts to stimulate teacher education reform that have been initiated by foundations, governmental agencies, or teacher educators themselves over the past fifty years.[2] Hundreds of millions of dollars, and years of hard work, have been devoted to implementing and studying many of the specific reforms that are now being proposed (Sarason, Davidson, and Blatt 1986). Although there have been several recent analyses of the development of teacher education programs within colleges and universities during the twentieth century that have illuminated many of the tensions and conflicts that have impeded the reform of university-based teacher education programs (Powell 1976, Schneider 1987, Clifford and Guthrie 1988, Herbst 1989), attempts to identify lessons from specific teacher education reform efforts, and from similar efforts in other professions, that could be instructive to contemporary teacher

3

educators are scarce (e.g., Sykes 1984, Coley and Thorpe 1986, Johnson 1987, Zeichner 1988, Perrone 1989).

A clear example of this amnesia in the current reform literature is with regard to one of the most difficult problems that has plagued teacher education programs since their establishment in colleges and universities: the relations between arts-and-sciences faculty and school-of-education faculty. There have been several major initiatives to establish the reality of an "all-university approach to teacher education" and to foster collaborative teacher education projects among traditionally quarreling groups (Lindsey 1961, Bigelow 1971). Nevertheless, in current efforts to address the problem—such as the widely publicized "Project 30" (Givens 1988)[3]—it is difficult to find any attempt to build upon what we might have learned from these ventures.

One consequence of this historical amnesia in the current teacher education reform movement is a lack of clarity about the theoretical and political commitments underlying specific reform proposals. Currently popular terms like "reflective teaching," "action research," "knowledge base," "subject matter" and "empowerment" are bandied about in the teacher education community with a great deal of confusion about the underlying commitments and assumptions that distinguish one proposal from another. In some cases (e.g., with "reflective teaching"), the use of particular terms has become almost meaningless because of the way in which teacher educators holding very diverse perspectives have expressed allegiance to the same slogans (Calderhead 1989).

The reform traditions

Throughout the twentieth century, specific efforts to reform teacher education programs have reflected, often implicitly, varying degrees of commitment and affiliation to several distinct reform traditions. Drawing on Kliebard's (1986) analysis of the various interest groups that have vied for control of the U.S. curriculum in the twentieth century and on several recent analyses of alternative conceptual orientations to teacher education (Joyce 1975, Zeichner 1983, Kirk 1986, and Feiman-Nemser 1990), we will outline and discuss four distinct traditions of reform in twentieth-century U.S. teacher education and then locate our own proposals for teacher education in relation to these traditions. These traditions are: (1) the academic tradition; (2) the social-efficiency tradition; (3) the developmentalist tradition; and (4) the social-reconstructionist tradition.[4] None of the contemporary proposals for the reform of teacher education, including our own, can be understood exclusively in relation to any one tradition. Throughout this century, specific teacher education programs and reform proposals have reflected particular patterns of resonance with these traditions. We present this framework of reform traditions to enable us to situate our own proposals in relation to the work of others in the past and present and to encourage the building of new reform initiatives based on an awareness of the failures and successes of those who have preceded us. Rather than merely debating the merits of specific proposals regarding the length of programs and the numbers of courses to be required in different areas and so on, we need to be able to link specific proposals to the broader schools of thought and sets of commitments from which they draw.

The academic tradition

Prior to the existence of formal programs of teacher education, a classical liberal education was equivalent to being prepared to teach (Borrowman 1965, Woodring 1975). During the twentieth century, as programs for the preparation of both elementary and secondary teachers became established in colleges and universities, the point of view persisted among many that a sound liberal arts education, complemented by an apprenticeship experience in a school, was the most sensible way to prepare teachers for their work. Throughout this period, the contributions of schools, colleges, and departments of education to an education for teaching (with the exception of student teaching) were severely criticized for their alleged inferior intellectual quality and for interfering with the liberal education of teachers. This orientation to teacher education emphasizes the teacher's role as a scholar and subject matter specialist and has taken different forms depending upon the particular view of the disciplines and subject matter knowledge that have supported specific reform proposals (Joyce 1975, Feiman-Nemser 1990).

One of the earliest critics of professional education courses for prospective teachers was Abraham Flexner, who is often noted for his contributions to the reform of medical education in the United States. In his work on European and American universities, Flexner (1930)

5

lodged a number of criticisms that have been raised repeatedly by advocates of the academic tradition. He argued, for example, that the mastery of subject matter is the most important thing in the education of a teacher and that education courses interfere with this fundamental goal. Flexner, like many who were to follow him, criticized education courses for their intellectual superficiality, education professors and their students for their meager intellectual resources, and educational scholarship for its insignificance. Accepting the value of a few legitimate areas of study within education such as educational philosophy and comparative educational studies, Flexner argued that all the rest of what teachers needed to learn beyond a sound liberal arts education could come from an apprenticeship experience in a school:

> Why should not an educated person, broadly and deeply versed
> in educational philosophy and experience, help himself from
> that point on? Why should his attention be diverted during
> these pregnant years to the trivialities and applications with
> which common sense can deal adequately when the time
> comes? (pp. 99–100)

Flexner complained that it took 26 pages alone to list the names of the staff of Teachers College Columbia and that most of the 200 pages of course listings in the T.C. catalog were devoted to "trivial, obvious, and inconsequential subjects, which could safely be left to the common sense or intelligence of any fairly educated person" (p. 100). Flexner's bias toward disciplinary knowledge is also revealed in his criticisms of the educational literature, including Ph.D. dissertations:

> The topics discussed in the current literature are so unimportant
> as compared with the subjects discussed by physicists, chem-
> ists, or political scientists that it may well seem as though they
> were designed to frighten off intelligence. (p. 102)

Since Flexner's critique, a number of highly visible and controversial analyses of teacher education have repeated these same themes about the inferior intellectual quality of education courses, students, and faculty. Among these critiques are those by Lynd (1950), Bestor (1953, 1956), Koerner (1963), and Conant (1963).[5] These reports, which are based on some direct study of teacher education institutions across the U.S., continued to raise the same kinds of issues and concerns about teacher education programs that had been raised in Flexner's earlier critique. For example, Lynd (1950) who was a school board member in Sharon, Massachusetts, complained about the proliferation of education courses that he found when he examined a large sample of college and university bulletins. He provided readers with lists of courses having similar titles to show how education faculty have covered "every imaginable topic and subtopic of pedagogy with a course" (p. 141). He also argued, as did James Koerner (1963) of the Council for Basic Education, that there was a great deal of duplication of content in these courses. Koerner's (1963) charge of repetitiveness was based in part on an analysis of seventy of the most frequently used education texts. He found a great deal of duplication both within and among the books he reviewed:

> Take, for example, the subject of how to use "resources" of the community for school purposes—its public and private institutions, its outstanding citizens, its recreational facilities, etc. The education student covers this material the first time in his textbook in educational psychology, again in his textbook on methods of teaching, again in his textbook on audio-visual aids, again in his textbook on curriculum development, again in his textbook on secondary, or elementary education. . . . The same is true of countless other subjects, such as classroom discipline, the importance of individual differences, motivating students. . . . By the time he has been through two or three such books, all he hears is echoes. (p. 71)

In addition to these charges that education courses were too many and too repetitive, Lynd, Koerner, and Bestor (a historian at the University of Illinois), criticized these courses for their alleged superficiality:

> Whatever they claim to do and be, they [education courses] deserve the ill-repute that has always been accorded them by members of the academic faculty, by teachers themselves, and by the general public. Most education courses are vague, insipid, time wasting adumbrations of the obvious, and probably irrelevant to academic teaching. (Koerner 1963, pp. 55–56)

Bestor (1953) argued that these courses could not help but be superficial because of the education and training of those who taught them:

7

University and graduate departments of education began as
agencies of genuine interdisciplinary investigation and teaching.
When, however, they began to recruit their faculties from
young men trained by themselves, they gradually lost their
original character. Several academic generations have now
passed and the overwhelming majority of present day professors of education have received virtually all their advanced
training in departments of education. Their knowledge of the
disciplines that are required to solve pedagogical problems is
for the most part elementary and secondhand. And this knowledge is passed on, increasingly diluted and increasingly out of
date, to new generations of professional educationists. (p. 108)

Ten years later, Koerner (1963) reiterated these same biases in reporting
his impressions after having talked with hundreds of education faculty
from across the U.S. Identifying the inferior intellectual quality of
education faculty as the fundamental limitation of the field, he reported
that

In all those timeless and imponderable ways in which compari-
sons and judgments are made in person to person situations—
involving clarity of discourse, subtlety, force, depth of knowledge, intellectual penetration . . . the education faculty comes
off poorly in relation to the academic professor on the same
campus. (pp. 36–37)

Very few of these kinds of criticisms over the years have been based
on direct observations of the classes in which the supposedly inferior
education was taking place (Zeichner, 1988a). Among the four reports
cited here only Koerner (1963) and Conant (1963) provided any evidence
in support of their criticisms that was based on firsthand experience with
courses. The observations to which they refer are alluded to in only the
most general way, with little specific detail provided to substantiate very
pointed condemnations of classes:

The classes I have visited are far too reminiscent of the less
satisfactory high school classes I have seen. The course is dominated by a textbook or a syllabus and the instructor seems to
be wedded to the dogma that a discussion must take place
whether the talk is lively or the class is bored. The pace and

the intellectual level seemed geared to students far less able than those in the top 30 per cent group from which we should recruit our teachers. (Conant 1963, p. 129)

There is little doubt that some of the charges leveled by these academic reformers have been and continue to be true in certain situations. There is some question, however, as to the extent to which these caricatures of the professional education component of teacher education are representative of education courses generally or exclusively. Recently, several scholars have argued that these academically based criticisms may have less to do with the actual quality of the people, courses, and programs than with a status based on gender and social-class differences between education faculty and students, and those in the arts and sciences (Lanier 1986, Ginsburg 1988). For example, there is little doubt that teacher education has been an easy target within the university—in part, because of the marginal status in the society of work associated with women and children (Clifford and Guthrie 1988). Although even the harshest of the critics such as Bestor have admitted that things have not been all well within the courses in the arts and sciences, the general assumption seemed to be and continues to be that courses within the arts and sciences are necessarily liberalizing while education courses are exclusively technical and vocational in the narrowest sense of the term (Borrowman 1956).

The programmatic implications of the academic tradition have changed somewhat over time depending upon particular views of a good liberal arts education and of the kinds of subject matter needed by teachers. Following the decline of the humanist position based firmly in a classical liberal arts education (Kliebard 1986) and periodic attempts to "professionalize" subject matter offerings by considering pedagogical implications in academic courses (Borrowman 1956), most manifestations of this position have, until recently, involved proposals for the preparation of teachers based firmly in the traditional academic disciplines as they are taught to all students, regardless of their intended vocations. It has been repeatedly argued that this approach will draw many academically talented students into teaching who would otherwise be repelled by requirements to take many education courses of doubtful intellectual value. Bestor (1953) succinctly summarizes this position regarding the most appropriate teacher education program as follows:

A new curriculum for the education of teachers, based firmly upon the liberal arts and sciences, rather than upon the mere

9

vocational skills of pedagogy will do more to restore the repute of the public schools than any other step that can be taken. Not only will teachers be adequately trained in the disciplines they undertake to teach, they will also be imbued with respect for those disciplines and will be prepared to resist the anti-intellectualism that currently threatens the schools. And when the tide begins to turn, young men and young women of genuine intellectual interest and capacity will be attracted in increasing numbers to the profession of public school teaching. They will not be repelled at the outset by being asked to lay aside their intellectual interests and fritter away their time in the courses of the pedagogues. (p. 147)

Until very recently, the academic tradition of reform in teacher education has had the most impact on the preparation of secondary teachers. With a few notable exceptions such as in the state of California (Hendrick 1967) and in liberal arts colleges (Travers and Sacks 1987), elementary education students have typically completed twice as many education courses as prospective secondary teachers and have rarely completed academic majors. One notable example of reforms was the efforts of the Ford Foundation and its Fund for the Advancement of Education to establish various forms of graduate teacher education as a replacement for traditional undergraduate preparation. In the 1950s and 1960s Ford sponsored several different graduate teacher education program models, including an attempt to convert an entire state (Arkansas) to an approach where all prospective teachers would receive four years of a liberal arts education with a reduced load of professional education courses at the graduate level. Throughout this period, Ford spent over $70 million on initiatives that included fifth-year programs specializing in the preparation of older liberal arts graduates for teaching, M.A.T. programs for secondary teachers that were jointly developed by education and arts-and-sciences faculties, and a special set of "Breakthrough" programs (Woodring 1957, Stone 1968).[6] These Ford programs became the models for many other graduate programs across the U.S., some of which continue to exist today, as well as for significant aspects of the National Teacher Corps program which lasted until 1980 (Saxe 1965, Corwin 1973).

Recently, several challenges have been raised to this emphasis on a traditionally defined liberal arts education and subject matter knowledge for teachers. One line of inquiry, from a feminist perspective, criticizes a traditionally defined liberal education for perpetuating the Platonic emphases "on mind not head, thought not action, production not repro-duction, and reason not emotion" (Martin 1987, p. 406). Martin (1985) among others (e.g., Laird 1989), have called for a rejection of these dualisms and a redefinition of the ideals of educated persons and a liberal education in a way where both sides of these dichotomies are equally valued:

> The project for teacher educators that I am recommending . . .
> is neither so simplistic nor so impoverished as one that merely
> replaces an emphasis on head with one on hand, one on
> thought with one on action, one on reason with one on feeling
> and emotion, one on separation of the self with one on connec-
> tion to others, one on the productive processes of society with
> one on its reproductive processes. It is a difficult project to
> carry out because it is possible to join together the two sides of
> the various Platonic dichotomies only if they are equally val-
> ued. . . . Once we understand the historic roots of liberal edu-
> cation, we will begin to see the inappropriateness for prospec-
> tive teachers today of the educational ideal Plato held up for
> the guardians of his just state and of the educational program
> he designed for them in light of it. (p. 406)

Contemporary examples of teacher education programs that have been influenced by recent feminist scholarship are the graduate M.A.T. program at Lewis and Clark College (Tetreault 1987, Tetreault and Braunger 1989) and the teacher education program at Wheaton College (Maher, 1991). Here teacher educators have infused the curriculum with issues focused on women and gender that challenge the Platonic dichotomies and have critiqued the pedagogy and social relations in their programs through lenses provided by feminist scholarship.

A second challenge to the dominance of conventional notions of the academic reform tradition has emerged from recent work on teachers' subject matter knowledge. Stimulated in part by Shulman's (1986, 1987) criticisms of the lack of attention to teachers' subject matter understand-ings by both researchers and teacher educators, investigators are explor-ing how teachers' understandings of subject matter content interact with other kinds of knowledge (e.g., "pedagogical content knowledge")[7] to influence instruction (Leinhardt and Smith 1985, Wilson, Shulman, and Richert 1986, Ball and McDiarmid 1989). One consequence of these efforts to explicate the dimensions of subject matter knowledge that are appropriate in a teacher's education is the emergence of a new "knowledge base" for teacher education that is much broader than the behavioristic "knowledge base" of the 1960s and early 1970s. (See Reynolds 1989.)

Feiman-Nemser (1990) describes one contemporary example of how this cognitive psychological perspective has been applied to teacher education in the Academic Learning Program at Michigan State University. This program emphasizes preparing elementary and secondary teachers to teach school subjects in ways that promote conceptual understanding and includes courses (e.g., in mathematics) that seek to help prospective teachers understand the conceptual foundations of the subject matter they will teach (Schram et al. 1988). Another contemporary example of this general approach is the work on "cognitively guided instruction" (CGI) that has been introduced into teacher education programs at the University of Wisconsin-Madison (Fennema, Carpenter, and Peterson, in press). In courses incorporating a "CGI" orientation, prospective teachers are given opportunities to understand how children think about mathematics and then to base their instruction on children's cognitions and knowledge. The goal for the C.G.I. program is to prepare teachers who can facilitate children's active mental involvement in worthwhile mathematics tasks. Although this approach avoids specific prescriptions for teacher action, both "instructional science" and "cognitive science" are said to provide a set of principles for teachers to consider when planning for instruction.

A third challenge to historically dominant notions of academically oriented reform in teacher education has focused on the western, white, middle-class biases in the liberal arts curriculum. There has also been criticism of the failure of many academically oriented teacher education reforms (e.g., M.A.T. programs) to respond to the needs for preparing teachers to work in economically depressed and culturally diverse inner cities (Coley and Thorpe 1986, Keppel 1986).

> It is not surprising that very few of the students from the Chicago program (and many other M.A.T. programs which were similarly designed) worked in inner city schools, or, in any but the college preparatory curricula in secondary schools. Both the curricula and the teacher training generated by the academic reform movement were almost necessarily developed for the aca-

demically talented . . . the intellectual scholar, not surprisingly, was oriented toward the education of the intellectually gifted student, the prototype of which was probably his own child. (Joyce 1975, p. 129)

One response to these elitist tendencies in U.S. teacher education has been attempts to incorporate multicultural perspectives into the curricula of teacher education programs (Gay 1986). This movement, which received a great deal of federal support in the 1960s and 1970s through the Teacher Corps and Trainers of Teacher Trainees (TTT) programs (Drummond and Andrews 1980), addresses issues related to both the preparation of teachers for our culturally and racially diverse society and to teaching in schools dominated by pupils of color. A great deal of effort has been devoted over the years to analyzing the extent to which multicultural perspectives have been incorporated into the curricula of U.S. teacher education programs (e.g., Gollnick 1978), to assessing the impact of multicultural perspectives that have been incorporated into programs (e.g., Grant and Koskella 1986), and to providing guidelines for action and program exemplars to the teacher education community (e.g., Baptiste, Baptiste, and Gollnick 1980; Gollnick, Osayande, and Levy 1980). Cabello and Dash (1988) and Grant and Secada (1990) discuss recent efforts to develop teacher education programs with a focus on cultural diversity.

Despite these challenges to historically dominant notions of what makes a good liberal education for teachers,[8] recent state policies such as the ones placing limits on the number of education courses in a teacher education program (Imig 1988) and the establishment of alternate routes allowing people to enter teaching with little or no professional education course work (Uhler 1987) reinforce the unfortunate confusion noted by Borrowman (1956) that a course is necessarily liberalizing if offered by academic faculty and is necessarily technical if offered in a school of education. Current efforts to arbitrarily limit the number of education credits in a teacher education program fail to address the issue of academic and professional quality in teacher education by ignoring the substance of what is offered within particular courses (Zeichner 1988a). Calls for a return to traditional forms of a liberal arts education for teachers that continue today (e.g., Damerell 1985) are unresponsive to the challenges that have been raised by three groups of critics.

13

The social-efficiency tradition

A second major reform tradition in twentieth-century U.S. teacher education, the social-efficiency tradition, has involved a faith in the power of the scientific study of teaching to provide the basis for building a teacher education curriculum. This tradition emerged largely within schools, departments, and colleges of education and has been seen by many as part of a strategy to strengthen educationists' claim to legitimacy within the university (Sykes 1984). Cremin (1953), in reflecting upon the development of teacher education in the early part of this century, observed:

> Growing out of this faith [in science] came innumerable attempts during the 1920s to break down and analyze the teaching task into its component parts and to build a teacher education program around such technical analysis. (p. 246)

One of the earliest and most prominent efforts at scientific curriculum making in U.S. teacher education was the Commonwealth Teacher Training Study (Charters and Waples 1929). Criticizing existing teacher education programs for lacking a clear definition of objectives and logical plans of procedure, Charters and Waples set out in 1925 with a grant of $42,000 from the Commonwealth Fund to demonstrate that a comprehensive description of the duties and traits of teachers would provide the necessary basis for systematically determining what teachers should be taught. Kliebard (1975) succinctly summarizes the procedures used in this study:

> As a first step, Charters and Waples "ascertained the traits that characterize excellent teachers." Adapting the consensus approach, the investigators used two methods: analyzing the professional literature and interviewing "expert judges." Working from a list of eighty-three traits, ranging alphabetically from Accuracy through Foresight and Magnetism all the way to Wittiness, "translators" were given the task of interpreting statements made in writing or in interviews. . . . Reliability among translators was determined by applying the Spearman prophecy formula. Finally, after some of the original traits were telescoped, scientifically determined lists were prepared indicating

that senior high school teachers should be characterized by twenty-six traits including Good Taste and Propriety, junior high school teachers by Conventionality (morality) and Open-mindedness . . . Next in adaptation of the job analysis technique, the investigators collected a master list of 1,001 teacher activities. (p. 35)

The teacher activities were based on the results of mailing surveys to experienced teachers in forty-two states. The final list of 1,001 activities of teaching was subdivided into seven major divisions (e.g., classroom instruction, school and classroom management). These teaching activities and the master list of eighty-three teacher traits of good teachers, broken down according to various levels of schooling (high school, junior high, intermediate grades, and kindergarten and primary grades) were to assist teacher educators in designing teacher preparation programs that were based firmly on the realities of schooling rather than on tradition or individual judgment. Although this study had little direct impact on teacher education programs, the idea of systematically building a curriculum of teacher education on the basis of a careful analysis of the work to be performed by teachers persisted.

One of the subsequent manifestations of this perspective in U.S. teacher education was the emergence of Competency/Performance-Based Teacher Education (C/PBTE) in the 1960s and 1970s.[9] C/PBTE was stimulated in part by applications of behavioristic psychology to the training of personnel in industry and the military during and after World War II (McDonald 1973), by the U.S. Department of Education's support for the development of plans for nine competency-based model elementary teacher education programs that applied procedures of systems analysis and job analysis to the design of a teacher education program curriculum (Clarke 1969), and by a subsequent requirement in the Teacher Corps that all projects develop competency-based programs (Houston & Howsam 1972). The idea of C/PBTE received so much attention in the literature that it has been described both within the U.S. and abroad (Atkin and Raths 1974; Turney 1977) as the single most influential and controversial trend in U.S. teacher education in this century.[10]

Despite all the attention that C/PBTE received in the literature and the popular press, actual practice in teacher education programs was affected by the movement only minimally. Sandefur and Nicklas (1981) concluded, for example, that full-scale implementation of C/PBTE programs occurred in only about 13 percent of the approximately 1,200 institutions associated with the American Association of Colleges for Teacher Education. Joyce, Howey and Yarger (1977) and the National Center for Education Statistics (1977) reached similar conclusions in two national surveys of practices in preservice teacher education programs. Two of the most prominent examples of institutions where C/PBTE did gain a foothold were at the University of Houston (Ginsburg 1988) and at the University of Toledo (Howey and Zimpher 1989).

This general approach to teacher education emphasizes the acquisition of specific and observable skills of teaching that are assumed to be related to pupil learning. By the 1960s educational research had progressed far beyond the relatively crude survey-and-analysis–techniques methods used in the Commonwealth study. This more recent version of the social-efficiency orientation sought to establish the intellectual legitimacy of teacher education through a grounding in classroom research linking observable teacher behaviors with student outcomes. Despite the increased sophistication in research methods, one of the major criticisms of the approach has been questions about the empirical validity of the competencies (e.g., Heath and Nielson 1974, Tom 1984). Even advocates of the approach were careful to admit that they had not yet attained the goal of empirically validated teaching competencies. They hoped, however, that increased commitment to the approach from the profession and from those who would support the necessary research would eventually yield such knowledge (Sykes 1984).

One key characteristic of the C/PBTE approach is that the knowledge and skills to be mastered by prospective teachers are specified in advance, usually in behavioral terms. Furthermore, the criteria by which successful mastery is to be measured are made explicit. Performance, rather than the completion of specified course work, is assumed to be the most valid measure of teaching competence (Houston and Howsam 1972, Gage and Winne 1975). Some of the attempts to design competency-based teacher education programs resulted in the specification of hundreds and frequently as many as thousands of separate competencies in a given program (Joyce 1975). Another important element in this approach is the development of instructional, management, and evaluation systems to monitor students' mastery of individual competencies. In the middle 1960s to early 1970s, a number of significant developments occurred in this area. First, microteaching was developed at Stanford University as a method for systematically imparting specific teaching skills to students (Allen and Ryan 1969). Complex and comprehensive teaching strategies were first broken down into discrete skills. The skills were then practiced by student teachers with relatively small groups of children for brief periods of time. Following the teaching, the student teacher received detailed feedback about his or her performance of the skills from a supervisor, often with the aid of video technology. The student teacher would then reteach the lesson to another small group of children if his or her performance fell below specified minimum standards.

Microteaching was later incorporated into more comprehensive teacher training curriculum packages called "minicourses" by staff at the Far West Laboratory in San Francisco (Borg 1970). Several minicourses were developed that, in addition to microteaching, included readings and films. These packages were to enable student teachers to master important skills of teaching such as effective questioning at the elementary level, tutoring in mathematics, and organizing the kindergarten for independent learning and small-group discussion. Closely related to these developments was the development of protocol materials and simulation materials for use in competency-based programs (Cruickshank 1984),[11] the development of systematic classroom observational systems that could enable the assessment of a variety of discrete teaching behaviors (Simon and Boyer 1967), and the development of models of skill training such as the "models of teaching" approach by Joyce and his colleagues at Teachers College (Joyce, Weil, and Wald 1974).

These developments caused a great deal of controversy in the teacher education community. A vast literature quickly emerged that raised several criticisms of the general orientation. One challenge, as mentioned above, came from those who questioned the empirical validity of the "knowledge base" upon which these programs rested. Some criticized the methods that had been used in conducting the "process-product" studies that were to establish the linkages between specific teacher behaviors and student outcomes, but retained faith that improved research would overcome the validity problems (e.g., Gage 1970). Others questioned whether the complex and uncertain nature of teaching would ever enable these problems to be overcome through research (Tom 1980) or argued that any attempt to do so would limit our conception of teaching to "telling" (Broudy 1973).

A second line of protest against the C/PBTE movement came from "humanistic" educators such as Art Combs and his colleagues at the University of Florida. This critique focused on the assumptions of the behavioristic psychology underlying most examples of the approach.

17

Combs (1972) even went so far as to argue that "requiring a teacher education program to define precisely the behaviors it hopes to produce may be the surest way to destroy the effectiveness of its products" (p. 288). It was felt that the approach undermined the growth in personal meaning that was thought to be necessary for becoming a better teacher.

A third major critique of the C/PBTE movement came from those such as Apple (1972) and Nash and Agne (1971) who criticized the conservative political tendencies that were thought to be associated with the approach. By basing the specification of competencies on current conceptions of the teacher's role in a system that was felt to be in need of fundamental reform, it was argued that C/PBTE necessarily undermined the reconstructionist ideals of many teacher educators and served to legitimate the status quo in school and society. One response to these charges of conservatism and technicism by those within the C/PBTE movement who espoused goals related to reform and equity was the development of competencies that they felt addressed the concerns of both the humanistic and reform-minded critics. For example, in one fascinating description of a C/PBTE program at SUNY-Cortland "Project Change," one can find examples of specific teaching competencies that address the personal growth of student teachers and their capabilities to initiate institutional change (Lickona 1976).

Despite the low rate of implementation of C/PBTE in teacher education programs across the U.S.,[12] the social-efficiency tradition has emerged once again in the current debates on teacher education reform, this time under the label of "research-based" teacher education. Many current proposals for the reform of teacher education (e.g., the Holmes Group 1986) have argued that the past decade of research on teaching has produced a "knowledge base" that can form the foundation for a teacher education curriculum.[13] According to Berliner (1984), "We have only recently developed a solid body of knowledge and a fresh set of conceptions about teaching on which to base teacher education. For the first time, teacher education has a scientific foundation" (p. 94).

> We have made unbelievable strides in understanding management concepts during the last decade. We have learned many of the teacher behaviors that result in the least amount of off-task behavior in classrooms and in the least amount of deviancy in classrooms. That work was first investigated in 1970 by Kounin. It was investigated by others throughout the 1970s and turned into teacher training materials during the early 1980s

(Emmer et al. 1984). These materials, based on empirical research, have been field tested recently. In New York and elsewhere, the results have been amazing. Teachers who have
failed to meet the criteria of good management were, for the
first time in their professional lives, in complete control of their
classes. One 20 year veteran of the New York City schools
said that the training produced nothing short of a miracle
(Rauth et al. 1983). This technology must be learned through
role playing, simulations, and other forms of practice. To have
technology and not train people to use it is not at all sensible.
(Berliner 1985, p. 5)

Feiman-Nemser (1990) describes two ways in which this position has
been interpreted by contemporary teacher education reformers. First,
she describes a technological version in which the intent is to teach
prospective teachers the skills and competencies that research has shown
to be associated with desirable pupil outcomes. This narrow interpretation is basically a reemergence of a behavioristic version of C/PBTE.
Joyce and Showers's (1984) work with the development of procedures
for skill training is cited by Feiman-Nemser (1990) as an example of
this trend.

A second contemporary trend in the application of the findings of
research on teaching to the design of teacher education curricula described by Feiman-Nemser (1990) is one in which the findings of research
are used by teachers as "principles of procedure" within a broader process
of decision making and problem solving. Advocates of this deliberative
orientation to the use of research on teaching to improve teacher education argue that the reality of teaching demands an approach to teacher
education that reflects the complex and uncertain nature of the work.
The crucial task, from this point of view, is to foster teachers' capabilities
to exercise judgment about the use of teaching skills:

Because they view good teaching as good deliberation, their
concern is not that teachers follow a set of rules, which could
never account for all circumstances anyway, but rather that
teachers view teaching as a process of constantly making
choices about the means and ends—choices that can be informed by process-product research, descriptive research, experience, intuition, and one's own values. (Zumwalt 1982, p.
226)

The Teacher as Decision-Maker program at Michigan State University is cited by Feiman-Nemser (1990) as an example of this cognitively oriented approach to the application of research findings to teacher education programs. Another contemporary example of this approach is certain aspects of the PROTEACH program at the University of Florida (Ross and Kyle 1987). Berliner (1984) outlines some of the research findings that are to be the basis for these deliberations about teaching. These include findings about the selection of content, the allocation of time in the classroom, grouping practices, questioning, and classroom management. Unlike the earlier C/PBTE movement that drew exclusively on correlational or process-product studies of teaching, current versions of the social-efficiency paradigm have also drawn upon recent descriptive studies of classrooms, research on teacher thinking (e.g., Clark 1988), or, as in Hunter's tremendously popular work (Gentile 1988), upon cause-and-effect relationships that have allegedly been established in research on human learning and behavior.

Although many of the devices for systematically training prospective teachers in the use of specific teaching skills like microteaching have disappeared from the literature, newer versions more compatible with the broader cognitive orientation of the approach have emerged to take their place—such as Cruickshank's (1987) "Reflective Teaching" program and skill training through microcomputer simulations (Strang, Badt and Kauffman 1987). Despite the variations among social-efficiency–based approaches throughout the century, the common thread that ties them together is their reliance on the scientific study of teaching as the major source for determining the teacher education curriculum.

The developmentalist tradition

The third major tradition of reform in twentieth-century U.S. teacher education, the developmentalist tradition, has its roots in the child study movement initiated by G. Stanley Hall and others near the turn of the century. According to Kliebard (1986), the most distinguishing characteristic of this tradition is the assumption that the natural order of the development of the learner provides the basis for determining what should be taught, both to pupils in the public schools and to their teachers. This natural order of child development was to be determined by research involving the careful observation and description of children's behavior at various stages of development. The most pressing need in educational research, argued Lucy Sprague Mitchell (1931), founder of Bank Street College of Education, was "a scientific study of children's behavior as conditioned by the stage of their development and a planning of a school environment (the curriculum) upon the basis of such a study of growth" (p. 254).

In the early part of the century this tradition was most visible in teacher education in the efforts of the "Bohemian progressives"[14] to prepare teachers to teach in the new child-oriented progressive schools springing up all over the country. It is this work that Vito Perrone (1989) refers to when he writes about the "Progressive Tradition" in U.S. teacher education. These advocates of what was often referred to as the "new" or "modern" education were very critical of the failure of regular teacher education institutions to supply them with creative and imaginative teachers who had a clear understanding of the developmentalist philosophy and children's patterns of growth and development. For as Pollitzer (1931) argued, "Only teachers imbued with a thorough understanding of that philosophy and a deep feeling for it can interpret its ideals in practice" (p. 247).

> Who is to provide the teachers for the new schools? The "regular" sources are certainly not producing them; . . . for the most part those who are doing anything worthwhile in the progressive schools are either the unconventional products of conventional preparation (if not downright rebels) or happy accidents with no training at all in the ordinary sense. (*Progressive Education* 1931, p. 280)

One critical element in these early developmentalist ideas about teacher education was that teachers for progressive schools offering the new child-centered education must be educated in the same kind of supportive and stimulating environment that they were expected to provide for children. Advocates of new "student-centered" teacher education institutions were often very critical of the mechanical methods they felt were used in most teacher education institutions because they felt that mechanical methods in teacher preparation led to mechanical and passionless teaching of children.[15]

> Still we go on preparing these young teachers of tomorrow by fifteenth century methods to achieve twentieth century aims.

> We continue to treat these youthful human souls as if they were
> machines; we polish the cogs with academic brickdust and the
> kelp of pedagogic taboos; we set them into working order, and
> in good, oiled, and empty futility we attempt to start these im-
> mortal locomotives. . . . We cultivate these young teachers'
> abilities but we give them no fire. . . . Their chief lack when
> we send them out to a completely irrational world for which we
> have prepared them in a wholly rational fashion is a flaming
> purpose. (Stroh 1931, p. 260)

According to Perrone (1989), three central metaphors were associated
with early manifestations of this progressive/developmentalist tradition
in teacher education: (1) the teacher as naturalist; (2) the teacher as artist;
and (3) the teacher as researcher. The teacher-as-naturalist dimension of
the movement stressed the importance of skill in the observation of
children's behavior and in building a curriculum and classroom environment consistent with patterns of child development and children's interests. Classroom practice was to be grounded in close observation and
study of children in natural settings or on a literature that grew out of
child study. Educating prospective teachers to conduct observations and
to learn from and plan activities for children on the basis of the observations were key features in developmentalist proposals for teacher education reform (Perrone 1989).

The teacher-as-artist aspect of the developmentalist tradition had two
dimensions. On the one hand, the artist/teacher has a deep understanding
of the psychology of child development and is able to excite children
about learning by providing them with carefully guided activities in a
rich and stimulating learning environment. To do this, however, the
teacher needs to be a wide-awake and fully functioning person in touch
with his or her own learning. A common developmentalist proposal for
teacher education was to provide prospective teachers with a variety of
experiences in dance, creative dramatics, writing, painting, and storytell-
ing so that they would be able to exemplify for their students an inquiring,
creative, and open-minded attitude. The comments of a director of one
progressive school about the qualities needed for successful teaching
illustrate the stress that was often placed upon the personal and artistic
development of the teacher in this tradition and also the influence of
Freudianism on child-centered pedagogy in the 1920s:

> I do not see how any person can teach in a progressive school
> who is not a real person and who has not lived some sort of in-

teresting, full life, or who is not living such a life. If one has
amounted to something and is living life to the full, I have
found little difficulty in giving the techniques necessary to
make an excellent teacher, provided it is in the person. Such a
one, who has an interest in life and is well balanced and emotionally free, has usually, by the very fact of his interest acquired the necessary sort of information and continues to keep
it up. I should think that the courses for teachers would include
dancing and physical education to relieve physical inhibitions;
plenty of social contacts with life and persons of the opposite
sex to relieve emotional inhibitions; a great deal of dramatic
work and expression to free the teacher from self consciousness; and a discovery of some vital interest in the teacher's life
and a pursuit of that interest as far as possible during the years
at normal school . . . Some of my best teachers have never
been trained at all but have lived in a world of reality. (Bonser
1929, p. 116)

The third guiding metaphor in the developmentalist tradition of teacher
education was the teacher-as-researcher. Here the focus was on fostering
the teacher's experimental attitude toward practice. Child study was to
become the basis for teachers' inquiries, and teacher educators were to
provide instruction to prospective teachers about how to initiate and
sustain ongoing inquiries in one's classroom about the learning of specific children. Lucy Sprague Mitchell's (1931) summary of the aims of
the Cooperative School for Student Teachers illustrates the importance
placed upon the development of an experimental attitude toward practice
and its relationship to the artistic and naturalistic themes:

Our aim is to turn out teachers whose attitude toward their
work and toward life is scientific. To us, this means an attitude
of eager, alert observation; a constant questioning of old procedure in the light of new observations; a use of the world, as
well as of books, as source material; an experimental open-
mindedness, and an effort to keep as reliable records as the situation permits, in order to base the future upon accurate knowledge of what has been done. Our aim is to equally turn out students whose attitude toward their work and toward life is that
of the artist. To us this means an attitude of relish, of emotional drive, a genuine participation in some creative phase of

work, and a sense that joy and beauty are legitimate posses-
sions of all human beings, young and old. If we can produce
teachers with an experimental, critical, and ardent approach to
their work, we are ready to leave the future of education to
them. (p. 251)[16]

Other than the Cooperative School for Student Teachers and subsequent work at Bank Street College and a few other institutions such as
Milwaukee State Teachers College (Ayer 1931), one does not find the
overall transformation of mainstream teacher education along developmentalist lines that was hoped for by the child-centered progressives.
An apprenticeship system has been and continues to be a major way
in which the developmentalist philosophy is awakened in prospective
teachers (Beatty 1933).[17]

During the late 1960s and early 1970s when child-centered pedagogy
and "open education" once again received widespread attention in the
U.S., a number of experimental teacher education programs were initiated that resembled those of the child-centered progressives of the 1920s
and 1930s. Crook (1974) analyzed four programs of this later era that
sought to translate the assumptions underlying "open education" into a
teacher education curriculum. These were the Center for Teaching and
Learning at the University of North Dakota, the American Primary
Experimental Program at the University of Vermont, the Educational
Program for Informal Classrooms at Ohio State, and the Integrated Day
Program at the University of Massachusetts. Despite the differences that
she found among these programs, Crook (1974) identified a number of
developmentalist themes that they all shared:

A commitment to involvement in one's own learning, an active
approach to learning in terms of direct experience with materials, an encouragement of children's communication and prospective teachers' communication with children using skills of
observing, reading, speaking and writing; early field experiences, offerings in the expressive arts as well as in academic
areas, and an understanding of children's development which
reflects the writings of Jean Piaget. (p. 1)

About this same time, several other versions of the developmentalist
tradition emerged in the literature. For example, Art Combs and his
colleagues at the University of Florida received a lot of attention for

their "humanistic" teacher education program (Combs et al. 1974, Wass et al. 1974). Their notion of "self as an instrument" (that a good teacher is primarily a person striving to fulfill him or herself) strongly resembles the earlier emphasis by Lucy Sprague Mitchell and her contemporaries on "the teacher as artist." Another prominent developmentally oriented program of this period was the "Personalized Teacher Education Program" at the University of Texas, which was grounded in Fuller's (1972, 1974) studies of teachers' concerns. Attempts were made to conduct this program in a manner so that the curriculum of the program addressed students' concerns as they experienced them. The assumption was that if the program was conducted in accordance with the developmental needs of students, the students would progress through various "stages of concerns" toward maturity as teachers.[18]

Another more recent example of a developmentalist-inspired teacher education program, "Deliberate Psychological Education," evolved at the University of Minnesota in the late 1970s and early 1980s under the direction of Norm Sprinthall, Lois Thies-Sprinthall, and their students. Here teacher educators applied cognitive-developmental stage theories to the design of teacher education program components and posited their goals for prospective teachers on the basis of the characteristics of the advanced stages of one or more stage theory. Glassberg and Sprinthall (1980), for example, redesigned a typical student teaching experience to include structured role-taking activities that were linked with a weekly seminar. Teacher educators associated with these University of Minnesota efforts claim that their experimental curriculum was able to stimulate teacher growth to higher developmental stages (see Sprinthall and Thies-Sprinthall 1975, for a summary of the research).

One of the most prominent contemporary examples of a developmentalist approach to teacher education is the "Developmental Teacher Education Program" at the University of California-Berkeley. This two-year graduate program culminating in a master's degree, was initiated by a small group of faculty who were dissatisfied with the limited emphasis given to knowledge of human development in teacher education programs (Amarel 1988). This program, which is a clear example of the developmentalist emphasis on teacher-as-naturalist is guided by the view that a grounded understanding of developmental principles is the best preparation for teaching. Students are exposed in their courses to theories of cognitive, social, moral, and language development and then focus in various practicums on the application of developmental principles to the teaching of mathematics, science, and literacy. During the two years, students complete placements in five different schools and complete an original research project on some aspect of development and education. In recent years the program has shifted from the application of content-free developmental principles to a concern with the development of domain-specific knowledge within each of the basic school subjects (Ammon and Black 1988).

The social-reconstructionist tradition

The fourth and final tradition of reform in U.S. teacher education, the social-reconstructionist tradition, defines both schooling and teacher education as crucial elements in a movement toward a more just society. According to Kliebard (1986), this tradition

> derived its central thrust from the undercurrent of discontent about the American economic and social system . . . and saw curriculum as the vehicle by which social injustice would be redressed and the evils of capitalism corrected. This "undercurrent" existed in the 1920s and before, and emerged in the 1930s. (p. 183)[19]

A critical mass of radical progressives was located at Teachers College in the 1930s.[20] Following Counts's (1932) forceful articulation of the reconstructionist position in *Dare the School Build a New Social Order?* (1932), challenging teachers to reach for political power and lead the nation to socialism, this reform perspective continued to be expressed and debated in the John Dewey Society for the Study of Education[21] and in the pages of *The Social Frontier* from 1934 to 1939 and its successor, *The Frontiers of Democracy,* 1939–1943.[22] This tradition, which was given strength by an economic depression and by widespread social unrest, stressed the role of the school, allied with other progressive forces, in planning for an intelligent reconstruction of U.S. society where there would be a more just and equitable distribution of the nation's wealth and the "common good" would take precedence over individual gain. Although collective ownership of the means of production was not essential to all social reconstructionists, most felt that the private economy must be regulated to help ensure full employment, economic opportunity, and adequate incomes for a fair standard of living (Stanley 1985).

Given the vast number of changes wrought by science and technology, these "frontier educators" argued that it was the task of education "to prepare individuals to take part intelligently in the management of conditions under which they will live, to bring them to an understanding of the forces which are moving and to equip them with the intellectual and practical tools by which they can themselves enter into the direction of these forces" (Kilpatrick 1933, p. 71).[23]

One of the major issues of debate among social reconstructionists was the degree to which teachers and teacher educators should consciously indoctrinate their students with socialist and collectivist values or rely on the method of experimentalism and reflective inquiry to lead to social improvements. Counts (1932) was representative of those who argued for deliberate indoctrination of socialist values and ideas. In *Dare the School Build a New Social Order?* he argued that given the inevitable partisanship of all educational activity and the dominance of capitalistic and individualistic values in all aspects of society, it was necessary for the teacher consciously to foster ideas and values supportive of the new social order (e.g., cooperation instead of competition). Holmes of Harvard (1932) and Bode (1935) of Ohio State were among those who rejected the notion that the school should be used to promote a previously determined social program. They placed their emphasis on cultivating students' ability to think critically about the social order. This tension between indoctrination and fostering critical intelligence has been characteristic of the reconstructionist tradition throughout its existence (Stanley 1985).

Because the teaching profession was being asked by the "frontier educators" to assume a leadership role in the reconstruction of American society, teacher education was viewed as playing a key role in the process:

> The duty of the teachers' colleges is thus clear. They must furnish over a period of years a staff of workers for the public schools who thoroughly understand the social, economic, and political problems with which this country is faced, who are zealous in the improvement of present conditions and who are capable of educating citizens disposed to study social problems earnestly, think critically about them, and act in accord with their nobelist impulses. (Brown 1938, p. 328)

If teachers were to fulfill their role in social reconstruction, however, teacher education itself would have to be reconstructed. In *The Educa-*

27

tional Frontier, Kilpatrick (1933) and his colleagues, who included John Dewey, criticized traditional forms of teacher education for their emphasis on technique divorced from consideration of broader purposes, and called for a new social emphasis in the preparation of teachers where the stress would be on helping prospective teachers develop an adequate social and educational philosophy and a "zeal for the betterment of our common civilization" (p. 270). This development of a thoughtful orientation among prospective teachers about schooling and society was thought to be critical to the ability of teachers to lead the intelligent redirection of the social order:

> More than anything else, so far as importance goes, does education mean the building of the life outlook, for when put to work, the life outlook includes and orders everything else. . . .
> Techniques and procedures become then subordinate, always so, to the general aims we set up for life and education. . . .
> Professional education must thus hold as its central and dominating feature the building of an inclusive and criticized outlook upon life and education. No step in the educative process can be weighed or judged except in the light of such a point of view, itself always growing as each new problem is most thoughtfully faced. The building and use of a philosophy of education thus becomes the key aim in professional education. (Kilpatrick 1933, pp. 261–62)

Unlike many contemporary reconstructionist plans for teacher education that focus exclusively on what needs to be done to develop social consciousness and reform capabilities among prospective teachers, these earlier "frontier educators" also recognized the dominant tendency toward conformity to the status quo among the "teachers of teachers"[24] and focused some of their efforts on awakening social consciousness among teacher educators. They recognized the difficulty of this task but also its necessity in their plans for the reconstruction of society:

> In the education of teachers probably no one factor is more important than the social attitude of the faculty of the professional institution. In general social outlook and attitude . . . the staff of our ordinary normal school or teachers' college is only too often severely lacking. A more adequate social outlook is an absolute necessity if prospective teachers are to catch the social

vision. The socially unenlightened teaching too often found in the ordinary college or normal school can hardly have any other result than turning out teachers ignorant in our social situation and with no intelligent concern about it. We must, then, as fast and as far as is humanly possible bring it about that all members of the professional staff hold an intelligent and positive social outlook. . . . How to effect a new attitude within the professional school is no simple matter. One chief hope must lie in the work of the greater schools where the staff members of the lesser professional schools are prepared. . . . Each staff member should be encouraged to know at first hand how the less-favored among us live and feel. First-hand contacts carry great potency. We easily disregard the needs of those we do not know. In every possible way we must work for the more intelligently social outlook within our staff of our teacher-preparing institutions. Without this, we can hardly hope for socially prepared teachers. (Kilpatrick 1933, p. 266)

Two prominent early examples of efforts to apply the proposals of these radical progressives to teacher education were New College, an experimental and demonstration teacher education program at Teachers College from 1932 to 1939, and the emergence of an integrated social-foundations component in teacher education programs. New College was designed to serve two major purposes: (1) to prepare "first-rate" elementary- and secondary-school teachers and (2) to serve as a teacher education laboratory for those graduate students who would staff the teachers' colleges of the nation.[25]

The New College experiment represented a conscious effort to apply to teacher education the idea that teachers could be prepared to be the leaders of societal reconstruction. The college's first announcement quoted from Counts's (1932) manifesto and reminded prospective students that "it is the peculiar privilege of the teacher to play a large part in the development of the social order of the next generation" (Cremin, Shannon, and Townsend 1954, p. 222). Important elements of the New College experience were its integrating seminars, "problems based" curriculum, and firsthand experiences with various aspects of community life. The New College faculty, in asserting that a teacher's work is community wide in scope, "held that a major task of professional preparation is the enlargement of the student's range of interest and the deepening of his insight into basic problems of human living so that he may see his specific job in terms of larger social needs" (New College 1936, p. 30).

The New College curriculum provided students with various opportunities for contact with life that would contribute to this development of a social outlook. All students were expected to develop skills of community planning, living, and leadership by spending at least a summer living and working on a student-operated farm in western North Carolina. They were also required to work in industry for a term, to study and travel abroad for at least a summer, and to participate in numerous field trips that involved them with the various cultural and commercial opportunities in New York City. Students were also required to complete a year-long teaching internship following a semester of student teaching.

Consistent with this emphasis on the value of direct experience in a teacher's education, the faculty constantly attempted to foster political activity among the students. For example, in 1937, the director announced the establishment of two scholarships that would be given to the two students who ". . . go the furthest beyond academic neutrality in active participation in life outside the walls of the university" (Cremin, Shannon, and Townsend 1954, p. 226). Many of the assemblies of students and faculty over the years became forums for the debate of political issues. According to Limbert (1934), the faculty was determined that no one be allowed to graduate from this teacher education program who was politically illiterate or indifferent. Limbert, in describing important happenings at the college during one four-month period, reported a variety of activities that were consistent with the emphasis on developing students' abilities to take an intelligent stand on important economic and political issues:

> . . . the holding of several anti-war meetings and the selection
> of representatives to a University conference, where drastic ac-
> tion was taken looking toward the divorcing of the University
> from the war system; an assembly of the entire student body
> and staff to hear a proposal, presented by one of the professors,
> for the formation of a new movement for the reconstruction of
> American society, revolutionary in purpose, but fundamentally
> in accord with American traditions; a spirited criticism of this
> proposal by instructors and students, leading to a demand for
> additional assemblies for the discussion of similar proposals for
> social change. (p. 118)

A second example of early attempts to apply the social-reconstruction-ist agenda to teacher education was the development, also at Teachers College Columbia, of the social foundations of education as a component of a teacher education program. According to Cohen (1976), Rugg and Kilpatrick spearheaded in 1934–1935 ". . . the most famous and influential innovation in American teacher education in the twentieth century" (p. 31), the initiation of the two-semester course Education 200F, Social Foundations of Education. According to Rugg (1952), the foundations of education, with its focus on the fundamental problems of school, the society, and culture, would aid in the development of a social and educational philosophy by prospective teachers that would enable them to assume a leadership role in the making of educational policy. According to the faculty who created the program, this coordina-tion of focus among previously isolated disciplines represented a signifi-cant shift from a mechanistic and atomistic outlook on life to an organic one (Borrowman 1956). This effort to develop an integrated social-foundations approach was complemented by attempts to reconstruct the general education of teachers in a manner that broke down conventional–subject-matter boundaries such as the efforts of Frank Baker at Milwau-kee State Teachers College (see Rugg 1952, pp. 236–37). The social foundations of education were to aid teachers in making wise educational decisions.

Although Education 200F was never popular among many Teachers College faculty who maintained a commitment to a discipline-based general education, the idea of social-foundations courses spread to teacher education institutions throughout the U.S. During the 1940s and 1950s leadership in the foundations movement shifted to the University of Illinois where William O. Stanley, Kenneth Benne, B. Othaniel Smith and Archibald Anderson formed the core of the social foundations group (Cohen 1976). These newly developed social-foundations components of teacher education programs and the "educationists" who taught them became the main targets for reformers of the academic tradition, like Bestor, Koerner, and Conant, who charged that their interdisciplinary focus destroyed the integrity of the disciplines.

Another aspect of the social-reconstructionist tradition has been the commitment evident in several federally funded programs such as Teacher Corps and TTT to alter societal inequities by focusing on the improvement of educational conditions for children of the poor. Here it was hoped that the cycle of educational failure, poverty, and despair for many rural and urban children could be broken through programs that prepared teachers and teacher educators to work in schools where the students were poverty-stricken.[26]

Among the contemporary examples of the social-reconstructionist tradition in teacher education is Landon Beyer's work at Knox and Cornell Colleges with the notion of "teacher education as praxis." Beyer (1988) describes his efforts to implement a "foundationally oriented" approach to teacher education as a project that is guided by the normative principles of democracy, equality, and autonomy, and which is committed to the development of practical wisdom. A key to his efforts has been the examination by students of a variety of issues and situations from multiple and interdisciplinary perspectives. Another key component is the intended union of reflective inquiry and practical action where students are given continuing opportunities to enact and then examine their ideas in practice. Beyer's (1988) commitment to the preparation of teachers who will be inclined toward and capable of contributing to the reconstruction of schools and society is clear:

> Teacher education must be committed to the development of critically oriented, compassionate, and impassioned, reflective and socially engaged practitioners who can aid in the process of educational improvement and social change. (p. 185)

Other contemporary proponents of a social-reconstructionist view of teacher education include Ira Shor, Henry Giroux and Peter McLaren. Shor (1987), for example, sets out an agenda for what he calls "egalitarian teacher education." He proposes a number of themes that he feels need to permeate the teaching-learning process in teacher education programs if teacher education is to contribute to social change (e.g., dialogic teaching, cross-cultural communication, and cultural literacy). Giroux and McLaren (1987), in contrast, propose a conceptual apparatus for thinking about teacher education as a democratizing or counterhegemonic force and teachers as "transformative intellectuals." According to Giroux and McLaren, if teacher education is to contribute toward a more just, humane, and equitable social order, then it needs to be viewed as a form of cultural politics based on the study of such themes as language, history, culture, and politics:

> The project of doing a teacher education program based on cultural politics consists of linking critical social theory to a set of stipulated practices through which student teachers are able to

dismantle and critically examine preferred educational and cultural traditions, many of which have fallen prey to instrumental rationality that either limits or ignores democratic ideals and principles. One of our main concerns focuses on developing a language of critique and demystification that is capable of analyzing the latent interests and ideologies that work to socialize students in a manner compatible with the dominant culture. We are equally concerned, however, with creating alternative teaching practices capable of empowering students both inside and outside schools. (Giroux and McLaren 1987, p. 173)

Other contemporary social-reconstructionist teacher education efforts in the U.S. include the following: the work of Adler and Goodman (1986), who have used social-studies methods courses to help prospective teachers develop curriculum analysis and development capabilities that will contribute toward more democratic school and societal contexts; the "emancipatory" supervision methods developed by Gitlin (Smyth and Gitlin 1989); our own work in developing an inquiry-oriented student teaching program (Zeichner and Liston 1987, Liston and Zeichner 1987); several feminist-inspired proposals for teacher education programs that seek the correction of gender inequities in schools and society (Maher & Rathbone 1986); Ginsburg's (1988) proposal for more progressive political activity by teacher educators; and Sears's (1985) proposal for teacher education, which is based on a historical analysis of reconstructionist teacher education efforts. Several examples of these social-reconstructionist teacher education projects will be discussed in more detail in chapter 6.

Beyond the common desire to prepare teachers who have critical perspectives on the relationships between schooling and societal inequities and a moral commitment to correcting those inequities through their daily classroom and school activities, there is a great deal of variation among these contemporary proposals of social-reconstructionist teacher educators. At various times, the focus has been on the content of programs, the skills of critical analysis and curriculum development, the nature of the pedagogical relationships between teachers and pupils and between teacher educators and their students, or on the connections between teacher education and other political projects which seek to address the many instances of suffering and injustice in our society.

Despite the existence of all these proposals, one of the most notable characteristics of the contemporary social-reconstructionist teacher education literature is its marginal status in relation to teacher education programs in the U.S. This marginal status is indicated in part by a general lack of examples of teacher education programs that translate conceptual proposals into either feasible programmatic components or teaching strategies. In several of the most prominent of these proposals (e.g., Giroux and McLaren 1987, Shor 1987, and Ginsburg 1988), for example, there is not a single reference to existing programmatic examples of the authors' proposals. This marginal status of the reconstructionist tradition in U.S. teacher education has been the case throughout most of the twentieth century. According to Kliebard (1986), the social-reconstructionist ideas of Counts and his contemporaries aroused the animosity of those on both the political left and right and had very little influence on school practices. Cremin (1988) concurs with this view and characterizes the social-reconstructionist commentary as an academic discussion that has had very little influence outside its own inner circle, including a lack of influence on mainstream U.S. teacher education. The marginal status of social-reconstructionist proposals for U.S. teacher education is one of the most critical issues that needs to be addressed by this group of reform-minded teacher educators.

Conclusion

We believe that the four reform traditions described in this chapter can serve as a heuristic for clarifying some of the similarities and differences among ideas and practices in teacher education which in some cases may appear on the surface to be alike. Teacher education programs, as well as proposals for reforming teacher education, reflect particular patterns of resonance with these traditions.[27]

Our own proposals for teacher education in the United States (which will be presented beginning in chapter 2) represent an effort to place social-reconstructionist perspectives in a more prominent location in the discourse about the education of teachers. Although in the last decade there has been a lot of discussion about reforming teacher education in the United States, very little of this discussion has focused on the social context of schooling in a democratic society—let alone on the societal transformations that will need to occur if a high-quality education for all children is to become a reality.

We have not set out to convert teacher educators and their students to any particular set of educational ideas and practices, or to our own particular vision of a more just and equitable social order. But we do recognize the inherently political nature of teacher education programs and maintain that it is essential for teacher education in the United States to make a contribution to the building of a more humane and just society. This will require a new resolve by those in the field to prepare teachers who are committed to teaching in those urban and rural schools where the problems of inequity are the greatest. There must be an ongoing commitment to prepare teachers who, wherever they teach, are dedicated to the realization of a top-quality education for everyone's children, and who recognize the importance and value of the diverse cultures and traditions that make up our nation.

In the next chapter, we begin presenting our arguments by highlighting the importance of initiating and sustaining a process of moral deliberation within our teacher education programs so that prospective teachers become more conscious about and capable of articulating the moral and ethical dimensions of their work. Although how they choose to act as teachers and as citizens is a matter that we cannot (and do not wish to) control in any final way, we can create in our teacher education programs educational situations that represent our commitment to certain values such as social justice rather than individual greed; to education rather than indoctrination; and to caring and compassion rather than to detached rationality. We must turn our students' attention to certain issues of educational injustice, and ask them to consider and evaluate their work on the basis of its moral and ethical quality—not simply its technical soundness. If as teacher educators we can do something to awaken the social consciousness of prospective teachers, and provide them with alternative and concrete possibilities for realizing the goal of a high-quality education for everyone's children, we will have accomplished a lot. Although teacher education cannot by itself create a better society, it can join in the struggle for bringing it about.

In articulating our social-reconstructionist–oriented agenda for teacher education in the United States, we are not suggesting that it is unimportant for teacher education programs to be concerned with the priorities emphasized in the other reform traditions (e.g., teachers' subject matter knowledge and their ability to represent this knowledge to their students in ways that promote understanding; a liberal education which empowers students to be active participants in processes of democratic deliberation in the society; the "knowledge base" about teaching generated through research; and the "knowledge base" about the learning and development of both teachers and their students, also generated through research). And of course, we are not opposed to academic rigor and technical competence as long as this rigor does not exclude care and compassion for the disenfranchised in our democratic society—and as long as this rigor extends our world view beyond white, male, Western views of the world that have dominated teacher education for so long. We care deeply about academic literacy, about technical competence, and about developmentally appropriate schooling, but we want to see the benefits of this schooling shared by all.

In the next chapter we outline what we believe ought to be the central aims of a teacher education program. We argue, in brief, that prospective teachers should be educated so that they can discern good reasons for their educational actions. This type of deliberation, this reason giving, is dependent on distinct conceptions of the teacher's role and the activity of teaching. We also argue that it is only in the social-reconstructionist tradition that teachers' social and political beliefs and teachers' knowledge of the social context of schooling figure significantly in deliberations about what counts as good reasons for educational action.

2

The Aims of Teacher Education

Introduction

It is frequently lamented that teacher education programs lack a formulated set of aims and purposes, consist of a collection of unrelated course work and disconnected fieldwork, and as a result end up haphazardly training rather than thoughtfully educating prospective teachers. Schools of education's mission statements are rarely followed. The institutional aims and purposes remain formal. The situation is not promising. At times it seems that there is an inexorable institutional logic which resists purposeful direction and that the aims of teacher education have not been given adequate thought by the participants. At other times it seems that state authorities and national accrediting agencies seriously constrain teacher educators' efforts.[1] In short, it appears that forces both within and external to institutions of higher education tend to subvert the process. In this chapter we begin to identify and elaborate a set of defensible aims. Our aims are designed to give further direction to the professional educational process and to provide a basis for the subsequent reform of teacher education in a manner consistent with a social-reconstructionist reform agenda. We hope that our arguments and claims will encourage teacher educators and prospective teachers to examine, clarify, and further articulate their own educational views and beliefs and to examine and scrutinize the social context of schooling and teacher education.

In the previous chapter we noted that social reconstructionist teacher education programs have attempted to:

> prepare individuals to take part intelligently in the management
> of conditions under which they live, to bring them to an under-

standing of the forces which are moving [them] and to equip
them with the intellectual and practical tools by which they can
themselves enter into the direction of these forces. (Kilpatrick
1933, p. 71)

In previously published work we have focused our analyses on conceptions of reflective teaching and reflective teacher education in an attempt
to guide and justify our work in teacher education. We have always
sensed that our efforts to elaborate, justify, and build reflective teacher
education programs, were consistent with and meant to further the spirit
of these earlier social-reconstructionist efforts. But given the discussions
of the last few years it is evident that the reflective stance in teacher
education has become so widely employed by so many distinct practitioners and theoreticians that the term now lacks what, for us, has
always been a very conscious social and political orientation. We want
to renew the "social" emphasis that Kilpatrick and others had supported.[2]
Our overriding aim is to enable prospective teachers to develop an
adequate social and educational orientation and, to reiterate the concern
of Kilpatrick and his colleagues, to develop a "zeal for the betterment
of our common civilization" (1933, p. 270).

Unfortunately the discourse among teacher educators has become
increasingly muddled as terms such as "empowerment," "reflection,"
and "critical" have been bandied about, oftentimes with little explicit
indication of the perspectives and commitments underlying them.[3] Lately
the sense within teacher education seems to be that as long as teachers
"reflect" on their actions and purposes, everything is all right. When this
is the case, calls for further reflection become groundless—that is, they
lack a substantial basis for discerning what will count as good reasons
for educational actions. Since teachers are (and we think should be)
responsible for key educational decisions and actions within the classroom, it is important that prospective teachers begin to consider what
will count as a good reason for effective educational action.

Teachers frequently face situations of conflict where it is not clear
what action or option ought to be taken. In fact, the classroom can be
accurately described as a locus point of numerous conflicts focusing at
times on instructional choices, curriculum development, administrative
directives, parental concerns, cultural differences, and socioeconomic
inequalities. If teachers are going to be able to approach these conflicts
in ways that do not rely blindly on authority or special interests, then
they must be able to discern good reasons for their educational actions.

Only the social reconstructionist gives much attention to the giving of reasons, the formation of purposes, and the examination of how the institutional, social, and political context affects the formation of those purposes or the framing of the reasons.[4] Only the social-reconstructionist approach seriously attempts to situate educational action within a larger social and political context.

We sense that teacher education ought to aim directly at developing teachers who are able to identify and articulate their purposes, who can choose the appropriate instructional strategies or appropriate means, who know and understand the content to be taught, who understand the social experiences and cognitive orientations of their students, and who can be counted on for giving good reasons for their actions. These justifications should take into account the activity of teaching, the larger communities of educators, and a greater understanding of the social and political context of schooling. Furthermore, such reason giving should have some basis on which to discern good from bad, and better from worse, reasons for particular educational actions. But before the aim of "reason giving" can be viewed as a credible or even justifiable aim, some context or criteria must be established that enables one to discern which reasons are good and which actions are effective.[5] While we don't think there exists a single set of immutable standards, we sense that a framework can be elaborated which would give a more substantial basis than anything now articulated and previously defended. Recently, Margret Buchmann (1986) and C.J.B. Macmillan (1987) have attempted to articulate a basis for discerning better from worse, and good from bad educational rationales. We will turn our attention to their discussion.

Reason giving in teaching

In "Role over Person: Morality and Authenticity in Teaching," Margret Buchmann (1986) argues that teachers' actions are based on choice and that their rationales for these choices cannot be based on personal reasons alone. In answering the question "What counts as good reasons in teaching?" Buchmann argues that personal reasons must be subordinate to external standards. She maintains that providing justification in teaching requires the existence of a professional community, a community that sets standards and identifies the role obligations of teachers as members of that community. In effect, she argues that the role of the teacher defines what will count as good reasons in teaching. Buchmann elaborates this point by indicating some of the immediate and more removed role constraints. She maintains that in a fairly immediate sense the teaching role obligates teachers to take an interest in student learning and to convey worthwhile knowledge. She states that "The view of students as learners underlies the distinctive obligations of teachers, and role orientation in teaching by definition means taking an interest in student learning. Thus, insofar as teachers are not social workers, career counselors, or simply adults who care for children, their work centers on the curriculum and presupposes knowledge of subject matter" (Buchmann 1986, p. 531). In a more removed sense Buchmann argues that the teaching role obligates teachers to respect the constraints imposed by the structures of the disciplines. Teachers are not free to use whatever methods, content, or organizational procedures they might feel appropriate. The structures of the disciplines constrain what is an appropriate mode of teaching or learning.

Buchmann is concerned with critiquing a general personalistic ethos which maintains that teaching is a personal affair, where creative efforts should flourish and personal meaning ought to predominate. In contrast to this personal approach she states that "Professional decisions are tied to the public realm where they are constrained by facts and norms, both forms of public knowledge. Put differently, justification needs to reach beyond the particulars of teachers' own actions and inclinations to consider larger organized contexts relevant to their work, such as the disciplines of knowledge, laws, and societal issues" (Buchmann 1986, p. 533). For Buchmann the basis of good reason giving is to be found in the role of the teacher. And for her, the role of the teacher is defined by the larger professional community of educators.

Macmillan (1987) lauds Buchmann's emphasis on reason giving and her critique of strictly personal and psychological "justifications," but he disputes her claim that the role of the teacher provides the justificatory basis. Instead he argues that the activity of teaching provides the central basis upon which we can discern sound and justified reason giving. In short, he argues that the activity (or practice) of teaching is logically prior to the role of the teacher. For Macmillan, "Both the ethics and the epistemology of teaching depend upon a clear conception of teaching apart from those settings [institutional and professional]. . . . the activities of teaching are logically prior to the role of the teacher" (Macmillan 1987, p. 366). Macmillan believes that Buchmann erred. For Macmillan, educational rationales should not be based solely on an understanding of the teacher's role as defined by the larger community of teachers but rather must be grounded first in the activity of teaching. Macmillan argues that "What is important about this is that the ethics of teaching as well as the limits of the activities are necessitated by the notion of teaching itself, quite apart from any social or institutional context. Rather than being contingent upon a place in a community, they are necessarily part of teaching regardless of its social context. When one teaches, one takes these limits and these ethics upon oneself, quite apart from any decision to take on the social role of the teacher" (Macmillan 1987, p. 367).

In the end Macmillan does admit that although the ethics of teaching are initially defined by the activity of teaching, the further development of this ethic "probably depends upon there being a community of committed persons" (Macmillan 1987, p. 370). But he steadfastly maintains that the activities of teaching are logically prior to the community-defined role of teachers. The implications of this discussion reach far beyond the realm of teacher education; they also strike at the heart of what we sense teacher education ought to be all about. With regard to the central question—"What is the basis of good reason giving in educational deliberation?"—Buchmann answers that it entails a clear understanding of the teacher's role in the professional community; Macmillan argues that it entails a sound understanding of the activity of teaching irrespective of the larger social context.

Certainly, we think, the activity of teaching limits and gives some direction to what will count as sound rationales in teaching. As Macmillan has argued, in teaching, we expect truth to count as a central value because teaching is the sort of activity that relies on the virtues of honesty and trust. Honesty and trust are inherent in the activity of teaching, irrespective of the context or time. If we found, as Macmillan argues, a society in which teaching lies was viewed as acceptable, we would have some basis for criticizing that society's educational practices (Macmillan 1987, p. 369). Teaching is also an activity in which just relations should predominate. If a teacher acts harshly toward a student because of whim or some other external distraction, that would seem to constitute a breach of the educational relationship. The sense of breach would come from our belief that the activity of teaching and the relationships entailed by that activity would require fair and just relations between participants. Now while most of us would recognize that the activity of teaching entails trusting, honest, and fair relations, there are many choices that a teacher must make that are not so "easily" resolved. That is, the activity

41

of teaching provides only a very minimal basis for assessing and giving direction to educational choices. The activity of teaching as such simply doesn't take into account pertinent contextual features of teaching. For example, as we noted above, the activity of teaching seems to entail relations of justice. But in a teaching situation where knowledge is being conveyed, it is not always clear what justice (as fairness to others) requires. For example, when students are grouped by "assessed ability" does justice "require" the teacher to spend more instructional time with the "lower" groups and therefore less time with other instructional groups in a specific skill or content area? Should the teacher make trade-offs among content areas giving the lower group more time in one area and offering the other groups enrichment activities in another area? Should the teacher question the justice of a distributional schema based on "assessed ability" and a small-group instructional format? It is not clear what the activity of teaching would countenance as good reasons in this example. It seems we must enlarge the basis beyond the activity of teaching.

Macmillan eventually agrees with Buchmann that the teacher's role, as defined by the professional community, provides a basis on which deliberation can occur. But Buchmann makes this thesis her central claim, while Macmillan utilizes it to complement his activity thesis. Nevertheless both would agree that the role of the teacher enlarges the basis of deliberation and that the notion of a role is conceptually and pragmatically dependent on our understanding of the relevant community. Both also seem to share the view that the relevant community is the "professional" community of teachers and that such a community is internally coherent and cohesive, at least to the degree that it can inform us on these crucial matters.

While it does seem that, in some sense, a "professional" community exists, we doubt that it is either coherent or cohesive enough to ground sufficiently the role of the teacher or the activity we call teaching. The unitary notion of a professional community overlooks deep divisions within the professional community. Conservative, progressive, and radical educators share certain views about teaching and, at times, the role of the teacher; however, their educational views differ in important and significant ways.[6] We sense that a more appropriately differentiated notion of the relevant community would provide a more sound basis for developing prospective teachers' understanding of the educational process. Certainly there does not exist a monolithic activity that we call education, and furthermore it seems that reasonable and differing conceptions of the teacher's and student's roles exists. If we are asking students to give good reasons for educational actions, and we expect their rationales to evince an understanding of the activity and role of teaching, then it seems we must be sensitive to the various ways these roles and the activity of teaching have been defined by relevant educational traditions and/or communities. In effect, our understanding of the role of the teacher and the activity of teaching is conceptually dependent on particular communities. Therefore it seems that if teacher education is to aim at the formulation of good reasons for educational action, then teacher educators should enable prospective teachers to articulate good reasons based on and formulated with an understanding of teaching and the roles of teaching as defined by the varied and established educational traditions.

Something of this sort (in the realm of moral deliberation) is proposed by Robin Lovin (1988) in a paper entitled "The School and the Articulation of Values." There he notes that a pervasive moral emotivism frequently precludes the possibility of reasonable assessments of moral claims or of giving sound reasons for particular actions. Lovin quotes Alasdair MacIntyre (1984) as capturing one of the central obstacles to a reasonable approach to moral deliberation:

> Emotivism is the doctrine that all evaluative judgements and more specifically all moral judgements are nothing but expressions of preference, expressions of attitude or feeling, insofar as they are moral or evaluative in character. (MacIntyre 1984, pp. 11–12)

According to this emotivist view, MacIntyre explains, "Factual judgments are true or false; and in the realm of fact there are rational criteria by means of which we may secure agreement as to what is true and what is false. But moral judgments, being expressions of attitude or feeling, are neither true nor false; and agreement in moral judgment is not to be secured by any rational method, for there are none" (MacIntyre 1984, p. 12). In contrast to this emotivist view, Lovin argues that it is possible for rational deliberation over value claims to occur. He argues that the rationality of value claims is not a strictly deductive enterprise whose only criteria are clarity and consistency but rather that

> . . . understanding the rationality of value claims requires attentiveness to the contexts in which they are formulated and as-

sessed. An important aspect of MacIntyre's criticism of emotivism is his emphasis on the communities and practices that give rise to values. To see values simply as products of individual experience and expressions of personal choice is descriptively inadequate, but, more important, the relationship between an individual's values and the ways of thinking that characterize the communities in which he or she participates provides a starting point from which critical assessment of values becomes possible. (Lovin 1988, p. 148)

Furthermore, he argues that:

To be articulate about one's values is to be able to locate them within these traditions and systems of belief and to be able to explore the implications that these larger contexts have for how values are to be applied and practiced. To be articulate is also to understand which of the several systems that may support a specific value position is decisive for one's own affirmation of the value and to be able to explain how that tradition relates both to others who affirm the same value for different reasons and to those who deny it. (Lovin 1988, p. 151)

Earlier we claimed that the giving of good reasons for educational action required an understanding of the activity of teaching and the role of the teacher. We also claimed that the role of the teacher is defined in important ways by the relevant community, by a particular tradition of educational thought. This comes down to claiming that the giving of reasons is dependent, in a significant way, on the context, on the particular tradition or community in which the discourse is located. It also means that teacher education ought to enable future teachers to develop rationales and justifications for educational actions that are both heartfelt and consistent with larger educational traditions. In effect, we are claiming that teacher education ought to aim at the articulation of those values and practices that are integral to the educational enterprise. As a part of this articulation students would be introduced to the central traditions of educational thought and practice and as a result of both academic and field experiences they would gradually develop their positions among and within these traditions.

A number of questions and concerns seem pertinent at this point in our discussion. First of all, one might wonder whether any significant and distinct educational traditions actually exist? And if such traditions can be identified, one might also question whether utilizing these traditions as a basis and context in which to formulate good reasons leaves us with a pernicious relativism, where we end up pitting one tradition against another and have little hope of achieving a sound and justifiable direction. From a distinctly different perspective one could also question whether our use of "educational traditions" commits us to a search for the quintessential, foundational, overarching educational rationale. Second, it seems reasonable to raise questions about the relationship between the prospective teacher's initial beliefs about education and the larger traditions of educational thought and practice. Does the goal of articulation entail a critical examination of the prospective teacher's own beliefs and/or a critical examination of the central tenets of that tradition? In the next section we address these questions.

Educational traditions

Thus far we have used the concept of tradition in a fairly loose fashion. We will stipulate what we mean by that term and how we intend to use it. As a sort of first approximation it seems that educational traditions consist of intergenerational bodies of thought and practices that are concerned with and are connected to particular educational aims and values. All too often people tend to view traditions as bodies of inert and internally confluent ideas and practices. This is not the position that we take. Instead we hold the view that a tradition is marked by a preoccupation with and pursuit of particular valued goods and that within a particular tradition there frequently is a core set of beliefs around which considerable disagreement may exist. Our overall sense accords with Alasdair MacIntyre's (1984) usage when he claims that "A living tradition . . . is an historically extended, socially embodied argument, and an argument precisely in part about the goods which constitute that tradition. Within a tradition the pursuit of goods extends through generations, sometimes through many generations. Hence the individual's search for his or her good is generally and characteristically conducted within a context defined by those traditions of which the individual's life is a part, and this is true both of those goods which are internal to practices and of the goods of a single life" (MacIntyre 1984, p. 222).

In educational scholarship it is possible to discern not only a number of traditions but also a number of ways of formulating identifiable educational traditions. In the previous chapter we identified four major reform traditions in U.S. teacher education: the academic, social-efficiency, developmentalist, and social-reconstructionist traditions. In that chapter we portrayed the reform traditions in a historically rich and empirically descriptive manner. We believed that this way of capturing the reform traditions was not only accurate but would also make sense to teacher educators, teachers, and academics acquainted with the practices and rationales of various teacher education programs. We also hoped that our analysis might enable teacher educators, teachers, and academics to articulate further their own sense of what is valuable and worthwhile in the various U.S. teacher education reform traditions.

For prospective teachers we think that a less historically descriptive but more conceptually focused approach is initially helpful. When we speak of having prospective teachers become acquainted with the ways in which distinct educational traditions construe the role of teachers and the activity of educating, a slightly different formulation is beneficial. In order for students to gain a clearer and more consistent conceptual understanding of the distinct ways of construing education and to help them articulate their own preferred and hopefully defensible views we have identified three general educational traditions: the conservative, progressive, and radical traditions. These three traditions serve as heuristic constructs, and as such represent one way to enable students to identify conceptually distinct views of the teacher's role and educational activity.

There is a rough correspondence between our two "sets" of traditions: the sort of correspondence one would expect between a conceptually focused elaboration and a historically descriptive account. Roughly, the conservative tradition corresponds to the academic reform agenda, the radical tradition corresponds to the social-reconstructionist reform movement, and the progressive tradition corresponds to both the developmentalist and social-efficiency reform movements. In time we would hope that prospective teachers would move back and forth from a conceptual articulation of their own views, formulated in relation to the three traditions, to an inspection of the more subtle, historically attuned sense of educational traditions, and then back to a further examination of the concepts and values. But, for our purposes, the three traditions seem initially to represent the more useful constructs.

Since we have claimed that the distinct educational traditions present different views about educational activity and the teacher's role, we briefly outline key tenets in each of the traditions. The reader should keep in mind, however, that these represent heuristic constructs whose purpose is to provide a context for and elaboration of distinct educational orientations. They are not intended as complete conceptual or empirical depictions.

In recent years Paul Hirst (1965), Alan Bloom (1987) and E. D. Hirsch (1988) have elaborated central strands of what we call the conservative tradition. These authors continue the work of such earlier writers as Robert Hutchins (1947), and Arthur Bestor (1955). The conservative tradition in educational thought appears to be concerned basically with conserving the established cultural and scientific heritage of Western civilization. For many of these individuals, our established heritage represents a vast body of achievement and understanding unsurpassed and unparalleled in the history of humankind. Their concern lies basically in education's ability to convey or transmit this heritage or to initiate students into the forms (disciplines) of knowledge that represent our distinct intellectual heritage. Essentially it seems that conservatives view the educational process as a means of cultural transmission. The teacher's role is to convey this knowledge, information, or distinct forms of inquiry to students so that they can become more fully rational and/or moral human beings. When prospective teachers examine the writings of either Robert Hutchins (1947), Paul Hirst (1965), or E. D. Hirsch (1988), it is possible to see both their common concerns and their distinct emphases. All are concerned with students' growing ability to reason, all three think it is the teacher's role to facilitate the enhancement of students' reasoning, and all believe that this educational process requires discipline and effort on the part of student and teacher alike.

But when one compares Hirsch and Hirst, distinctive emphases and concerns appear. Hirst (1965) provides a rationale for the initiation of students into distinct forms of knowledge, whereas Hirsch (1988) is most concerned with reestablishing something of a common cultural heritage shared by all "Americans." When prospective elementary teachers and undergraduates read Hirsch, they note his emphasis on shared "canonical knowledge" with the goal of cultural literacy for all.[7] They read justifications for pedagogical methods of drill and rote memorization. And they begin to think aloud about whether we have, or desire, this shared canonical knowledge, what it would take to create such an emphasis in our public schools, if this emphasis on a common cultural background further disadvantages those who are already "disadvantaged," and if a rote approach to cultural literacy constitutes learning? Some students find Hirsch's call for cultural literacy appealing, and they gain from Hirsch arguments to support his claims. Other students maintain that Hirsch's program is practically unfeasible and politically undesirable. For these students a common culture does not exist, and they fear that the construction of one for educational purposes would amount to a type of cultural imperialism. Certainly these are not the only questions or issues that could be raised, but they definitely highlight prominent problems and issues in the conservative tradition. Students find these discussions invigorating, and troubling. The discussions clarify further particular aspects of the conservative tradition and enable students to begin to place themselves partly inside or partly outside this body of educational concerns and practices.

John Dewey (1902, 1916, and 1938), of course, is one of if not the central voice in the progressive tradition. But one could also include a number of past and present educators including Boyd Bode (1938), Lucy Sprague Mitchell (1931), John Childs (1956), Vito Perrone (1989), and Vivian Gussin Paley (1981). For those in the progressive tradition, the central aim of education is for students to become competent inquirers, capable of reflecting on and critically examining their everyday world and involved in a continual reconstruction of their experience. Dewey wrote that education is

the reconstruction or reorganization of experience which adds to the meaning of experience, and which increases the ability to direct the course of subsequent experience. (Dewey 1916, p. 89)

To accomplish this progressive aim, a few additional assumptions are made. First of all it is believed that students become competent inquirers by focusing on problems rooted in their experience. For the committed progressive, students should not be fed information or drilled into a way of thinking. Instead, their inquiry ought to arise out of their "interests." Second, the subject matter to be learned will be mastered by students as a result of their inquiries. In the course of problem solving, they will have need of subject matter, and it is through using the subject matter to solve problems that the students master the content to be learned. Pedagogically, the role of the teacher is one who structures the educational situation so that the student attends to particular problems, develops an inquiring disposition, and has the need for further information. Very roughly, the progressive teacher's role is to construct educational situations whereby the student is in need of knowledge to solve problems and to ensure that the required knowledge and information is available. When students begin to examine Dewey's *Experience and Education* (1938) they question the role of a democratic ethos in classroom organization, they find the notion of interests intriguing but elusive, and they wonder if a teacher can or ought to be as neutral as progressives sometimes portray them. Many students find Dewey's view of the child attractive, his call for subject matter to be "psychologized," and accounts of the laboratory school impressive.[8] For some students the progressive tradition provides the context through which they can articulate and examine their own intuitive educational views.

Finally there is the radical tradition. Historically this view was promulgated by George Counts (1932), Theodore Brameld (1955), and Harold Rugg (1931). More recently Paulo Freire (1974), Jonathon Kozol (1980), Jane Roland Martin (1985), Michael Apple (1986), Henry Giroux (1988), and Susan Laird (1988) have elaborated and extended the radical educational tradition. Radical educators generally maintain that men and women are capable of being free and equal members of a just, democratic, and caring society. They tend to start from a position of critique arguing that our public schools do not support or develop these capacities equally for all children. Children of minority populations, and members of the working and under class do not receive good-quality educations or educations comparable to upper- and middle-class white children. But, they maintain, one of the roles of education is to alter the current situation. Schools, and the education contained therein, have the power of positively affecting individuals and bringing about social change. Theodore Brameld argued some forty years ago that the radical tradition is

> infused with a profound conviction that we are in the midst of a revolutionary period out of which would emerge nothing less than control of the industrial system, of public services, and of cultural and natural resources by and for the common people who, throughout the ages, have struggled for a life of security, decency, and peace for them and their children. (Brameld 1947, p. 452)

While contemporary radicals are perhaps not as optimistic as some of the earlier proponents, many sense that our democratic way of life and that democratic forms of schooling are continually undermined by forces both internal and external to the institution of schooling. They encourage students (and we will encourage prospective teachers and teacher educators) to elaborate and clarify their social beliefs and assumptions and to examine the ways in which larger societal forces obstruct and undermine our democratic way of life. When prospective teachers read the radical literature they highlight and question what seems, to them, to be indoctrinatory features of the radical project, they raise questions about the radical proposition that school knowledge is connected to class, racial, and gendered interests, and they wonder if such an approach would ever be appropriate for public schools. But many students also find in the radical tradition support for their sense that schools are connected to a larger social structure, one that affects unjustly the futures of many public school students. They find attractive the radical claim that teachers should be aware of these forces and they wonder if radical alterations in the schools could be accomplished by coalitions of teachers, parents, administrators, and community members.

Clearly these approaches form distinct sets of educational beliefs and practices and, for us, they constitute useful heuristics which capture diverse educational traditions. Other categorizations are certainly possible. We think that within each of our three traditions there exists the necessary degree of shared concern about specific goods. And, as we have already stated, further more historically refined and empirically attuned elaborations of each tradition are necessary and desirable. Certainly there are marked differences within traditions, but our sense is that even given the disparate voices in each tradition there exists a concern for a core set of shared values. For example, within the radical tradition the neo-Marxist and feminist frameworks are markedly distinct in their conceptual categories and their foci, and yet within both of these frameworks there is an overriding concern to explain and eradicate arbitrary domination and oppression, and a view of education as liberating. Accepting the plurality of traditions acknowledges the differing conceptions of the teacher's role and the activity of teaching. This is in sharp contrast to the notion of a professional community that overlooks these distinct conceptions. But an acceptance of this diversity is not without problems. Some will object that embracing this diversity will only lead to a pernicious relativism, a situation in which none of the traditions can justify adequately their aims or warrant their claims. According to this view, the goal of articulation—since it assumes a plurality rather than a single all-encompassing tradition—results in relativism. There are a variety of ways this charge of relativism can be formulated. We will look at two.

Relativism and educational rationales

For some the thesis of distinct traditions, with its accompanying notion of distinct teacher roles and educational rationales, violates a premise that credible rationales should appeal to universal claims and not be bound by context or tradition. Here the central claim would be that good reasons are good reasons, no matter what the tradition or context might be. Educational rationales and the giving of reasons are not dependent on their place within a tradition but must be judged by universal standards. Our response to this is a qualified yes and no, and relies on a distinction noted earlier. In our previous discussion we maintained that the criteria for discerning what counted as good reasons in educational deliberation were determined in an important sense both by the activity of teaching and by the role of the teacher. It seems reasonable to claim that certain reasons based on the activity of teaching might well have universal appeal. For instance, we noted that honesty is required by the activity of teaching. Teaching lies is oxymoronic. Teaching seems to require the virtue of honesty no matter how one construes the teacher's role. It seems that when we examine the activity of teaching there is certainly reason to claim that some justifications can and ought to be universally acceptable.[9] But to argue that all educational deliberation should satisfy universal criteria simply ignores very real and distinct educational aims and purposes. Recognizing and accepting this diversity does not mean that we cannot communicate with people from other traditions, or that no purposes can be shared. It does mean that distinct aims, values, and sets of background assumptions significantly alter the terrain upon which reason giving operates. Furthermore, it means that when people differ over the aims and values guiding the educational enterprise, then significant differences exist—and these differences cannot be resolved by appeal to a set of universal criteria.

An example might help. Suppose we asked a member from each of our traditions what pertinent concerns and issues would be raised over the issue of curriculum selection. In answering the question "What ought I teach?" members of each tradition would venture in distinct directions guided by diverse concerns. Within the progressive tradition answers to questions about curriculum selection assume a need to "psychologize" bodies of knowledge and reflect the view that significant learning is an outcome of students' problem solving. Within the conservative tradition answers to questions about curriculum selection tend to assume a need to maintain a cohesive cultural unity and reflect the view that learning is an initiation into culturally established forms of knowledge. Within the radical tradition answers to questions about curriculum selection assume the need to achieve praxis, to link thought with action, and that worthwhile and valuable learning occurs best when controversial issues are addressed and when students help to influence and are directly engaged by the learning process. Very distinct concerns are raised within each tradition because of each tradition's particular aims, purposes, and sets of background assumptions. For someone to assert that one set of universal aims ought to predominate ignores very real differences. These differences do not entail an inability to communicate with others, or, put another way, a thesis of incommensurability among educational traditions. Members and students of these distinct traditions can and ought to communicate with others. Clarity, coherency, and consistency are intellectual values to which all traditions can and should adhere. Realistically the universalist will probably not be satisfied with our claims. For the universalist any notion of tradition-bound inquiry restricts the universal claims of reason. We sense, however, that (1) any assertion that one set of educational aims and practices deserve universal status has yet to be substantiated, and in our opinion cannot attain such status, and (2) these universal claims ignore substantial moral and practical differences among educational practitioners and scholars.

A second objection might be heard from members of a particular tradition claiming that the goal of articulation undermines their tradition's claim to preeminence. As Lovin (1988) has noted:

> For those who are strongly convinced that one faith, one political system [one educational tradition], or one cultural heritage alone possesses the truth, the effort to identify their ideas with those found in other traditions or to locate these ideas in some larger framework of thought bespeaks in itself a relativism.
> . . . Whether this takes the strong form of a claim that all ideas that differ from the received tradition are false or the more modest claim that certain ideas can only be understood within a faith commitment . . . the exclusive affirmation of a particular moral tradition will [find] . . . values articulation "relativistic." (p. 154)

This is not an uncommon response from members of all three of our educational traditions. Conservative, radical, and progressive thinkers frequently argue the "correctness" of their own position. It is not uncommon to hear members of each tradition complain that students are misled and miseducated by the other traditions. Conservatives rail against the antiintellectual orientation of the progressive tradition, and they deride the utopianism and foggy thinking of the radical tradition. Progressives accuse conservatives of seeing only the intellectual powers of children and thereby misconstruing students' engagement in learning, and they criticize radicals for their indoctrinatory practices. Radicals condemn conservatives for their ideological obfuscation and elitist politics, and they chide progressives for their romantic view of the child and liberal view of society. At times the language and debates are quite emotionally charged and accusatory. However, to argue that prospective teachers ought to be introduced to only one perspective raises the specter of either a grossly limited or indoctrinatory education. It seems extremely presumptuous, protectionist, insular, and misguided to claim that one educational tradition is correct. Certainly none of the traditions has actually achieved such acclaimed status, and it seems mistaken to encourage future teachers to think that this is so. Recognizing and educating prospective teachers about the intellectual and pedagogical differences among these traditions does not amount to a pernicious relativism where all claims are without warrantable status. It seems apparent to us that warranted claims can be made within traditions, and at times these claims can be shared by other distinct traditions. The aim of articulation recognizes these distinct values. It encourages future teachers to recognize the distinctions and to come to terms with their own beliefs and practices within the context of these distinct traditions.

For many readers, our response to the charge of relativism may not be satisfactory. Some may think we have skirted numerous difficult issues, and at least one central question might remain for certain readers: How do we resolve the differences of aims, procedures, and practices among these traditions? Our own sense is that such differences should be relished not banished, and that they should be more fully articulated not reduced. Teachers who are educated to appreciate these differences, and who can come to terms with the variety and richness of the different traditions' frameworks and practices while developing a sense of their own, will (we believe) become stronger and more reasonable teachers.

A democratic basis

It should be obvious by now that our aim of articulation does not attempt to legitimate one set of educational aims.[10] It does not support a single

53

set of universal aims or a preferred set of aims elaborated by *the* "correct" tradition. In effect, we are not searching, or asking prospective teachers to search, for the quintessential, foundational, or overarching rationale. Such a goal, as we have already stated, seems simply unfeasible. But that does not mean that any practice or every rationale is acceptable. While a search for the foundational approach seems rationally unfeasible, we think that there are limits to what would constitute acceptable educational aims and rationales in a democratic society. A commitment to a democratic way of life limits what are acceptable educational aims. It is our belief that the aim of articulation must recognize these limits. While we recognize that distinct individuals have offered various interpretations as to what constitutes a "democratic" education, we have found Amy Gutmann's (1987) elaboration persuasive and justifiable. For Gutmann, a democratic education honors three basic principles. A democratic education (1) must develop a deliberative, democratic character in students; (2) cannot repress rational deliberation and (3) cannot discriminate against any group of children.

Gutmann's reasoning is as follows: She argues that within a democracy we are committed to

> collectively re-creating the society that we share. Although we are not collectively committed to any set of educational aims, we are committed to arriving at an agreement on our educational aims (an agreement that could take the form of justifying a diverse set of educational aims and authorities). The substance of this core commitment is conscious social reproduction. As citizens, we aspire to a set of educational practices and authorities of which the following can be said: these are the practices and authority of which we, acting collectively as a society, have consciously agreed. It follows that a society that supports conscious social reproduction must educate all educable children to be capable of participating in collectively shaping their society. (Gutmann 1987, p. 39)

According to Gutmann a central feature of conscious social reproduction is the development of "deliberative" or "democratic" character. At an individual level deliberation is construed as "careful consideration with a view to a decision" (Gutmann 1987, p. 52). At an institutional level, deliberation is seen as the "consideration and discussion of the reasons for and against a measure by a number of councilors" (Gutmann 1987,

p. 52). A society that is committed to conscious social reproduction, and therefore to the educational aim of critical deliberation, must recognize some principled limits on the articulation of its educational aims. Gutmann identifies two such principles. She states that

> One limit is that of nonrepression. The principle of nonrepression prevents the state, and any group within it, from using education to restrict rational deliberation of competing conceptions of the good life and the good society. (Gutmann 1987, p. 44)

Gutmann's reasoning in support of this principle is as follows:

> Because conscious social reproduction is the primary ideal of democratic education, communities must be prevented from using education to stifle rational deliberation. . . . (Gutmann 1987, p. 45)

A second principled limit is nondiscrimination. As Gutmann states:

> For democratic education to support conscious social reproduction, all educable children must be educated. Nondiscrimination extends the logic of nonrepression, since states and families can be selectively repressive by excluding entire groups of children from schooling or denying them an education conducive to deliberation among conceptions of the good life and the good society. (Gutmann 1987, p. 45)

Following Gutmann we claim that irrespective of the tradition or context in which an individual articulates his/her aims, it must be the case that the aims (and their practical consequences) be neither repressive nor discriminatory and that they be directed toward developing students' deliberative character. Therefore, in addition to taking into account the tradition-specific claims, prospective teachers should recognize these democratic principled limits in their educational rationales. Some democratic basis, however minimal, exists upon which to discern and distinguish the merits of distinct educational proposals. In chapter 4 we will extend our discussion of the implications of these democratic principles. For now we simply want to highlight that under our schema of teacher education—that is, teacher education as the articulation of values, beliefs, and practices integral to various educational traditions—all aims are not acceptable and certain elements of specific traditions may be unacceptable.

Challenging cherished beliefs

Thus far we have been concerned with defending our proposal against criticisms that it either lapses into a gross relativism or searches for an indubitable foundational basis. But we want to elaborate how this goal of articulation relates to prospective teachers' initial beliefs and ideas about the educational and schooling process. We believe it is crucial that this reflective articulation of educational traditions both challenge and support future teachers' understandings of themselves as educators, the educational process, and the social and political context of schooling. The articulation of teacher roles within distinct traditions cannot be a simple affirmation of previously held conceptions and prejudices. Rather it must challenge prospective teachers' cherished notions and beliefs about teaching and schooling, and it must provide a context in which their future development as teachers can take place. All this brings us to another set of concerns: What is the relationship between the prospective teacher's initial beliefs about education *and* the traditions of educational thought and practice? Does the goal of articulation entail a critical examination of the prospective teacher's beliefs or of the tenets of his/ her preferred tradition?

It is clear to us that prospective teachers come to their professional education with a history of educational experiences as students. They have initial ideas about what it means to be a good teacher, what content ought to be taught, how it ought to be taught, and the kind of classroom ethos they would like to create. They do not walk into professional programs as blank slates but rather as former (and current) students and as individuals who have intuitions, ideas, and at times a lot of doubt about their own and others' educational ideas and practices. They come to learn how to teach, what to teach, and how to create an environment in which learning can take place. Somehow their professional education must eventually accord with their own reflectively examined felt sense of what it means to be a teacher. Many students have experienced teachers who engage in conservative, progressive, or, ever so often, radical educational practices. They have experienced what it means to be a student in these teachers' classes, and they frequently come to teacher education programs with particular teachers, if not particular orientations, in mind. We sense that the goal of articulation in educational deliberation requires an attentiveness to an individual's felt sense of what it means to be a teacher within the context of these traditions.

But this attention to the individual's felt sense is just the beginning. As we noted earlier it is important that prospective teachers see their beliefs and values not simply as expressions of individual choice or as the outcome of personal experience but rather as existing in relation to the communities or traditions of which he/she is a part. Many students come to their teacher education programs as "moral emotivists." That is, many prospective teachers sense that people's beliefs and values are simply expressions of preferences, attitudes, or feelings. Therefore it is initially important that students see the relationship between their individual values and the various communities and traditions of which they are a part. It is crucial for prospective teachers to come to see and believe that reasoned deliberation over educational values, beliefs, and practices can, and ought to, occur. Prospective teachers need to understand that they can examine their own and others' educational views and in the process gain an enhanced understanding of both their own and others' educational rationales. This sort of examination serves, then, as the "starting point from which [a] critical assessment of values becomes possible" (Lovin 1988, p. 148).

Students come to teacher education programs with a diverse set of values formulated in part by their family and local customs, religious and political traditions, and school experiences. In order to be able to develop their reason-giving abilities they need to relate their "personal convictions to the ideas and values of others who stand within the same tradition of thought" (Lovin 1988, p. 148). As Lovin maintains, "Values education must take as its starting point the mastery of this kind of thinking, in which one learns not to formulate and express individual preferences, but to identify the claims that a larger tradition of moral reflection makes on one's understanding and to assess one's plans and choices in light of those claims" (Lovin 1988, p. 148). This does not translate into an automatic affirmation of a tradition's particular beliefs, but instead requires a critical reflection and examination of individual beliefs in light of the tradition's claims *and* a critical examination of the tradition's precepts. Echoing John Rawls's (1971) notion of moral deliberation as a process of reflective equilibrium, Lovin states that

learning to assess one's plans and choices in the light of tradition does not mean that the tradition will always trump the

57

choices. The ways of thinking by which we arrive at our values involve a complex equilibrium between larger bodies of belief and more specific applications to cases. In that process, the tradition is more than an inert body of data. It can also be transformed in light of current experience, and one's stance toward it may turn out to be that of the prophetic revisionist rather than the dutiful disciple. . . .

A critical assessment of a person's moral beliefs will include not only the question of whether they are formed consistently within a tradition or traditions, but also the question of how they relate to the claims of other traditions that the person rejects or ignores. (Lovin 1988, pp. 149, 150)

It should be clear that the articulation of educational traditions is not a process of prejudice affirmation but rather can and should encourage a reflective examination of one's beliefs within and among traditions.

Conclusion

Finally we need to address, if only to anticipate subsequent chapters, the implications of the aim of articulation for our social-reconstructionist reform agenda in teacher education. We have argued that teacher education programs ought to enable prospective teachers to give sound reasons for their educational actions. Earlier we maintained that the social-reconstructionist reform tradition is the only reform agenda that gives adequate attention to the giving of reasons, the formulation of purposes, and the examination of how the institutional, social, and political context affects the formation of those purposes and the framing of the reasons. In this work we emphasize what the social-reconstructionist reform agenda has to offer the teacher educator and the prospective (and practicing) teacher. We do not propose that the social-reconstructionist focus be the only emphasis in a teacher education program. But we do maintain that it is a generally neglected perspective, and one that is sorely needed for today's teacher. Certainly a prospective teacher's education ought to include and highlight the differences among the various educational traditions. Our efforts are an attempt to reformulate, articulate, and legitimate central components of the social-reconstructionist agenda in teacher education.

From our perspective it is crucial that the prospective teacher be encouraged to reflect on his/her reasons, giving due and adequate attention to his/her implicit social beliefs and assumptions and proper recognition to our current understanding of the social and political context of schooling. This reflective examination needs to be accomplished both in the students' university course work and in their field experiences.[11] In programs of teacher education, university course work can further the goal of articulation and give a renewed emphasis to the social context of schooling. Teacher educators have at their disposal a wealth of knowledge and theoretical perspectives focused on the social and political context of schooling. Encouraging prospective teachers to examine this literature would, we believe, enable them to think not only about their own implicit social beliefs but also about the reality of schooling. In chapter 4 we will describe and outline a set of concerns on specific issues that we think ought to be examined by prospective teachers.

The other central component of teacher education programs, students' field experiences, can also focus students' attention on the implications of their social beliefs and encourage them to examine the social and political reality of schooling. In recent years it has become popular to ask prospective teachers to reflect on their practice. Two models of reflective inquiry, Gary Fenstermacher's (1986) practical argument model and Donald Schon's (1983) model of reflection on knowing-in-action, are frequently cited. Our sense is that neither model is adequately designed to enable prospective teachers to reflect on how the institutional, social, and political context affects teachers' actions or rationales. Individuals involved in social-reconstructionist reform efforts should be aware of how these models of reflective inquiry affect examinations of the social context of schooling and how they could be used to further such examinations. In the next chapter (chapter 3) we will examine the uses of these models of inquiry.

3

Teachers' Knowledge, Models of Inquiry, and the Social Context of Schooling

Introduction

Teaching is a messy affair, and learning to teach seems even messier. In the previous chapter we argued that teacher educators ought to aim at the articulation of prospective teachers' values and beliefs, and relate these values and beliefs to central educational traditions. If teacher educators are to enable future teachers to act wisely and ruminate about what constitutes good reasons for their educational actions, then reflection upon and inspection of personal beliefs, passions, values, images, and prejudices should occur. This inspection and reflection would be enhanced, we think, if it focused on one's location and participation within a particular educational tradition and challenged one's own beliefs through a comparison with distinctly different traditions. This articulation would facilitate an inspection of central educational values and, in doing so, would raise a host of other questions, dilemmas, and issues. As a result of this articulation one would begin to think about the descriptive, evaluative, and prescriptive assumptions that are brought to the educational endeavor.

The justification of educational actions, or plans of actions, depends not only on our values but also on our understanding of the pertinent "facts," the relevant contexts, the particular features of the setting at hand, and the conflicting demands felt at a particular juncture. Since the education of teachers ought to strive for some critical awareness of these features, it seems we cannot stop with the general goal of values articulation but should continue on. A reflective examination of our educational practices inevitably raises questions about our descriptive understanding of both particular and general educational situations.

When we reflect on our teaching, it is appropriate for questions about the students, the curriculum, the institutional setting, and the larger social role of schools to surface. Therefore, it seems that another central task for the teacher educator is to encourage the examination of and conversation about how our descriptive views of children, schools, and the larger community affect our educational actions.

Our view is that prospective and practicing teachers bring to the classroom implicit and unarticulated assumptions, beliefs, and values about the social context of schooling. This social knowledge (that is, teachers' knowledge and beliefs about the social, political, and historical context of schools and the communities that surround them) tends to be inadequately addressed in most accounts of teacher knowledge, is rarely examined in teacher education curricula, and is awkwardly handled in the prominent models for cultivating reflective thinking and action in teachers. It seems commonplace these days to accept the proposition that the social, political, and historical contexts of schooling have influenced classroom practices and school policies. It seems just as acceptable to claim that prospective and practicing teachers bring into their classrooms their own particular understanding of the students they teach and the social, political, and historical contexts of schooling. A teacher education program committed to the justification of educational actions would seemingly encourage both an inspection and reflection of teachers' implicit social and cultural beliefs, and an acquaintance with our present views and theories of the social context of schooling.

In this chapter we maintain that much of the research on teachers' knowledge tends inadequately to explore teachers' social beliefs. We take two fairly standard but somewhat opposing accounts of teachers' knowledge (what we term the "dismal" and "laudatory" views) and show that neither one gives much attention to teachers' social knowledge. We also show that the dismal view seems to overestimate while the laudatory view underestimates the effect of the institutional and larger societal contexts on how teachers teach. We then examine two prominent models of reflective thought and practice (Gary Fenstermacher's [1986 and 1987] notion of a practical argument and Donald Schon's [1983 and 1987] conception of reflection) showing that neither model seems to mine capably teachers' implicit assumptions and beliefs about the social conditions of schooling. If prospective teachers are going to be encouraged to give good reasons for their educational actions, they need to reflect on the social beliefs that undergird their teaching. Neither model examined in this chapter seems to be designed to focus on teachers' implicit social beliefs. But either could be used, if changes were made or their respective limitations were recognized. In the final section of this chapter we argue for the value of a teacher education program that encourages the examination of prospective teachers' social beliefs and for creating a teacher education curriculum that places greater emphasis on our current knowledge about the social, political, and historical contexts and conditions of schooling.

One final caveat is in order. Our work is concerned centrally with improving the practice of teacher education. In this endeavor we may be perceived as being preoccupied with an emphasis on knowledge as the salvific response to the woes of teacher education and teaching. Given this probable interpretation, we want to highlight our belief that knowledge is but one facet of intelligent or wise educational action. Passion, persistence, an enlivening vision, and at times a blindness to the acclaimed "facts," are all features of wise action. But since it seems that teacher educators and the research on teaching all too often ignore the social context of schooling to the detriment of teachers, teaching, and the educational process, we think our emphasis on knowledge is justified.

Teachers' knowledge

Teachers, as a group and a profession, are not known for their substantive or accumulated knowledge base. Dan Lortie (1975) and Phillip Jackson (1968) have argued that teachers lack technical expertise and professional knowledge. Many commentators view teachers as individuals who base their judgments and views on personal feelings and limited subjective experience. In this "dismal" view of teachers' knowledge, the teaching culture is said to be insular, reliant on custom and whim, and immune to thoughtful reflection. Margret Buchmann's (1987b) elaboration of the folkways of teaching is a recent and rather sophisticated delineation of this general perspective.

In contrast to the "dismal" view of teachers' knowledge, others such as Freema Elbaz (1983) and Michael Connelly and Jean Clandinin (1988) present a laudatory view of teachers' knowledge—one that maintains that teachers' practical and personal knowledge is rich, substantial, and reliable. They hold that the dismal view puts too great a value on scientific, research-oriented knowledge and not enough on teachers' practical knowledge and personal experiences. While these two views differ substantially in their respective appraisals of teachers' knowledge, both recognize the "subjective," interpersonal, and highly practical nature of teachers' knowledge. Neither spends much time elaborating or investigating teachers' implicit social beliefs and conceptions. We briefly elaborate both Buchmann's analysis of the "folkways" of teaching and Elbaz, Clandinin, and Connelley's descriptions of teachers' practical knowledge. With these descriptions as a basis for understanding current perspectives on teachers' knowledge, we can then move on to consider Gary Fenstermacher's (1986 and 1987) and Donald Schon's (1983 and 1987) proposals for reflective teaching.

In a recent article entitled "Teaching Knowledge: The Lights That Teachers Live By," Margret Buchmann (1987b) describes teachers' knowledge as essentially curtailed by and dependent on the folkways of teaching. In her view, teachers learn their craft through reliance on imitation, custom, habit, and tradition. This process is half-conscious and connects the biography of the individual teacher to the collective tradition of teaching. According to Buchmann, the folkways of teaching have the "practicality of common sense: prudence and astuteness in sizing up persons and situations and in adopting means to (given) ends without much cogitation. This practicality implies an 'objective chance of success' that makes people feel secure and capable" (Buchmann 1987b, p. 156). Quoting the phenomenologist Alfred Schutz, Buchmann relates that the folkways of teaching are akin to those cultural patterns whose function is to "eliminate troublesome inquiries by offering ready-made directions for use, to replace truth hard to attain by comfortable truisms, and to substitute the self-explanatory for the questionable" (Buchmann 1987b, p. 156).

Buchmann is not optimistic about altering the folkways of teaching, even though she contrasts it with the corrective of "teaching expertise." In her view, teaching expertise can build on the folkways but goes beyond the folkways by including " . . . (1) judgments of appropriateness, testing of consequences, and consideration of ends, not just means; and (2) less typical modes of practice, such as explanation, discussion and the deliberate management of value dilemmas by the teacher" (Buchmann 1987b, p. 154). Buchmann notes, however, that instances of teaching expertise seem to occur only on rare occasions, the result of character not cultivation. She also maintains that the frequency of teaching expertise is diminished by teachers' education and their workplaces. Teacher education does not hold much promise. In the past, it has not improved the chances that teaching expertise will flourish. Commonsensical orientations dominate professional courses for teachers and are balanced only with "useless" theory courses. Further induction into the folkways through student teaching and the workplace only serves to affirm the value of simplistic and routine solutions to complex problems. Summarizing her appraisal Buchmann notes that

> as things stand, opportunities for acquiring teaching expertise in the United States are scarce, and they are not institutionalized.
> The case of teaching is therefore shut for most intending teachers and likely to remain so. To be sure, they will learn more about teaching at the workplace and, for the most part, develop their private views. But these categories of teaching knowledge tend to arise by the methods and within the confines of the folkways. Expertise, as I have defined it, is as inaccessible to the majority of American teachers as the opportunity to become rich or to climb up the social ladder. (Buchmann 1987b, pp. 161–62)

In contrast to Buchmann's rather dim view of teachers' knowledge, Freema Elbaz (1983) and Michael Connelly and Jean Clandinin (1988) present what seems to be an almost laudatory view of teachers' knowledge. Reacting to the dismal view of teachers' knowledge, they maintain that teachers have a vast repertoire of "practical knowledge" based on personal and professional experiences, rooted in the problematics of everyday teaching, and integrated with theoretical knowledge about children and learning. They emphasize the need to see teachers as thinking and deliberative agents. Once this perspective is taken, they argue, not only is teachers' practical knowledge emphasized but the possibility for school reform is enhanced. When teachers are seen as dullards, dullness is likely to prevail. When teachers are construed as reflective and knowledgeable agents, change is more likely to occur. Although these authors' perspective on practical knowledge is rich and varied, they tend to emphasize a few key concepts. We focus on their concepts of "image" and "personal narrative."

Connelly and Clandinin explain that in designating the teachers' image as an essential element in teachers' practical knowledge, they are pointing to an image as

> . . . something within our experience, embodied in us as persons and expressed and enacted in our practices and actions.

Situations call forth our images from our narratives of experience, and these images are available to us as guides to future
action. An image reaches into the past, gathering up experien-
tial threads meaningfully connected to the present. And it
reaches intentionally into the future and creates new meaningfully connected threads as situations are experienced and new
situations anticipated from the perspective of the image. Thus
images are part of our past, called forth by situations in which
we act in the present, and are guides to our future. Images as
they are embodied in us entail emotion, morality and aesthet-
ics. (Connelly and Clandinin 1988, p. 60)

Some of the operating images that they found include viewing the
instructional process as the "planting of seeds," construing the classroom
as a "home," and viewing the school as a "community." Teachers and
principals acted with these images in mind. As a result of viewing
instruction as the "planting of seeds," one teacher derived both practical
principles and rules of action. She felt justified allowing children to
choose their own activities because she "knew they would learn in a
more interesting way" (Connelly and Clandinin 1988, pp. 65–66), and
she felt comfortable giving students ideas but not making them do the
work. Another teacher who viewed the classroom as a home felt that
classrooms and homes ought to have gardens where plant life can flourish. Both her own home and the classroom became places where "growing things" became an integral part of the daily life (Connelly and
Clandinin 1988, p. 61). And with one particular principal they

. . . came to understand him as having an image of "community" in which the school itself is a community as well as part
of the larger community with which it is in dynamic relationship. This image of "community" is an expression of a narrative unity in Phil's [the principal's] life. The image is not the
narrative unity. The narrative unity is composed of the threads
that connect Phil's image of "community" to his ongoing narrative. The threads are found in Phil's childhood and school experiences in inner-city Toronto, in his experiences on the Toronto islands as a child and as an adult in his first teaching
experience in the Island School. (Connelly and Clandinin 1988,
p. 76)

For these authors practical knowledge is a complex set of practically oriented understandings of self, instruction, subject matter, curriculum development and, at times, the larger social context.[1]

While the differences between Buchmann's and Connelly and Clandinin's and Elbaz's accounts are great, both perspectives view teachers' knowledge (at least in part) as an outcome of teachers' daily practices. And both perspectives see the value and potential (for Buchmann, admittedly a very limited potential) in asking teachers to reflect on their understandings and practices. And yet in neither account does the reader come away with any strong sense that these teachers have implicit or explicit beliefs and assumptions about their work in bureaucratic institutions, how that institutional context affects their teaching, or how their students' class or ethnic backgrounds affect how they teach. For the most part, teachers are not presented as having significant social, cultural, or political beliefs or assumptions. In addition, Buchmann's analysis portrays prospective and practicing teachers as lacking an important degree of resourcefulness and as being fully socialized into a habitual dullness by their inadequate professional preparation and workplace norms. In Clandinin and Connelly's depictions one gets the sense that the effect of these institutional forces is negligible, that teachers are very resourceful people.

As first approximations we sense that both views might very well present accurate descriptions of a range of teachers' practical knowledge and resourcefulness. Certainly there are teachers who utilize recipe approaches to complex problems, and there also are those teachers whose practical knowledge is quite sophisticated and thoughtful. And surely there are teachers who seem to have been "successfully socialized" by their professional preparation and workplace norms while others seem to be "untouched" by institutional constraints. But it seems odd that the research has shed little light on how teachers' implicit and explicit social, political, and cultural beliefs affect their educational deliberations. And it seems questionable to maintain that teachers are either total "dupes" of or fairly free from institutional constraints of work or their prior education. In a very real sense these are empirical questions, and ones worth pursuing.[2] But since our concern is with elaborating a program for teacher education reform, we will outline our basic assumptions and move on to examine Fenstermacher's and Schon's reflective models.

It seems clear to us that practicing and prospective teachers are rarely encouraged to examine their social beliefs nor are they encouraged to examine the institutional and societal constraints under which they work or the social conditions of schooling. If teachers and future teachers are to reflect on their educational actions, much of this reflection will certainly focus on events occurring within the classroom. But as almost any practicing teacher knows, the classroom is not an island unto itself. Consider these aspects of school life. Students walk into the classroom with biographies, cultural backgrounds, and a set of educational expectations in hand. In effect, students enter the schools all wrapped up in the conflicts, exigencies, and dilemmas of the world beyond the school walls. Most teachers seem aware that the adequacy or inadequacy of curriculum materials, building safety, and basic supplies can make or break an otherwise effective teacher. Frequently beginning teachers do not find their first jobs in schools that receive adequate funding, where pupils are "performing" at or above grade level, or where the match between home and school is a comfortable one. Furthermore, the school climate significantly affects teachers' work environments. Hostile, indifferent, or supportive staff relationships make for very different working conditions. First-year teachers can be overwhelmed by the complexities and politics of the workplace. Teachers' relationships with parents and the immediate community can enhance or obstruct the transitions between home and school life. All these factors, ones that are quite prominent in teachers' lives, usually appear only on the peripheries of academic accounts of teachers' knowledge. We want to give these aspects of teaching a greater pride of place, both within our general understanding of teachers and within the practices of teacher education. If prospective teachers are going to be able to provide good reasons for their educational actions, they must begin to account for and examine the constraints under which they will operate. If teacher educators are going to be honest about prospective teachers' futures, they need to recognize what the work of teaching entails.[3]

Unfortunately, most accounts of teachers' practical knowledge seem to give little emphasis to these cultural, social, historical, or political beliefs. If one examines the work of authors concerned with bridging educational knowledge and action (e.g., Joseph Schwab [1978], Alan Tom [1984], Gary Fenstermacher [1986] or Donald Schon [1983]) it becomes evident that little if any attention is paid to teachers' social beliefs. Certainly a lack of prominence does not constitute an inability to make connections between teachers' social beliefs and educational action, but the absence of any prominent concern bespeaks, we believe, an underestimation of the importance of teachers' social knowledge in educational action.

In the next section we describe briefly both Gary Fenstermacher's (1986 and 1987) and Donald Schon's (1983 and 1987) proposals for enhancing teachers' reflective examinations of their own practices, and we highlight the ways in which their proposals tend to underestimate the complexity of reflecting on the social context of teaching and schooling. While neither Fenstermacher nor Schon pays much attention to these contextual features, we think that both of their approaches (once their limitations are recognized) can be used to focus on the contextual aspects of teaching and teacher education.

Models of reflective inquiry

Fenstermacher's practical argument model

Gary Fenstermacher explains that his interest in practical arguments grew out of a search for a "plausible account of how the findings of educational research might relate to practice" (Fenstermacher 1988, p. 41). As a result of his work in this area he also came to believe that practical arguments represented "an excellent analytic device for helping teachers become more reflective practitioners" (Fenstermacher 1988, p. 45). Practical arguments, for Fenstermacher, became both the means to bridge research-produced knowledge with teachers' practice, and a tool for reflecting on that practice. Before we sketch Fenstermacher's view of practical arguments, their utilization of research knowledge, and their usefulness for reflection, we want to highlight key assumptions undergirding Fenstermacher's project. Fenstermacher maintains a sharp distinction between knowledge production and knowledge use. Specifically, he claims that researchers produce scientific knowledge which teachers can then use. In an earlier work (1986) he seemed to imply that most worthwhile knowledge is produced by scientific researchers, and it was the role of teachers to utilize that knowledge. But in a later work (1987), he had made it clear that both researchers and teachers produce knowledge, albeit knowledge of distinct types. For Fenstermacher, practitioner knowledge is knowledge born of practical experience, not knowledge created through "controlled" scientific research. But generally Fenstermacher's concern lies not with practitioner knowledge but with scientific research knowledge, that is, knowledge produced under conditions of "controlled inquiry, subject to publicly defensible cannons of epistemic adequacy" (Fenstermacher 1988, p. 44).

Fenstermacher's interest, then, is to examine the "links" between research-produced knowledge and teachers' actions and to enhance the ways in which teachers can reflect on their practice. Central to both of these endeavors is his notion of a practical argument:

By practical argument is meant a reasonably coherent claim of reasoning leading from the expression of some desired end state, through various types of premises to an intention to act in a particular way. Among the types of premises intervening between the expressions of an end state and an intention to act are those that are empirical, and those that are primarily situational in character. While there may be other types of premises these two types are sufficient to explain the notion of a practical argument." (Fenstermacher 1988, p. 41)

He goes on to state that situational premises describe specific circumstances, are context dependent, and are "required in order to complete the chain of reasoning from a desired end state to intention to act" (Fenstermacher 1988, p. 41). Empirical premises, on the other hand "express testable claims that teachers make about the way students learn. . . . and a host of other conceptions the teacher has that could be or have already been submitted to some form of empirical scrutiny" (Fenstermacher 1988, pp. 41–42). The empirical premises form the link between educational research and teachers' practices. Fenstermacher (who cites Thomas Green's work [1976]) states that the ". . . value of educational research for educational practice is the help it provides in 'identifying what is required to change the truth value of the premises of the practical argument in the mind of the [teacher], or to complete or modify those premises, or to introduce an altogether new premise into the practical argument in the mind of the [teacher]' " (Fenstermacher 1986, p. 43). For Fenstermacher, ". . . research bears on practice as it alters the truth or falsity of beliefs that teachers have, as it changes the nature of these beliefs, and as it adds new beliefs" (Fenstermacher 1986, p. 43). He gives the following example as an illustration of a practical argument.

1. As a teacher, I want to teach in ways that yield as much student learning as possible.

2. Well-managed classrooms yield gains in learning.
3. Direct instruction is a proven way to manage classrooms.
4. My students and I are together in this classroom.
   ACTION:
   I am organizing my class according to the principles of direct instruction.

Statement 1 is an expression of a general desired end state. Statements 2 and 3 are empirical premises. And statement 4 is a situational premise. The line of reasoning ends with an intention to act (Fenstermacher 1986, p. 43). Fenstermacher notes that in the example cited above the veracity of the empirical premises is not of interest, he is simply offering us an example.

Fenstermacher values practical arguments not only as a way to link educational research and practice, but also as a tool to enable teachers to reflect on their practice. Practical arguments, according to Fenstermacher, are useful in that they help "teachers gain a sense of the basis for their actions, and for helping teachers use defensible theory and good research to advance their pedagogical competence" (Fenstermacher 1987, p. 416). He adds that

. . . this happens when, for example, an inquirer in the classroom observes the teacher at length, trying to account for what the teacher does. From observations of and conversations with the teacher, the initial premises are developed. The teacher is encouraged to analyze them, in discussion with the inquirer, until a reasonably complete and coherent account of the teacher's thinking about the observed activity is in hand. Then the inquirer might raise questions with the teacher about the completeness of the argument, about its overarching moral goals, about the accuracy and soundness of its empirical claims, or about the teacher's description of the present situation. Such questions are intended to alert the teacher to possible re-interpretations, to different ways of perceiving the situation, to new evidence that might bear on the goals, or to value conflicts in the aspirations the teacher has for the students. (Fenstermacher 1987, p. 416)

Our present interest in Fenstermacher's notion of a practical argument lies in its potential use in teacher education: (1) to link research-produced knowledge about the social context of schooling to teachers' action, and (2) as a heuristic to examine the social beliefs and assumptions that inform prospective teachers' educational actions. With respect to these two uses, Fenstermacher seems to make two distinct claims. Regarding the linkages between research and teachers, he maintains that practical arguments—via the empirical premises—enable an examination of the truth value of empirical claims implicit in teachers' thinking. Purportedly, if educational research is to best benefit practice, it will accomplish this through improving the truth value of the empirical premises in teachers' minds. As a result of teachers examining the empirical premises in their practical arguments, they may begin to question the accuracy of their empirical claims. Fenstermacher's second claim is that practical arguments facilitate a general reflective examination of the moral, descriptive, and interpretive assumptions within teachers' thinking and give to their thinking a coherent form and ordering. In order to consider these uses and claims, we offer an example of a practical argument that contains implicit and explicit social assumptions.

It is not unusual in schools of education to encounter white, middle-class, prospective teachers whose rationales for educating urban African-American children follow this loosely formulated logic:

1. I want to treat my fourth-grade students equally and educate them so they are prepared to meet the demands of the adult world.
2. I teach language arts, and a significant number of my students are black.
3. These children do not speak standard English, and standard English is not encouraged at home.
4. This inability creates learning difficulties, and if these difficulties aren't resolved they will experience grave problems meeting the demands of an adult world.

ACTION:

I will correct my students' misuse of language in conversations and written assignments.

In the practical argument formulated above, statement 1 expresses a generally desired end state, statement 2 represents a situational premise, and statements 3 and 4 are empirical (and predictive) premises.

First we consider the merits of Fenstermacher's initial claim. The empirical propositions in the third and fourth premises could be interpreted in a variety of fashions. Further discussion with the prospective or practicing teacher would have to fill in the content of the premises. It may be that the student teacher has an implicit cultural-deprivation, cultural-difference, or bicultural understanding of the urban African-American culture.[4] According to the deprivation view, the black family evinces serious inadequacies: the communication between mother and child is deficient, and black students tend to be poorly motivated and unable to delay gratification. Such a view also tends to value "standard English" as the acceptable norm and one to which non-standard English speakers ought to be held. Grossly black culture is seen as deficient, and the implications are that black students need to reject important aspects of their culture and accept the norms and practices of the school.

According to the difference model, urban African-American and white middle-class cultures are distinct. The African-American language is seen as a "structurally differentiated variant" of the English language, and one that is coherent, rich, and highly expressive. Within this perspective, the African-American culture and relationships among individual family members are viewed not as deficient or pathological, but rather as different in kind (but not in value) from white middle-class culture.

The bicultural model shares many of the same interpretations and empirical claims of the difference model but maintains that cultural difference does not entail cultural monism. That is, people can live and operate in two distinct cultures. People can be bicultural. Adult African-Americans know and can operate in both their own and the white middle-class cultures.

These brief sketches are indeed oversimplifications of the respective social theories, but they should suffice to serve our purposes. It seems evident that the empirical premises within the practical argument noted above are not univocal; they could be interpreted to be in line with any one of the three generally elaborated social theories. Discussion with prospective teachers should make it clearer what position is being taken. But more important, it seems evident that when social beliefs are evoked in the empirical premises of practical arguments, they come enmeshed within interpretive frameworks. As such these "empirical" claims (teachers' social beliefs and assumptions) frequently contain both moral and political assessments. For example, deviations from standard English in the deprivation model tend to evoke claims of individual and group insufficiency, and result in proposals for the remediation of deviant individuals. In the difference model, the same phenomenon could easily be viewed as distinct but coherent and respectable language expressions from a member of a culture other than white middle class, and might result in a respectful recognition of difference with little need for any changes. Finally, from the bicultural perspective, the same phenomenon might be viewed as a distinct cultural expression and one that does not necessitate rejection in order to learn other language expressions.

Fenstermacher's claim that practical arguments highlight the presence of testable empirical claims within the empirical premises seems to overlook the nature and use of social beliefs within these empirical premises. Social beliefs are not amenable to easy tests of accuracy. Steven Lukes (1978) reminds us that "Social theories come in overall though not incommensurable, packages, involving [not only] method-ological and epistemological but also moral and political positions, which are therefore also at issue. . . ." (p. 98). African-American chil-dren's language use does not appear in a descriptively neutral way in most prospective teachers' practical arguments. And certainly very little social knowledge arrives in value-neutral packages. When knowledge claims and beliefs are part of larger social theories, then it seems that Fenstermacher's claim about the testability of empirical premises is not so easily satisfied.

In short, it seems clear that Fenstermacher values the practical argu-ment form for its ability to pinpoint and further scrutinize the veracity of the empirical premises in teachers' thinking. We sense that practical arguments are capable of highlighting teachers' social and political beliefs that bear on their practice (e.g., our examination of urban African-American language use). But it seems that the practical argument model cannot readily serve up teachers' implicit social beliefs for tests of accuracy. The examination of empirical claims about the social world is a complex process and one not facilitated by practical arguments. Rather than leading teachers to examine directly the accuracy of their implicit assumptions, the practical argument model may enable teachers to begin to consider how their moral, political, and epistemological assumptions affect their teaching and their work in schools.

Fenstermacher's second claim is that practical arguments are helpful analytical tools for highlighting the assumptions upon which teachers base their actions and that they render these assumptions in a coherent and understandable form. Practical arguments bring out the moral as-sumptions, the evaluative claims, and the implicit aims of the teacher's actions for reflective discussions. Our own sense, as we've already related, is that practical arguments can initiate a reflective examination of and highlight prospective teachers' underlying assumptions, but that potentially significant limitations result from the use of the practical argument model. In brief, we have reservations about the uses of practical arguments with prospective teachers.

Our reservations issue from two sources. From our experience, it seems that discussions taking the format and flavor of a debate or argument tend to put prospective teachers, especially student teachers, on the defensive. If an observer takes even a slightly aggressive stance, raising questions about underlying moral assumptions, implicit aims, or empirical assumptions, little reflective examination occurs. The student feels compelled to defend, rather than contemplate or discuss, his/her thoughts and actions. Teacher educators have noted how difficult it is to encourage even experienced teachers to examine their assumptions.[5] It seems possible that prospective teachers might find a conversational format rather than a probing elaboration of underlying assumptions more conducive to discussing their views. At issue here is whether the practical argument model is pedagogically appropriate. Given our experiences in teacher education and the recent literature focused on distinct and gendered ways of knowing, we think it reasonable to question the appropriateness of the practical argument format.[6] Students could view practical arguments as an adversarial form of inquiry, one in which an observer enters into the classroom to assail their logic and attack their use of evidence. Instead, what these students seem most open to is someone who empathetically understands their views and is willing to discuss their assumptions in a situation of trust. Certainly there is nothing "inherent" in the practical argument model itself that creates defensive reactions, but such reactions seem likely to arise and should be taken into account.

Our second reservation arises from our belief that practical arguments may not capture the complexity, ambiguity, and much of the conflict that underlies many teachers' thoughts about teaching. At times practical arguments seem to represent post hoc reconstructions whose purpose is to convince ourselves and others of the reasonable and justifiable quality of our rationales and actions rather than capturing the difficult, tenuous, and, at times, ambiguous nature of practical deliberation. When we teach and when we think about our teaching, we find ourselves caught in dilemmas, amidst conflicting educational aims, and between competing moral goals. Practical arguments do not seem to mine well this arena of conflict and ambiguity.[7] Further, if there are teachers whose practical knowledge relies—as Connelly and Clandinin (1988) and others maintain—on images and personal narratives, then it seems that the practical argument model does not capture adequately the "logic" of their deliberations. The narrative ordering of significant images is quite distinct from the logic of a practical argument. Again we are raising a pedagogical consideration. It seems that the use of the practical argument model may reasonably be viewed by prospective and practicing teachers as a hindrance rather than an aid. Certainly there are times when a logical ordering of claims and an emphasis on empirical premises can be illuminating. However, a singular reliance on the practical argument form would seem questionable.

Since one of our central concerns in this analysis has been to scrutinize the ability of practical arguments to encourage a reflective examination of social beliefs and assumptions, a summary assessment is in order. Fenstermacher's truth-testing claim seems to simplify and therefore misconstrue the complexity of the relationship between social beliefs and social theories. Frequently the empirical statements within the empirical premises of a practical argument are embedded within social theories. These frameworks give to the empirical claims particular interpretations, and these interpretations are usually infused with moral and political overtones. As such, the empirical premises are not amenable to simple tests or clear-cut examinations of accuracy. Fenstermacher's second reflective claim certainly has merit, but we have reservations about the use of practical arguments in clinical situations. As indicated in our example about cultural language use, practical arguments certainly can highlight the underlying social, moral, and political assumptions. But the potential effects of practical arguments on prospective teachers, and the ability of practical arguments to mine adequately the complexity of teachers' deliberations, merits some concern. Any reflective strategy will have its strengths and weaknesses. Certainly we value Fenstermacher's model of practical argumentation. As a heuristic tool it brings to the surface implicit assumptions and orders those assumptions in a logically coherent manner. Having noted both strengths and weaknesses of Fenstermacher's model we now turn to Donald Schon's conception of reflective practice.

Schon's reflection on knowledge-in-action

Whereas Fenstermacher focuses on research-produced knowledge, bracketing practitioner-produced knowledge, Schon (1983 and 1987) focuses almost exclusively on practitioner knowledge (or, as he prefers to call it, knowledge-in-action). And whereas Fenstermacher's practical argument model encounters problems handling adequately the ambiguity, conflicting aims, and moral dilemmas of educational action, Schon's "model" of reflection-in-action is designed with these particular features of practice in mind. Schon begins his clarification of knowledge-in-action by first creating a distinction between technical expertise and reflective practice. In order to understand the basic elements of his reflective model, it will be helpful first to sketch his view of technical expertise.

According to Schon technical practice is the most commonly accepted way of conceiving the relationship of professional knowledge to practice. In this view, the problems of educational practice are those that can be "solved through the selection from available means of the one best suited to established ends" (Schon 1983, pp. 39–40). Technical practice presumes the presence of a scientific fund of knowledge that serves as a basis for professional action. Knowledge is related to practice through both an engineering component and a skills and attitudinal component. In this approach, knowledge should be applied skillfully with attention paid to the demands of the situation and carefully with attention paid to the human factors.

Schon argues that this technical perspective misconstrues the reality of knowledge-in-action. It ignores the process of problem setting, focusing exclusively on problem solving. It also mistakenly assumes that the ends of practical action are "fixed and clear" (Schon 1983, p. 41). Elaborating further, he argues that the emphasis on problem solving ignores

. . . the process by which we define the decisions to be made, the ends to be achieved, the means which may be chosen. In real-world practice, problems do not present themselves to the practitioners as givens. They must be constructed from the materials of the problematic situations which are puzzling, troubling, and uncertain. (Schon 1983, pp. 39–40)

With respect to the ends of action he maintains that

When ends are fixed and clear, then the decision to act can present itself as an instrumental problem. But when ends are confused and conflicting, there is as yet no "problem" to solve. A conflict of ends cannot be resolved by the use of techniques derived from applied research. It is rather through the non-technical process of framing the problematic situations that we organize and clarify both the ends to be achieved and the possible means of achieving them. (Schon 1983, p. 41)

Schon then characterizes the dilemma that any professional practitioner must face:

> In the varied topography of professional practice, there is a high, hard ground where practitioners can make effective use of research-based theory and technique, and there is a swampy lowland where situations are confusing "messes" incapable of technical solution. The difficulty is that the problems of the high ground, however great their technical interest, are often relatively unimportant to clients or to the larger society, while in the swamp are the problems of the greatest human concern. Shall the practitioner stay on the high, hard ground where he is constrained to deal with problems of relatively little social importance? Or shall he descend to the swamp where he can engage the most important and challenging problems if he is willing to forsake technical rigor? (Schon 1983, p. 42)

Schon's answer is, of course, that we need to enter the swampy lowlands.

Schon's alternative to technical expertise is reflective practice, but even more specifically, reflection on knowing-in-action. He begins with the assumption that much of our everyday knowledge is tacit and implicit. We follow routines that work and we tend to have some sense about why they work. Reflecting on knowing-in-action usually begins when something troubling or puzzling occurs, and the individual tries to make sense of it. According to Schon, ". . . as he [the reflective practitioner] tries to makes sense of it, he also reflects on the understandings which have been implicit in his action, understandings which he surfaces, criticizes, restructures and embodies in further action" (Schon 1983, p. 50). When these problems appear the practitioner is called upon to "set the problem," to try to find out what is wrong in the situation, what makes sense, what coherence can be imposed on the situation, and how to act next. "Problem setting is a process in which, interactively, we name the things to which we will attend and frame the context in which we will attend to them" (Schon 1983, p. 40). In Schon's view practitioners build up repertoires of "examples, images, understandings and actions" which they utilize to both set and frame the problem at hand (Schon 1983, p. 38).

When a practitioner makes sense of a situation he perceives to be unique, he sees it as something already present in his repertoire. To see this site as that one is not to subsume the first under a familiar category or rule. It is, rather, to see the unfamiliar unique situation as both similar to and different from the familiar one. . . . From the repertoires of examples, images, descriptions, they have derived (by seeing-as) a way of framing the present, unique situation. They try then to shape the situation to the frame; and they evaluate the entire process by . . . whether they can solve the problem they have set; whether they value what they get when they solve it (or what they can make of what they get); whether they achieve in the situation a coherent artifact and idea, a congruence with their fundamental theories and values; whether they can keep inquiry moving. (Schon 1983, p. 141)

Integral to furthering this process of inquiry are a variety of "experiments": exploratory, move-testing, and hypothesis-testing experiments. In these experiments the practitioner tries out different ways of construing and setting the problem, acts in the situation, and then "listens" to how the situation responds. We need not distinguish these different types of experiments; for our purposes, it suffices to note that throughout all these moves, the central concern for the practitioner is to change the situation, to transform the ". . . situation from what it is to something he likes better." Frequently Schon portrays this desire for transformation as a need for immediate transformability—that is, the process he describes focuses on a single individual whose purpose is to change the immediate situation (Schon 1983, pp. 152–53).

At this point an example might prove helpful. Schon relates an incident in the Teachers Project at the Massachusetts Institute of Technology in which teachers were encouraged to explore their own thoughts about simple topics in subjects they taught—for example, math, physics, and music (Schon 1983, pp. 66–68). As a result, the teachers allowed themselves to become confused about subjects they supposedly "understood," and subsequently they tried to work their way out of this confusion. One outcome of this process was that teachers began ". . . to think differently about learning and teaching." Schon relates a specific example in which two teachers were asked to view and react to a videotape of two boys playing a game. The game involved one boy relating to a second boy the pattern and configuration of blocks that lay before him. The two boys were separated by an opaque screen, and the second boy had blocks in front of him but in no particular order. As the boys progressed it soon became apparent that the boy who was to receive the instructions had "gone astray." In their initial viewing of the video the teachers noted that there seemed to be a "communication problem" between the boys, that the boy giving the instructions had 'well-developed verbal skills,' while the boy receiving the instructions had been "unable to follow directions." Then one of the researchers pointed out that she had heard the first boy tell the second one to pick up a green square (none of the squares were green—all squares were orange and all green blocks were triangles). When the teachers viewed the videotape again, they were amazed. They now saw that one minor mistake had set off all the resulting confusion. The teachers no longer saw the second boy receiving the instructions as inept or unable to follow directions. Where previously they had perceived the boy as "unable to follow directions," they now were able to discern the reasons for the boy's errors. Initially the teachers framed the problem as one of individual inability, but then they allowed themselves, like Schon's reflective practitioner, to

> . . . experience surprise, puzzlement, or confusion in a situation which he finds uncertain or unique. He reflects on the phenomena before him, and on the prior understandings which have been implicit in his behavior. He carries out an experiment to generate both a new understanding of the phenomena and a change in the situation. (Schon 1983, p. 68)

As a result of the researcher's observation of the problematic instructions, the teachers reframed the situation and saw the interaction differently.

Donald Schon's approach to reflective practice takes into account the contingent, dilemma-filled, and conflict-ridden features of educational action. His approach touches on and illuminates many features of teachers' knowing-in-action and their potential reflection on that knowing-in-action. The concepts of teachers' repertoires, and the notions of problem setting and framing are rich. They appear to illuminate much of what we know about our own and others' practices. However one of our central concerns has been to examine the power of Schon's approach to enable prospective and practicing teachers to reflect on their implicit social beliefs and assumptions and to encourage the examination of knowledge focused on the social context of schooling. With respect to these concerns our assessment is mixed.

Schon's reflective model seems much too narrowly focused. For Schon there are four "constants" in reflection, four sets of background assumptions that are relatively stable and provide practitioners with the "solid references from which, in reflection-in-action" they can examine their theories and frames (Schon 1983, p. 270). These constants include:

- the media, languages, and repertoires that practitioners use to describe reality and conduct experiments
- the appreciative systems they bring to the problem setting, to the evaluation of inquiry, and to reflective conversation
- the overarching theories by which they make sense of phenomena
- the role frames within which they set their tasks and through which they bound their institutional settings. (Schon 1983, p. 270)

In Schon's account of reflective inquiry these four constants provide the backdrop to reflection on knowledge-in-action. While Schon maintains that they are amenable to change through reflection, he does not elaborate further the evolution or alteration of these "constants" (Schon 1983, p. 275). From our vantage point, these constants represent unquestioned assumptions that frequently contain significant implicit social beliefs and preconceptions. For example, by excluding from reflection the languages that practitioners use to describe reality, we effectively exclude an examination of the language of individualism that pervades many professional discussions. By treating as a background constant the overarching theories through which practitioners make sense of phenomena, we cannot examine, as we did utilizing Fenstermacher's model, prospective teachers' implicit deficit, difference, or bicultural views of African-American language. And finally, by excluding the role frames within which practitioners define their tasks and their institutional setting, we do not have available alternative views of the teacher's tasks and responsibilities. For those teachers who view teaching as essentially action confined to the classroom, we cannot consider the teacher's role as either an institutional change agent or a community activist.

Not only does Schon overlook the value of inspecting these constants but he also tends not to examine his own. As we noted, one of Schon's four constants is the way people construe their role within an institution. In our example we contrasted two role frames (teacher as classroom actor versus teacher as institutional change agent or community activist). Throughout Schon's work he tends to view practitioners as individuals engaged in a reflective practice over which they, as individuals, have the power to change. In essence, Schon operates and presents us with a role frame that is quite narrowly focused. Its focus is on the individual and assumes situations amenable to fairly immediate change. Such a focus is much too narrow. Competent reflective practice presupposes both an institutional setting conducive to a reflective orientation and a role frame that values collective reflection and collective action oriented toward altering not only the interactions within the classroom and the school, but also between the school and the immediate community, and the school and larger societal structures.

Schon is not oblivious of the institutional component. In fact, he states that "A practitioner who reflects-in-action tends to question the definition of his task, the theories-in-action that he brings to it, and the measures of performance by which he is controlled. And as he questions these things, he also questions elements of the organizational knowledge structure in which his functions are embedded" (Schon 1983, p. 337). Schon also states that "Life in the bureaucratic system of a school would be included, as teachers begin to experience the difficulties of (for example) seriously listening to children in an actual classroom" (Schon 1987, p. 323). But even though Schon recognizes that reflective practices will ultimately confront institutional constraints, his reflective process (as currently elaborated) cannot adequately examine those constraints. To adequately reflect on these constraints, practitioners need to question their role frames, appreciative systems, and overarching theories. Given Schon's penchant for individual action and his tendency to treat the four "constants" as backdrops to reflection, it seems unlikely that these social and institutional constraints can become proper objects of reflection.

To be capable of examining these institutional obstacles, Schon's individualistic and action-oriented role frame would have to expand to include more collaborative action and deliberation and less of an emphasis on only those changes that teachers can make within the classroom. In order for Schon's approach to be used to reflect on the social context of schooling, the four "constants" could no longer be treated as constants. They, too, would have to become objects of reflection. Admittedly

Schon was not attempting to outline a process for social and institutional change. His concerns focus more on individual practices, and in these areas he seems quite insightful. But our sense is that in order for competent reflective practice to occur within schools, the conditions of schooling would have to be examined and ultimately changed. In the final section of this chapter we argue that in teacher education there is much social knowledge to take into account and there are good reasons for doing so.

Social beliefs, interpretive frameworks and teacher education

Thus far (in chapters 2 and 3) we have argued that teacher educators ought to aim at the articulation of prospective teachers' educational values and beliefs so that they can formulate good reasons for their educational actions. As a part of this articulation we have claimed that prospective teachers' assumptions and beliefs about the social context of schooling should become more explicit and that alternative interpretive frameworks ought to be examined. We have maintained that research into teachers' knowledge does not mine adequately teachers' social beliefs and that the current models of reflective inquiry do not seem effectively designed for such investigations.

As a part of this critical examination of social beliefs, three concerns seem particularly pertinent: How accurate are these assumptions and beliefs? How do they cohere and articulate with other beliefs, values, and assumptions? and How morally and politically justifiable are these beliefs and values? The goal of this examination is not a totally coherent and fully integrated belief system, absolutely free of ambiguity and contradiction. That would not be feasible. Instead the goal is for prospective and practicing teachers to gain some sense of what their beliefs are, to examine their degree of accuracy and justifiability, to consider alternatives, and to gain a sense and appreciation of their own and others' implicit and explicit social views. This task becomes particularly important with prospective teachers. Prospective teachers come to their professional education with years of experience within the educational system and plenty of familiarity with teachers. This experience and familiarity is conducive to taking the existing system of schooling and interaction within the classroom for granted.[8] It is not conducive to a critical examination of the existing system. As Susan Florio-Ruane argues, "To become a professional teacher requires reexamination and transformation of what is already known. It is necessary to know, assess, and [perhaps] change one's tacit knowledge about schooling if one is to make reasoned pedagogical choices in creating a classroom community" (Florio-Ruane 1989, pp. 164). A corollary to this reexamination of beliefs, we think, is the recognition that classrooms and schools are not islands unto themselves. Sara Lawrence Lightfoot (1978) reminds us of this fact when she states:

> The teacher, although establishing a central and dominant role in the classroom, lives within the constraints and boundaries of the institutional norms of the school and has very minimal autonomy and self-defining power. Her ability to transform her classroom environment and to change deeply established patterns of interaction are always limited by the explicit rules and implicit assumptions of the school's collective life. (Lightfoot 1978, p. 4)

She adds that:

> the social system and the life of the school are shaped by the sociopolitical and economic structure of the community of which it is a part. Great disparities exist in the education and schooling offered to children from various communities that are reflective of differences in race, ethnicity, and social class. These glaring disparities not only represent economic inequities but also differences in political realities, cultural idioms, and ethnic histories. These powerful structural and societal forces surround schools and deeply touch the lives of teachers and children. (Lightfoot 1978, pp. 4–5)

This reflection on our understanding of the social, cultural, and political context of schooling is important for both educational and instrumental reasons. First we elaborate the educational reasons and then we move on to the instrumental ones. If we expect students to develop reasoned and reasonable justifications for their educational actions, then the beliefs or assumptions about the social world that undergird their current justifications ought to be inspected. For example (and as we noted earlier) many prospective and beginning teachers believe that African-American urban school children's language use needs to be corrected. They maintain, very generally, that these children do not speak standard English, that standard English is not encouraged at home, and that this lack of acquaintance and familiarity with standard English creates learning difficulties. In addition, they tend to claim that if these learning difficulties are not resolved the children will experience grave problems meeting the demands of an adult world. Now, as we related earlier, such students might hold widely divergent views of African-American urban cultures. It may be that the student has an implicit cultural deprivation, cultural difference, or bicultural understanding of these urban cultures. These are very distinct views. Prospective teachers ought to be aware of the implications of their own assumptions and cognizant of alternative frameworks.

Reflecting on and choosing among alternative social and political interpretive frameworks (theories) is not simply a matter of the accuracy of the respective theories (although accuracy must be among the key concerns), or a matter of which framework seems generally more appealing, but more crucially the choice seems to turn on considerations about the type of teacher and person an individual wants to become, the type of education he/she wants to offer, and the type of school in which he/she wants to work. All too often, it seems, prospective teachers and teacher educators view social, cultural, and political theories as mere window dressing for the real focus of classroom action. These theories are seen as potentially interesting interpretive frameworks but not connected in any meaningful way to classroom action, much less teachers' lives. Unfortunately this view misconstrues the very real sense in which one's social beliefs affect and reflect the image of who one is and who one wants to become both within the classroom and the larger social world. We walk around in this world with implicit interpretive frameworks, what Sara Lawrence Lightfoot calls "cultural images" (1978). Lightfoot maintains that "No matter how teachers might try to separate and isolate the classroom environment from the surrounding community life, the sociocultural and political perspectives of teachers (and children) pervade the atmosphere and [partially but importantly] shape the course of events" (Lightfoot 1978, pp. 7–8). She also states that we must begin to appreciate

the determining power and momentum of social and cultural imagery. The individuals involved in negotiating the bridges and boundaries of families and schools are greatly influenced by the socio-historical and cultural forces that incorporate their lives. This is not to say that parents, teachers and children are the helpless victims of a predetermined fate or that individual initiative and interpersonal exchange are meaningless and hopeless gestures, but rather that interpersonal and intrapsychic issues exist within the context of encompassing belief systems and enduring [societal and political] structures. (Lightfoot 1978, p. 176)

If one of the characteristics of educated teachers is a concern for the coherence, accuracy, consequences, and justifiability of their belief systems, then it would seem that reflection on such matters is important. And if one of the educational goals of teacher education is to enable future teachers to construct reasonable and justifiable professional identities, then it seems that their implicit social beliefs should be identified and scrutinized. There are numerous curricular and programmatic avenues for such reflection and construction, and in subsequent chapters (chapters 4 and 6) we address these avenues more substantively.

Obviously we think it important that students be presented with alternative visions of what schools and teaching could be like. However we do not think that this reflection should focus only on prospective teachers' implicit social beliefs with the sole goal of enabling them to choose and articulate their educational position in a more clear, substantive, and justifiable manner. We also think it instrumentally valuable for prospective teachers to examine our extant knowledge about the social conditions of schooling so that they might begin to consider if, and if so how, institutional and societal dynamics affect the implementation of their aims and educational programs. If novice teachers are to begin to master the basic rudiments of the craft and act as professionals in the service of the twin values of excellence and equality, then it seems that these teachers must be acquainted with, and be able to analyze and eventually alter, particular institutional instructional arrangements and working conditions. They should also be capable of acting in concert with other teachers and community members to alter significant societal or political dynamics. In short, it seems advantageous for future teachers to understand how the institutional and larger societal context encourages or obstructs their chosen educational aims.

If a prospective elementary teacher intends to utilize ability grouping in her reading instruction, she ought to be aware of the practices connected with, the critiques, and the unintended consequences of such grouping. For example, the prospective teacher ought to know that researchers (e.g., Hallinan 1984) have found that the type of instruction differs across ability groups and tracks. In lower groups more time is spent on noninstructional tasks, the material is covered at a much slower pace, and the teachers spend less time preparing for these groups. Furthermore it has been found that "student social status differs across and within tracks and ability groups" (Hallinan 1984, p. 231). Students in higher-level ability groups tend to be more popular than their peers, and students in the lower-level ability groups are held in less esteem. Prospective teachers should also know that ability groups is a "deterrent to learning for such students assigned to lower groups" (Hallinan 1984, p. 232). In addition to these claims, which focus on ability grouping as a classroom phenomenon, research has been conducted that connects ability grouping to the larger social order. Relating tracking to social class, Jeannie Oakes (1985) has argued that as a result of tracking (1) students of distinct social-class positions are presented with qualitatively distinct curricula, (2) students of privileged backgrounds receive curriculum that is of a higher status, and (3) this differential distribution of knowledge allows these students greater access to social and economic power. If prospective teachers choose ability grouping as an instructional approach, they ought to be aware of these findings and ought to be capable of examining their own school sites.

On the other hand, if a prospective teacher comes to believe that ability grouping is a major impediment to high-quality and fair instruction, then he/she should know that many teachers believe ability grouping to be an efficient means of distributing educational resources to students of differential ability—even though, at times, they may feel uncomfortable grouping students. The prospective teacher should also know that institutionally, ability grouping allows students to be tracked through a school-wide or district-wide reading program. Bureaucratically this is said to be an advantage. And furthermore he/she should know that, historically, ability grouping has lent credence to the notion that schools operate meritocratically and has helped to legitimate schools as social sorters. If a new teacher wanted to alter the practice of ability grouping in his/her classroom (or school), an understanding of these features would certainly be pertinent. In short, it seems instrumentally advantageous for future teachers to understand how the existing institutional practices and politics encourage or obstruct their chosen educational aims.

We have outlined instrumental and educational reasons for why prospective teachers should examine their own implicit social beliefs and our extant knowledge about the social context of schooling. Our educational and instrumental rationales, while analytically distinct, are pragmatically intertwined. A teacher education program that takes seriously the social context of schooling would have students examine current theories about the social context of schooling and would expect both a reflective inspection (and articulation of) individual beliefs and assumptions, and an examination of potential obstacles. During student teaching and other practice teaching experiences, students should be asked to reflect on their own assumptions and beliefs with a view to further articulating and justifying their views, and efforts should be made to link available knowledge about the social context to their experiences in order to highlight potential obstacles to their chosen educational orientation. When prospective teachers begin to examine our extant knowledge about the social context of schooling, either with an eye to a further articulation of their own beliefs or to an examination of institutional and societal constraints, they will be confronted with questions of empirical accuracy, moral persuasiveness, and political acceptability. We do not think there is a simple or easy calculus through which prospective teachers can discern the respective value of distinct social or educational theories. But we do think that the examination is not only worthwhile, but also necessary. Before we close this chapter, we will present an abbreviated example of one such comparison.

As we noted earlier, it is possible to find various interpretations about the effects and sources of tracking. For example, Maureen Hallinan (1984) argues that although ability grouping, as currently practiced, seems to incur deleterious effects, tracking does not necessarily create harmful consequences. The problem seems to lie with the way in which teachers have implemented it. She argues that ability grouping is a reasonable instructional design and can be effectively and fairly implemented. Jeannie Oakes (1985), on the other hand, takes a somewhat opposite stance. She argues that ability grouping is academically and politically unjust, and connected to the inequities of a larger social order. The problem, for Oakes, does not lie simply with the way in which teachers have implemented ability grouping but rather with the social context of schooling.

A prospective teacher examining these two views should be taught a way to compare them effectively. The differences between Hallinan and Oakes seem to lie not so much in their respective judgments that tracking (as currently practiced) harms and enables distinct children, but rather in how widely they construe the relevant context, their different moral views concerning what constitutes a just instructional design, and their sense about the teacher's role in all of this. Hallinan (1984) appears to view tracking as a strictly institutional, if not solely classroom, phenomenon. She does not consider the ways in which tracking may be connected to larger societal forces. She also maintains that while tracking currently produces harmful and unjust consequences, it need not be that way. She seems to imply that individual merit and individual abilities deserve their proper educational reward. If someone is more talented than someone else, ability grouping allows that individual to succeed. As a result, Hallinan construes teachers as being capable of rectifying the negative effects of tracking. Oakes (1985) clearly considers a much wider social and political context than Hallinan, linking the negative effects of tracking to an unequal and unjust social and political order. She seems to support a view of justice which claims that any form of instructional design that perpetuates invidious distinctions, based on social advantage or even individual "merit," requires wholesale rejection. For Oakes, ability grouping ought to be abandoned. Teachers, while they can support and encourage such rejection, would clearly have to convince others—an effort that would involve (most probably) teachers, parents, administrators, and community members.

For prospective and practicing teachers who have not looked at schools with an eye to their social context, the results can be both enlightening and disturbing. In effect, by claiming to tell us what is really going on, these theories can challenge and upset our "normal self-descriptions, either through identifying an unperceived causal context of our action, or by showing that it has a significance that we fail to appreciate" (Taylor 1983, p. 68). Such effects can be both educational and instrumental. In the next chapter we will describe curricular content, focusing on the social context of schooling, which would facilitate both educational and instrumental considerations.

4

Bringing the Social Context of Schooling into Teacher Education

Introduction

In the previous chapter we argued that Gary Fenstermacher's and Donald Schon's proposals are not adequately designed to examine the contextual features of schooling and teaching. Fenstermacher's focus on the assessment of teachers' empirical knowledge appears to us to be too simplistic when we examine prospective teachers' social and political beliefs. Schon's model of reflecting on knowing-in-action treats social knowledge as a set of background assumptions, not as the proposed focus of reflection. Neither approach seems designed to give adequate attention to prospective teachers' beliefs about the social, political, and cultural context of schooling. It is clear that both Fenstermacher's and Schon's models of inquiry were designed to engage teachers in a reflective examination of their practice. In teacher education, these models of inquiry would be used to enable prospective teachers to examine their own educational actions in their field or practicum settings. While we have noted that both models are limited in their ability to reflect on teachers' social and political beliefs, we have also maintained that both models of inquiry (once they are appropriately altered) could encourage a reflective examination of teachers' understanding of the social context of schooling. But there remains another central component of teacher education programs, university course work, that could also enhance further inquiry into the social and political context of schooling. Since most teacher education programs do not give much attention to the social, political, and cultural context of schooling—because most programs are by our standards much too narrowly focused—we believe this area deserves further attention (Borman 1990).

This sort of narrow focus is not unusual. Commentators have noted the tendency of educational scholars and teachers (and some might add, the general population) to examine situations within narrow rather than wider purviews. Seymour Sarason (1971) wrote twenty years ago that "so many of us are intellectually reared on a psychology of the individual: that is, we learn, formally or informally, to think and act in terms of what goes on inside the heads of individuals. In that process it becomes increasingly difficult to become aware that individuals operate in various social settings that have a structure not comprehensible by our existing theories of individual personality" (Sarason 1971, p. 12). Many of us seem to rely on such individualistic orientations. We operate with a folk psychology that attempts to understand educational phenomena through examining the actions and intentions of individuals while giving only a limited recognition to the influences of the social context. If we can explain an occurrence in the classroom by appealing to the actions and intentions of the teacher, student, or any other relevant actor, then we feel as if we have understood and adequately explained the situation.

It seems we have an interest in examining problems in this individualistic manner. If we can understand a situation in terms of the individuals involved, then we sense that we are able to "explain ourselves to ourselves; to see what it feels like to be in someone else's shoes" (James 1984, p. 156). As social actors (especially as teachers) we like to think that we are autonomous, capable of "bringing about events and states of affairs which would not otherwise have occurred" (James 1984, p. 156). And it seems that in order to be effective teachers, we have to feel that we can make a difference. We want to believe that we can contribute, in some positive way, to our students' educational growth.

Many prospective teachers are attracted to teaching because they think they can make that difference (Zimpher 1989). They think they can "make their mark" on students by closing the classroom door and keeping the students to themselves. Many of us who have gone into elementary and secondary teaching felt initially that we could protect ourselves and our students from the world beyond the school. But we soon realized that we could neither insulate ourselves nor our students. It is as if the social realities of the world seep in under the door and enter through the public-address system. It is simply impossible to isolate classroom life from the school's institutional dynamics, the ever-present tensions within the community, and the larger societal forces. As former elementary teachers and now as teachers of teachers, we rarely have found the individualistic orientation to provide an adequate account of classroom life. In order to act effectively we have had to recognize the influence of the social context. In order to bring about a desired state of affairs, we have had to examine the societal structures in which students live and teachers work. And while we have come to understand that the individualistic account is woefully inadequate, we have also come to realize that little else is offered to prospective teachers.

In commenting on their own preparation for teaching, Sara Freedman, Jane Jackson, and Katherine Boles (1986) have written that it

> emphasized the individual contribution by caring teachers whose dedication could significantly alter and improve schools. These books [written by the radical romantics of the 1960s] had inspired us as we entered teaching and provided a standard by which we had been judging ourselves and our fellow-teachers. Nothing in these books mentioned the powerful influences of the structure of schools on the relationship between the teacher and the child, principal, parent, or specialist. (Freedman et al. 1986, p. 3)

They add that

> Teachers who one by one enter the profession remain largely unaware of the institutional nature of school systems and are, therefore, ill-prepared to handle conflicts that arise from the nature of that institutional structure. The teacher's position within the school system as a whole is not seen as a professional concern and the institutional conflicts inherent in the role of the teacher remain unchallenged. (Freedman et al. 1986, p. 57)

Theoretically and pragmatically many prospective teachers sense that they must choose either an individualistic orientation that gives them a sense of autonomy and hope, or acquiesce in a sense of cynicism and despair that results from looking holistically at the constraining and "determining" societal context. When posed in this way, it is easy to see what any reasonable teacher would choose. The individualistic orientation gives teachers some hope. But as in most dichotomous depictions, we think there are other ways of construing the situation. In this chapter we view the teacher as one of many actors involved in the educational lives of their students, educational actors who respond to social and institutional constraints and attempt to affect changes in their own and their students' lives. Theoretically, the relation of the individual to societal processes has not been "solved" by anyone in the social sciences. We certainly do not presume to come up with any magical solution. In the next chapter (chapter 5) we will outline a research orientation that might help to examine this situation. In the present chapter we simply present a set of larger concerns and more specific issues which we believe will encourage prospective teachers and teacher educators to think about the context of schooling in ways that will enable them to develop more powerful educational plans and rationales. If one of the central aims of a teacher education program is to enable future teachers to give good reasons for their educational plans, and if these plans must take into account the social realities of schooling, then teacher educators must figure out sound ways to encourage a reflective examination of these realities. We think what follows is a sound, suggestive, and powerful approach for teacher educators. First we develop a brief rationale for our proposal, and then we present examples of the type of concerns and issues a teacher education curriculum focused on the social context of schooling might include.

A curricular rationale

In any reasonable educational agenda, decisions concerning curriculum selection and organization have to be made. Decisions about what knowledge should be included and, as a result, what knowledge will be excluded become prominent. Concerns about how the curriculum ought to be organized should be addressed. And a rationale for the chosen curricular organization and selection ought to be formulated. It seems reasonable to expect that this process should be guided by an understanding of articulated educational aims. With respect to these expectations, a teacher education proposal is like any other educational plan. Therefore, we need to sketch a bit of our rationale.

Thus far, we have argued that teacher educators ought to aim at the articulation of prospective teachers' educational values and beliefs. As a part of this articulation of beliefs and values, we have claimed that prospective teachers' beliefs about the social context of schooling should be made explicit and alternative frameworks examined. This examination, we have claimed, is important for both educational and instrumental reasons. The examination of social beliefs and frameworks enables prospective teachers to become more critically aware of their own assumptions and cognizant of alternative frameworks. Such an examination also enables them to see more clearly and alter, if they choose, the social beliefs integral to their professional identity. In a more instrumental vein it is advantageous for future teachers to see how the social context of schooling, teachers' work conditions, and the schools' institutional policies might facilitate or obstruct their chosen educational aims.

In chapter 2 we stressed that there seemed to be a great deal of acceptable diversity among educational aims and values (e.g., the central tenets of the three educational traditions). But we also maintained that our commitment to a democratic way of life constrains our educational aims (and therefore our curricular selection) in three important ways. Our aims cannot support either repressive or discriminatory educational proposals; they must attempt to encourage the development of a democratic, deliberative character in students. These democratic tenets also affect our examination of the social context of schooling. If prospective teachers clearly hold social beliefs that are conducive to repressive or discriminatory educational practices or if they deny the deliberative character goal, then those beliefs ought to be examined. If the social conditions of schooling clearly include features that contribute to either repressive or discriminatory educational practices, then those features ought to be recognized and altered. Minimally it seems that teacher educators must enable prospective teachers not only to formulate good reasons for their educational plans but also to identify those social beliefs and conditions of schooling that are obstacles to a democratic education. In this chapter we examine the social context of schooling, utilizing our democratic criteria. We present three analyses of particular social conditions (e.g., highlighting racial discrimination, gendered repression, and the poor working conditions of teachers) that obstruct democratic aims. Now it would seem that for each articulation of educational aims (e.g., conservative, progressive, and radical aims) there will be particular professional beliefs and social conditions that require some attention. For example, an educator committed to the progressive goal of an integrated, project-oriented curriculum would want to know what obstacles might obstruct the creation and implementation of a subject-integrated curriculum. A teacher with a more "conservative" orientation would want to know what obstacles she might confront in implementing a curriculum that stressed a set of "common" cultural facts and beliefs. A more radically oriented teacher would want to know what institutional norms and rules might obstruct greater student participation in school governance. Teacher educators committed to the articulation of educational values and beliefs, and cognizant of the importance of the social context, would want to explore further how the real world might constrain their prospective teachers' articulated aims. In this chapter we focus on a "prior" task. We present an analysis of three "sets" of social conditions that, we believe, would obstruct any teacher's commitment to democratic education.

Our analysis will unfold in the following manner. First we examine teaching as work, as a labor process. We discuss the working conditions of teachers and teachers' labor processes at both the personal and institutional levels. We then focus on the dynamics of race and gender relations, examining each set of relations (when appropriate) at the personal, institutional, and societal levels. We examine assumptions and knowledge about minority achievement in schools. We also look at the dynamics of gender relations and how that affects teaching in the public schools. In our substantive analyses of teachers' working conditions and racial and gender relations we have not tried to present sophisticated or fully developed analyses. Instead we have formulated fruitful but incomplete examples of the type of content we think is needed in teacher education curricula.

One caveat is in order. In the next three sections we examine at length particular authors' views on teachers' work, minorities' school experiences, and gender and teaching. We present these focused discussions for a few reasons. We want to convey the value of each particular analysis and we want to persuade others of the value of our general emphasis on the social context of schooling within teacher education. But we also want to remind the reader that we present these analyses as examples of the type of concerns and issues that ought to be included in the curriculum of teacher education.

Teachers' work

Teaching in the public schools is work. Teachers are involved in a labor process (teaching) where the work conditions can facilitate or obstruct their educational efforts. In a very real sense, teachers are workers. While analyzing teaching as work seems almost commonsensical to us, very few prospective teachers ever consider their perspective nor do teacher education programs emphasize this way of looking at teaching.

There seems to be a reticence among many prospective teachers and teacher educators about analyzing teaching as work or teachers as workers. For some, teaching is akin to a calling; for others, it is a professional career. At times it seems that the teaching-as-work perspective strikes educators as professional heresy. Analyzing teaching as work purportedly focuses the concern exclusively on the teachers (e.g., *their* work conditions, pay, and benefits) and detracts from a concern for the students. Looking at teaching as a labor process need not entail this self-centered orientation. Certainly, if one examines the history of the American Federation of Teachers it is clear that it was neither originally nor solely conceived in this self-centered manner (Eaton 1975).[1] If, as we argue, there are certain features of teachers' working conditions that obstruct rather than facilitate their democratic educational aims, then prospective teachers ought to be aware of these conditions. If viewing teaching as a labor process enables future teachers to see and analyze teaching in a way that would encourage the creation of a nonrepressive and nondiscriminatory educational environment, then it seems that this is a good way to explore the question. And if such an orientation enables prospective teachers to begin to make connections between their professional work lives and the larger social context, then it would seem advantageous. We argue that viewing teaching as work, as a labor process, is likely to accomplish these goals.

Amy Gutmann (1987), in her *Democratic Education,* articulates clearly the reasons why democratic educators ought to be concerned about the conditions under which teachers work. She begins with the premise that it is the "professional responsibility of teachers . . . to uphold the principle of nonrepression by cultivating the capacity for democratic deliberation" (p. 76). That is, it is the teacher's job to ensure that restrictions not be placed on students' rational deliberation and that students be able to consider critically different ways of living. But, Gutmann observes, teachers' ability to cultivate this capacity is continually obstructed by the working conditions in most public schools. The structure of teachers' work contributes to what Gutmann calls the "ossification" of office (p. 77). That is, teachers have too little autonomy, and as a result teaching in the public schools becomes rigid, settled, and fixed. This lack of autonomy issues, according to Gutmann, from "structural" sources: teachers have "little control over work, low pay, and low social status" (p. 78). Compared to other professions, the rewards of teaching are fewer, and the salary and status much less. Citing Seymour Sarason (1971), Myron Brenton (1970), Dan Lortie

95

(1975), and Gertrude McPherson (1972), Gutmann maintains that "most teachers who begin with a sense of intellectual mission lose it after several years of teaching, and either continue to teach in an uninspired, routinized way or leave the profession to avoid intellectual stultification and emotional despair" (p. 77). Quoting Sara Lawrence Lightfoot (1983), she writes that schools tend to encourage ossification by discouraging intellectual creativity:

> In the worst schools, teachers are demeaned and infantilized by administrators who view them as custodians, guardians, or uninspired technicians. In less grotesque settings, teachers are left alone with little adult interaction and minimal attention is given to their needs for support, reward, and criticism. (Lightfoot 1983, p. 334, cited by Gutmann 1987, p. 79)

And as a result of all of this Gutmann surmises that

> teachers make compromises in their professional standards for causes that are often entirely beyond their personal control: too many students, too little preparation time for teaching, too much administrative work, too little money to support their families. (p. 79)

Gutmann does not think all these causes are beyond teachers' control. Teachers, collectively, may be in a position to rectify some of the inadequate working conditions. Organized into unions, teachers may be able to achieve a more satisfactory level of autonomy. But, Gutmann asserts, the democratic purpose of teachers' unions needs to be underscored: Teachers' unions ought to "pressure democratic communities to create the conditions under which teachers can cultivate the capacity among students for critical reflection on democratic culture" (p. 79).

Gutmann's line of reasoning seems clear and reasonable. She presents a view of how teachers' working conditions can obstruct students' democratic education. If teachers are overworked, emotionally drained, and lack the time and support to be intellectually engaged in their educational tasks, it is highly unlikely that we have the minimal conditions for engendering students' deliberative capacities. A number of recent reports and analyses highlight a concern for teachers' work conditions and list numerous features of teaching (at times under the rubric of the "cultures of teaching"), some of which might obstruct democratic educational aims. It would seem both educationally and instrumentally advantageous for prospective teachers to consider the nature and effect of these sorts of work conditions and workplace norms.

For example, Sharon Feiman-Nemser and Bob Floden (1986) have summarized a number of features of the cultures of teaching that are worthy of consideration. They have noted that teachers work in isolation, they "have peers but no colleagues" (p. 508). Architecturally many elementary schools are "egg crate" structures, where individual classrooms are self-contained. Teachers spend most of their time with students in their own classrooms and as a result interact little with other teachers. When teachers do interact, there tends to be a norm against asking one another for help: to do so admits of failure. In their interactions with administrators, teachers tend to see themselves in an ambiguous position. Teachers desire little interference from the principal in their classroom activities, but at the same time they want the principal to act as a buffer between themselves and the outside world. As depicted by Feiman-Nemser and Floden, the culture of teaching seems highly individualistic and blatantly noncollaborative. Such features are not conducive to a democratic educational environment.

In another study entitled "Working in Urban Schools," the authors convey a general sense that many urban teachers face "intolerable" conditions. Examining teachers' working conditions in five urban school districts (Denver, Detroit, Indianapolis, New Orleans, and Rochester, N.Y.), Thomas Corcoran, Lisa Walker, and Lynne White convey the following.[2] The physical conditions of many schools are described as "substandard." The availability of resources is said to be sorely lacking. Teachers experience insufficient staffing of support personnel and counselors for students. A lack of such basic supplies as textbooks and blackboards exists. Teachers found the procedures used to distribute supplies "demeaning and unprofessional." Students are described as ill equipped for school and are viewed by teachers as having negative attitudes toward school and poor attendance. Teachers complain of a lack of parental support and a general sense of conflict between the expectations of schooling and the cultural background of students' families. And in regard to their own professional autonomy, teachers report "an increasing loss of control over what they taught" and "less influence over school policy decisions and few chances to work collaboratively" (Olson 1988, p. 22). These are depressing and dismal findings, ones that are rarely examined or discussed in programs of teacher education. If teacher educators are to prepare teachers capable of cultivating students' democratic deliberative capacities, it would seem advantageous for prospective teachers to be aware of, and to inquire further into, the nature and force of these work conditions.[3] Minimally it would seem that teachers should have the time to plan, implement, and evaluate their educational plans, should have the opportunity to work in a collegial and cooperative setting, and be able to secure the advice and comments of other informed participants inside and outside of the school (Weinshank et al. 1983).

Another feature of teachers' work that is rarely discussed with any analytical perspicuity is the manner in which these conditions affect the teacher. Intolerable work conditions would seem to be intolerable no matter what the task. But a further examination of the nature of teachers' work underscores the intensity and the manner in which these conditions are experienced. R. W. Connell's (1985) analysis is very helpful on this score. He makes two central points. One is that in many ways, teaching is a labor process without an easily discernible object. He states

> . . . it is always difficult to specify the object of teachers' labour, the raw material they are supposed to be working on. In consequence, the definition of the task can expand and contract in quite alarming ways. (Connell 1985, pp. 70–71)

The limit to teachers' work tends not to be the students' capacity to learn, but instead "the limit is purely and simply the other demands on [the teacher's] time and energy" (Connell 1985, p. 73). In most schools one can find teachers who arrive at 8:00 A.M. and leave at 3:00 P.M. and other teachers who seem to do nothing but live, breathe, and sleep teaching. Teachers eventually define and delimit their work in different ways. But the fact remains that the tasks of educating do not end, but instead seem to expand on and on.

The second point that Connell makes is that teachers' work is emotionally infused. When teachers teach students, they have to utilize and manage their own and their students' emotions. In doing so, teachers create emotional "relationships" with their students. According to Connell, managing these relationships "is a large part of her [the teacher's] labour process. Keeping order, and getting the kids to learn, both require operating on the emotions of the kids through the emotions of the teacher" (Connell 1985, p. 117). When teachers utilize their own and their students' emotions, they invest themselves in their work in a very personal way. In choosing a particular instructional or managerial strategy, teachers engage and invest in a particular set of emotions. This has an effect on the teacher's professional and personal identity. Connell notes this when he states that a beginning teacher

> facing the problem of keeping order lives on her nerves until she has worked out a strategy of survival. . . . A more experienced teacher is likely to be less vulnerable, but is not therefore less involved. For whatever strategy of control is adopted always requires an emotional commitment in a particular direction. By pursuing a particular strategy one becomes a particular kind of teacher and a particular kind of person. (Connell 1985, p. 118)

When one construes teaching, in part, as an emotionally diffuse labor process in which two central limitations are the teachers' time and energy, then the teacher's "emotional economy" becomes a prominent feature of teaching. This is important in a number of ways. When a teacher committed to democratic education (or his/her set of articulated and justified educational aims) encounters intolerable work conditions, the result is not simply the experience of one more "encumbrance," but rather a sense of personal and professional frustration. When a teacher encounters situations in which the effort it takes to create his/her educational relationships is continually frustrated, it takes a toll on the teacher. And when a teacher reacts to those situations with new educational strategies and approaches, the teacher's professional identity is at stake.

Viewing teachers' work as an emotionally infused labor process, prospective teachers should gain an enhanced understanding of teachers' work, their own experience as teachers, and insight into their relationships with students. Examining the working conditions of teachers allows prospective teachers insight into the institutional context of their work and how it affects their ability to teach. Initial reactions to the idea that such content should be included in teacher education curricula usually border on skepticism and disbelief. Analyzing teachers' work and the conditions of their work will, the skeptics argue, only result in cynicism, despair, and the abandonment of teaching. The realities are considered a bit too harsh for a "neophyte." The content should be experienced after some professional training and preparation. Others might argue that we have painted a particularly bleak picture and that life in the schools really is not that bad. Obviously we think that prospective teachers need to examine their probable working conditions and in doing this there is a danger that some students may despair and leave teaching altogether. But our hope is that by examining teachers' work conditions we will prepare teachers to become more realistic about their probable working situations. It seems that to work successfully in schools, teachers need to maintain a kind of "personally engaged but reasonably critical" view of schooling.[4] This sort of disposition is not easily attained. But without some idea of what teachers' work is like before their initial immersion, we fear that the most likely results will be accommodation and eventual acceptance of the current situation or cynicism, despair, and withdrawal from teaching. An ostrichlike response to teachers' work just does not seem appropriate.

Minority cultures and majority schooling

A crucial aspect of our social-reconstructionist orientation is a concern for altering, through education, relations of domination and subordination. It seems difficult to deny that in today's world being black and living in a large metropolitan area in the U.S. greatly increases the odds that one will receive an inferior education and most probably experience a life of subordination. Most prospective teachers have little prior experience with minority cultures and tend, like many white middle-class individuals, to utilize a cultural-deficit model to understand racial inequalities. Given that discrimination against blacks in schools still exists, that prospective teachers have little knowledge about African-American culture, and that the cultural-deficit model seems to be the dominant framework in most people's minds, this focus appears timely and appropriate. One of our central educational tenets is that as teachers we must be able to know and understand students' perspectives and we must be able to see and feel from students' perspectives. When we teach, we must be able to enter into the lives of our students and understand how they construe their worlds. Few teacher education programs present extended analyses of the discrimination and repression experienced by African-American people in the United States.[5] Many prospective teachers have little if any knowledge of African-American culture and the diversity within that culture. It is not that prospective teachers are uncaring individuals. But it seems the fear of being called a racist stems many a fruitful discussion and that, in general, prospective teachers follow the dictum that prescribes: Treat and approach all children as individuals, not as members of social, racial, or economic groups. Unfortunately, this fear and individualistic orientation obscures an understanding of the general features of children's lives. It creates barriers to understanding children of color. A focus on race relations, therefore, is likely to challenge and enlarge teachers' personal beliefs about African-American children and possibly provide insights into the institutional dynamics and larger social forces affecting African-American children's experiences and achievement in school.

Our focus on race relations begins with the teacher. Having argued that teaching is an emotionally infused labor process, and given the emotionally charged nature of black-white relations, we think it advantageous to think about white teachers' relationships with and responses to black children. Vivian Gussin Paley's (1989) reflections in *White Teacher* provide a wealth of examples for this segment of our analysis. After looking at Paley's reactions, we then move on to examine these racial relations at an institutional level. In this second section we highlight the ways in which teachers' language use at schools may conflict with African-American children's language experiences at home. Utilizing Shirley Brice Heath's (1982 and 1983) research we note ways in which these conflicts have been examined and accommodated. Finally we look at minority achievement from a larger sociohistorical perspective. Relying on John Ogbu's (1987) research we offer one interpretation of why many African-American children experience failure in the public schools.

In *White Teacher* Vivian Paley (1989), a white, Jewish, middle-aged woman, captures beautifully the complexity of her reactions to teaching urban black early-elementary children. Her observations and reactions are certainly her own, but we also sense that her experiences are not idiosyncratic. Her observations seem telling, and her approach is unusually honest and refreshing. She begins her work by noting that when the child comes to school he has already

> learned which of his characteristics are seen as weaknesses by
> those who take care of him at home. Suddenly a stranger called
> "teacher" is trying to find out not who he is but what he
> knows. The further away the teacher is from the child's cultural
> or temperamental background, the more likely it is that the
> wrong questions will be asked. The child instinctively knows
> the questions are inappropriate but soon figures out that he
> must be the one who is inappropriate. Thus he begins the en-

ergy consuming task of trying to cover up his differences. (Paley 1989, pp. xiii–xiv)

Students are not the only ones who are engaged in covering up differences. Some teachers seem to think that justice and fairness entail the denial of differences.[6] Paley notes that when she first started teaching she and her fellow white teachers "showed respect by completely ignoring black people as black people. Color blindness was the essence of the creed" (Paley 1989, p. 9). But the denial of differences didn't seem to take Paley very far; her understanding and knowledge of her students was curtailed drastically. The denial of differences obscured the need for knowledge of how her black children's cultural backgrounds might be quite different from those of some of her white children. This cultural knowledge, she argues, is an essential part of the educational picture. She writes:

I think it is a matter of clues. With most white children the smallest clue reveals a totality of characteristics I recognize. I am not aware, for example, of all the implications of a black child's saying "I don't eat pig. Only white people eat pig."

When Barbara, who organized "the Jewish club" two years before, said her family ate kosher food, I knew a lot about Barbara and her family. From her comments about meat and dairy dishes I received instant messages about her intelligence that a non-Jewish teacher might have missed. I think I am missing part of the picture presented by many black children by not being familiar with the context within which certain simple statements are made. (Paley 1989, p. 77)

For Paley, this lack of familiarity obstructs her understanding of the child, and therefore the instructional process.

These cultural differences between teacher and child not only affect the teacher and her educational actions but also the child's reactions to school. Paley notes that one summer she observed a group of black boys who regularly came to the schoolyard to practice their acrobatic movements. The youngest boy, Kenny, tried persistently to execute a double flip and was encouraged and supported by his friends. Paley was impressed by the cooperation, concentration, and self-regulation of all the boys. Paley then relates how she didn't recognize Kenny, the youngest child, when his father first brought him to school. In fact it was several weeks later when she realized that Kenny was the "remarkable little gymnast on the blue mattress" (Paley 1989, p. 122). She then asks, somewhat rhetorically:

> But what had happened to his confidence? Where was his daring manner and proud masking of bumps and bruises? Kenny cried if someone pushed him. He became speechless if required to perform some small task in front of the whole class. During table activity his eyes clouded over and he whispered "I can't do it." On that blue mattress he had looked as if he could conquer Mt. Everest. School had made Kenny a timid boy. (Paley 1989, pp. 121–22)

School didn't make all Paley's minority children timid. But it certainly had this effect on Kenny. Paley goes on to discuss how, with this understanding, she then encouraged Kenny to become less timid. For Paley, cultural differences affect both teacher and child.

Sometimes these cultural differences manifest themselves as racial antagonisms. Paley writes about her surprise and dismay at hearing one of her black students use the term "white" toward her derisively. She writes:

> But the truth was, I felt attacked. How could this be? Was I reacting to this affront to my authority as a teacher or to my authority as a white? I asked myself these questions during the following days, but I really knew the answers. If Steven had said, "I won't listen to you," this would have been an ordinary situation. I was of course, reacting to the hostile use of "white" by this black child. (Paley 1989, p. 14)

She goes on to explain:

> If he had yelled "Jew" instead of "white" I would have been more upset. This thought gave me courage. I do feel more Jewish than white. My ego seems to be tied up in Jewish images and insecurities. . . . But Steven Sherman sees me only as a white lady. I can't crawl into my Jewish role. I must react as a white, so Steven will know I'm not worried about our differences. But I *was* reacting as a white and I *was* worried about our difference. (Paley 1989, pp. 14–15)

Paley also writes about how she tried to convince herself that discussions of these differences should not occur because she wanted to "spare" people's feelings. Kim, one of Paley's black students, had torn up a picture of her house she had drawn that did not include her 'absentee' father. Another black student, Alma, seemed to be trying to figure her way in a white world. Paley writes:

> [Kim's] father got no picture and no explanation of why she tore her picture up. I had wanted to spare his feelings. I did not talk with Kim later because I wished to spare *her* feelings. I didn't talk about being black with Alma for the same reason. It was obvious that I hoped to ignore feelings, not spare them. My silence communicated the impression that there might be something wrong about being black or living apart from one's father. (Paley 1989, pp. 129–30)

As one reads Paley's reflections, it is hard not to be impressed by her emotional durability and cognitive insight. Having grown up a white Jewish woman in a gentile world she is aware of what it feels like to be different, and this seems to help her understand other types of differences. Eventually she becomes open to talking about these differences in a loving and nonjudgmental sort of way. There is a great deal that a prospective teacher could cull from Paley's experiences. But if we had to highlight a few central aspects, we would want to emphasize Paley's initial reluctance to acknowledge differences between her own white middle-class (Jewish) background and those of her urban black children. We would also point to her subsequent awareness of the necessity to know more about these children's cultural backgrounds. It seems that if teacher educators allow prospective teachers to ignore the cultural differences that do exist, these teachers will be ill-equipped to teach children whose cultural/social class background does not match their own. But learning about other cultures is not a simple endeavor. One needs to be sensitive to and aware of past and present patterns of prejudice and discrimination and attempt to see the school experience from the perspective of the "cultural other." Paley's work underscores what this effort to know looks and feels like to one teacher. Her work presents a telling and moving story about how these cultural differences affected both her and her students.

Differences between minority and majority populations can become institutionalized in such a way that they obstruct minority students' school achievement. And it is essential, we think, that prospective teachers explore the ways in which the institution of schooling (i.e., the predominant norms and policies and recurrent practices), and not solely the individual teacher's cultural views, can turn cultural differences into educational obstacles for minority students. For it is not only individuals' attitudes and beliefs that hinder minority achievement in schools but also the norms and practices of the institutions of schooling that create obstacles. In an ethnographic study that focuses partly on the experiences of working-class black students in a desegregated white middle-class setting (located in the southeastern section of the United States), Shirley Brice Heath (1982 and 1983) illustrates how the differential use of language, especially questions, between the black community and the white schools curtailed black students' involvement and achievement in school. She began her study when residents of the black community (Trackton) asked her to talk with their children to find out why they were not doing better in school. Having worked with many segments of the community, Heath enjoyed the trust of the Trackton residents and teachers in the public schools.

Schools, Heath notes, are supposed to convey knowledge and skills to students. Teachers rely on questions in their instructional efforts, and it seems that teacher-initiated questions dominate classroom talk. Classroom questions, Heath discovered, had functions and meanings rarely used by the black working-class students of Trackton. When the Trackton students walked into the classrooms, they entered a world of question-asking which did not match the kinds of questions they were asked at home. This cultural incongruence was not recognized initially by the teachers. The teachers, according to Heath,

> initially held a variety of stereotypes about how black children learned language: black parents don't care about how their children talk; black children don't have adequate exposure to language because their parents are probably as nonverbal as the kids are at school; black parents don't spend enough time with their children to train them to talk right. (Heath 1982, p. 114)

But, Heath notes, even though the teachers had a sense that something was awry, they assumed that the Trackton kids would respond to their school language use just as all the other children did.

However it soon became evident to the teachers and the Trackton parents that the Trackton students were not faring well. Heath found that

105

the questions the teachers used at home with their own preschoolers were very similar to the kinds of questions they and their colleagues used in school. Basically she found that teachers used questions

> . . . to teach their children what they should attend to when looking at a book. . . . The children were taught to label, to search out pieces of pictures, to name parts of the whole, and to talk about these out of context. As the children grew older, adults used questions to add power to their directives . . . and to call attention to the infraction committed. . . . Adults saw questions as necessary to train children, to cause them to respond verbally, and to be trained as conversational partners. (Heath 1982, p. 113)

In contrast to these teachers' practices with their children, Trackton children, when at home, were not viewed as conversational partners or as information givers. Early on, the children were taught not to respond to strangers' inquiries about friends' or neighbors' behavior. Questions in the Trackton community had very different functions. When Trackton children were asked questions Heath found a number of distinct types, including story starter, analogical, and accusatory questions. Story-starter questions were used by adults to ask for "an explanation of events leading to first questioner's question" (Heath 1982, p. 116). The initiator might ask the child, "Did you see Lem's dog yesterday," with the expectation that the child would then respond, "No, what happened to Lem's dog?" A story would then ensue. Analogical questions were asked of children for a "nonspecific comparison of one item, event, or person with another" (Heath 1982, p. 116). Thus, a child might be asked, "What's that like?" (referring to a flat tire on a neighbor's car), and the answer might be something like "Doug's car, never fixed." Accusatory questions were issued when some sort of infraction was committed and the expected reaction was either a "nonverbal response and a lowered head or a story creative enough to take the questioner's attention away from the original infraction" (Heath 1982, p. 116).

But such questions did not prepare the Trackton children to cope with three major characteristics of the very questions used in classrooms. "First, they had not learned how to respond to utterances which were interrogative in form but directive in pragmatic function (e.g., 'Why don't you use the one on the back shelf?' = 'Get the one on the back shelf'). Second . . . questions which expected students to feed back information already known to the teacher were outside the general experience of Trackton students. Third, they had little or no experience with questions which asked for display of specific skills and content information acquired primarily from a familiarity with books and ways of talking about books (e.g., 'Can you find Tim's name?' 'Who will come help Tim find his way home?'). In short, school questions were unfamiliar in their frequency, purpose, and types, and in the domains of content knowledge and skills display they assumed on the part of students" (Heath 1982, p. 123).

Heath's project was not solely a descriptive and explanatory endeavor; her ethnographic work became central to efforts to lessen the incongruity between these two different groups of language users. She notes that traditionally educational researchers and interventionists have prescribed changes for the parents of children who are not successful in school. Knowledge followed a "one-way" path from the school to the home. The idea behind these efforts seemed to be that students' home talk should become more like school talk (Heath 1982, p. 125). She indicates that no one either in teacher education programs or in the daily practice of education seemed able to tap the uses of language and ways of "talking about things" of the culturally different and to bring these skills into the classroom (Heath 1982, p. 126).

In order to accomplish this task, Heath argues that two components are necessary: Teachers must become active inquirers, and they need to have "credible data from both the classroom and the students' communities" (Heath 1982, p. 126). Heath accomplished both. She engaged teachers, voluntarily, to study both their own linguistic uses and patterns, and she gathered data about the students' community which the teachers could then use to alter their practices within the classroom (for more on this, see chapter 5).

John Ogbu, a Nigerian-born educational anthropologist, provides further insight into the role of cultural differences in educational endeavors. He highlights the role that larger societal forces play, especially the historical, cultural, and political-economic factors, in creating obstacles for minority children's academic performance. For prospective teachers, this sort of analysis adds immensely to the accounts that stress individual actions and institutional dynamics. Ogbu argues that the real obstacle for minority children's academic performance is not simply that these children exhibit different language, dialect, or cognitive styles but rather that the real issues are threefold: "first, whether the children come from a segment of society where people have traditionally experienced unequal opportunity to use their education or school credentials in a socially and economically meaningful and rewarding manner; second, whether or not the relationship between the minorities and the dominant-group members who control the public schools has encouraged the minorities to perceive and define school learning as an instrument for replacing their cultural identity with the cultural identity of their "oppressors" without full reward or assimilation; and third, whether or not the relationship between the minorities and the schools generates the trust that encourages minorities to accept school rules and practices that enhance academic success" (Ogbu 1987, p. 334).

According to Ogbu, most black Americans feel the negative side on all three of these issues. First, Ogbu maintains that blacks are part of an involuntary minority (or what Ogbu calls a castelike minority group) originally brought to the United States by force and under duress. Historically black Americans have been denied access to meaningful jobs in adult life through both an inferior education and established job ceilings. For generations blacks have been discouraged from pursuing educational and economic achievements, and this historical factor has probably "discouraged the minorities from developing a strong tradition of academic achievement" (Ogbu 1987, p. 318). Second, involuntary minorities tend to develop an oppositional cultural identity, in reaction to the dominant group social identity. Ogbu maintains that with involuntary minorities a type of "cultural inversion" usually occurs and "results in the coexistence of two opposing cultural frames of reference or ideal ways of orienting behaviors, one considered by the minorities as appropriate for themselves and the other as appropriate for white Americans" (Ogbu 1987, p. 323). The identity offered to black Americans by white schools is not viewed as an acceptable one. And finally, Ogbu relates that many black Americans tend to distrust the public schools. There are "many episodes throughout their (black's) history that seem to have left them with the feeling that white people and the institutions they control cannot be trusted" (Ogbu 1987, p. 326). Black parents tend not to trust inner-city public schools to give their black children the right kind of education. In effect, Ogbu argues that black children have not fared well in school due to a long history of racial exploitation and subordination *and* also due to their own expressive and instrumental rejection of white culture and public schools (Ogbu 1987, p. 317).

Given the complexity of the picture Ogbu paints, it seems that efforts to alter these discriminatory structures and practices cannot occur solely at the level of individual actions. In contrast to Heath's sociolinguistic thesis, Ogbu's explanatory sketch highlights the role political and economic power play in discriminatory educational practices. It would seem that if we accept Ogbu's initial explanation, then a strategy for effective action should recognize the source and nature of this power. While we cannot outline a satisfactory strategy, we can point to possibilities. Michael Williams (1989), in his *Neighborhood Organizing for Urban School Reform*, highlights the potential role neighborhood organizations can play in affecting minority achievement. Throughout his work he stresses the importance of local communities working together with teachers and school officials to create a more trusting and effective educational environment. He, along with Sara Lawrence Lightfoot, underlines the importance of increasing the communication between school and home, between the school and the local community. Recognizing the social history of discrimination and distrust, Williams utilizes Joyce, Hersh, and McKibbin's (1983) "Responsible Party Model" to create a school governance structure that includes all relevant parties, thereby giving parents and community members a greater role than before. As he writes:

> The main thrust of the neighborhood organization is to get the school under control—though not under its control—and in doing so create a new climate and mechanisms whereby its membership especially parents and students can gain increased voice in the school operation. (Williams 1989, p. 69)

Through these sorts of changes in school governance, Williams argues that black families may begin to view the public schools with less distrust and a greater sense of "ownership." Although schools and their communities cannot change two centuries of racial discrimination and job ceilings, they might become sites for struggle and educational change.

The notion of difference has resonated throughout our discussion of race and culture. White teachers and black children are different in significant ways. Teachers and students react to those differences. Schools institutionalize and solidify the differences between cultures. And these schools educate children in a society that historically has discriminated against those who are "different." In their respective work, Vivian Paley (1989) and Shirley Brice Heath (1982 and 1983) convey their attention to and care for the people and children around them. Both saw children who were different being harmed. And both expressed a need to alter this situation through a greater sensitivity to and knowledge of school practices and cultural context. If teaching is a labor process in which the management of the students' emotions plays a key role, then one needs to understand those emotions. Frequently our emotions are complex reactions to the cultural meanings that inhere in our worlds. Without an understanding of students' cultures and contexts, it seems that the prospects for nondiscriminatory educational success are minimal.

Understanding the complexity of past and present discriminatory practices certainly does not assure the effective transformation of those practices. But if teacher educators are going to encourage prospective teachers to formulate sound reasons and justifications for their educational plans, then it seems we need to look more carefully at the children affected by those plans, and the kinds of assumptions about schools and the cultural contexts contained within those plans. An educational plan that does not recognize that cultural differences frequently result in educational discrimination seems questionable. Prospective teachers who are not open to talking about how those differences affect their teaching and the children around them would seem to be impaired in their ability to accommodate those differences. Such discussions are not simple or easy matters. Talking about racial and cultural differences is fraught with ambiguity and uncertainty. But it seems that without such conversations the potential for democratic education is drastically diminished. Except for a general sense that we ought to value rather than devalue cultural differences and our commitment to democratic education, we want to make clear that we are in no way advancing a "party line." We do not think that there is one correct approach to these issues. But we do maintain that increased and enhanced communication among school personnel and between school personnel and community members is a necessary feature of democratic education. We think it doubtful that teacher educators who ignore these facets of school life can think of themselves as educators. Without a recognition of past and current discrimination, the prognosis for the future of public education is bleak.

Gender and teaching

Our focus on gender derives, in part, from our experiences as men working as elementary teachers (in what is frequently termed a woman's profession), our perceived need to problematize and discuss gender relations with many of our prospective teachers, and the desire to mine the provocative contributions of recent feminist thought on children, women, and education. As male elementary teachers and now as (male) teachers of (predominantly female) prospective teachers we have observed subtle and overt reactions to men's participation in "women's work." Many of our prospective women teachers express surprise that a man would want to be an elementary teacher. Many of our male college mentors thought we should choose more appropriate careers. And, more recently, many of our colleagues have advised us to focus on matters other than teacher education. Somehow teaching, especially at the elementary level, is not a job for a man. There seems, for many, to be a "natural order" in gender relations. For the most part, it is women who teach the children in our public elementary schools and it tends to be men, as principals, who manage the women teachers. For quite some time this arrangement has been viewed as "natural." Women purportedly have the nurturant qualities and abilities that sustain young lives but need the structure and direction provided by a male principal. In schools, and some might say in society in general, women "tend" the children while men "manage" the women. Obviously discussions of gender relations and gender domination are very personal matters. Whether the issue be economic discrimination, the lack of men's participation in domestic labor, gender roles and child rearing, or gendered ways of knowing, the discussion resonates in very personal ways. Few prospective teachers initially question the gendered nature of the division of labor in schools, the possibility of a gender bias in the elementary, secondary, or university curriculum, or the probable effect of a teaching career on their personal and professional lives. Committed as we are to a nondiscriminatory and nonrepressive educational agenda, the strong possibility that gender dynamics in schools and society may contribute to antidemocratic biases seems good enough reason to examine these relations.

One way to highlight a number of issues relating gender and teaching is to examine, as Susan Laird (1988) has, the various meanings attached to the slogan of teaching as "woman's true profession." Following Laird, we identify and describe five distinct ways of construing "woman's true profession"—interpretations that should shed further light on gender relations and teaching. Discussions of these interpretations should encourage prospective teachers to consider alternative ways of looking at the relationship between gender and teaching.

Laird identifies five distinct theses, or five distinct sets of interpretations. Although we will rely on her general framework, our analysis (while similar in spirit) will diverge from hers. As she relates, the theses are as follows:

1. The descriptive thesis: that the vast majority of American schoolteachers are women.
2. The normative thesis: that school teaching, on account of its nature and women's nature, should be women's work.
3. The problematic thesis: that intelligent women somehow become devalued by school teaching.
4. The negative thesis: that school teaching somehow becomes devalued through its identification with women.
5. The critical thesis: that schoolteachers' own public, collaborative, self-definitive responses to the other four theses are crucial to a reconception of teaching that can address our current teaching crisis. (Laird 1988, pp. 452–53)

The descriptive thesis

According to Emily Feistritzer (1985), the typical American teacher is female, married, white, and a middle-aged mother of two children. She is generally an inactive member of the Democratic party, has taught for an average of fifteen years, and works in a school where the principal is in all likelihood male and women comprise the teaching staff (Feistritzer 1985, pp. xix–xx).

The fact needs to be underscored that it is predominantly women who mother and teach. Teachers and mothers are viewed as the central actors, the major forces, in the child's socialization process. As Sara Lawrence Lightfoot has noted, "Mothers are thought to be the dominant shapers of the child's primary socialization, and teachers are perceived as being the most important primary force in determining the child's transition to the adult world" (Lightfoot 1978, p. 43). And as Lightfoot also notes, when something appears to go awry in the socialization process, it is the women (who mother and teach) who are blamed (p. 44).

The fact that many women teachers are also mothers is another descriptive feature that ought to be highlighted. It seems important to note that in our contemporary society professional women eventually confront the tension between having a career or having a child. R. W. Connell (1985) found in his empirical study of teachers that "whether [or not] to have children is a lively issue for younger women teachers" (Connell 1985, p. 154). If a teacher chooses to have children it is interpreted by some as a "lack of commitment" to teaching. After the baby(ies) arrive(s) the responsibilities entailed in raising a family frequently amount to a continual juggling of familial chores and professional tasks. Most men take little responsibility for the domestic chores that come with family life and the domestic economy. Women teachers who choose to have children seem to bear a disproportionate share of the domestic chores.[7]

The normative thesis

According to proponents of the normative thesis, the fact that so many teachers are women reflects a "natural order." Teachers' work and women's nature correspond. In order to teach, especially younger children, teachers need to be nurturant, sensitive, patient, and capable of adapting to children's needs. The qualities that constitute "the" feminine character ideal correspond to the demands of teaching. As Geraldine Clifford (1987) has written:

> Women's weaknesses, in men's eyes—their emotionality, sensitivity, subjectivity, manipulative powers, and "faculty of gaining the affection of children"—become strengths in reaching children in the schoolroom as well as in the nursery. (Clifford 1987, p. 8)

Women, it seems, are destined for the roles of mother and teacher.

The problematic thesis

While proponents of the normative thesis postulate a congenital fit between women's nature and the tasks of teaching, purveyors of the problematic thesis maintain that teaching is the sort of endeavor that does an intelligent woman no good. There are at least two general reasons for why teaching is viewed as harmful to women: There is the view that we live in a patriarchal society that devalues women and their work and there is the analysis that stresses that the working conditions of teaching are dehumanizing.

The patriarchal view maintains that women's work is not valued in our society. Women are involved in social-reproductive processes of society, not the productive world of work. Mothers and teachers rear children to a point of independence. Their work, as Lightfoot (1978) notes, has "use-value" but not "exchange-value" (p. 62). Women's qualities of "resourcefulness, patience, understanding, expressiveness are . . . thought only to be functional in the context of home and family [and school]. They are seen as antithetical to the aggressive, instrumental roles needed in the world of men and work" (Lightfoot 1978, p. 62). Walk into the teaching role and your value as a productive and respected member of society drops precipitously.

A second, and perhaps not unrelated, explanation for why teaching harms women is simply that teachers' working conditions obstruct meaningful work and educational success. Whether one utilizes Michael Apple's (1982) deskilling thesis, or Arthur Wise's (1979) view of schools as hyperrationalized bureaucratic institutions, it seems that teachers confront obstacles that make good teaching difficult if not impossible.

The negative thesis

Another view that connects gender and teaching is the sense that teaching is somehow devalued due to its identification as women's work. Susan Laird (1988) argues that the Carnegie Foundation's Task Force on Teaching as a Profession, in their *A Nation Prepared,* "juxtaposes two distinct conceptions of teaching as an economic activity, 'feminized occupation' and 'professional work,' in opposition to each other" (Laird 1988, p. 458). She goes on to state that "The professional whom these reformers hope to attract to teaching will doubtless include women, but the implication is clear in both reports [Carnegie and Holmes] that 'professional' values traditionally defined by men rather than the so-called 'feminine' values associated with childrearing must become sovereign in schoolteaching" (Laird 1988, p. 458). Under these reform efforts the preferred approach to teaching is construed as a more rigorous intellectual undertaking. Laird notes that these proposals appear to echo the educational philosopher Thomas Green's (1971) assertion that "we cannot allow the education of men to abandon the seriousness and rigors of reason for the gentler disciplines of love, unless men thereby acknowledge the love that is so much a part of serious and careful thought" (Laird 1988, p. 460). If we draw from this view a scenario for teacher education, we see that the attitudes and qualities characterized by Jane Roland Martin (1987) as the three *C*'s of care, concern, and connection "figure nowhere in the reformers' conceptions of what children's teachers need, not merely to exercise, but also somehow to study, learn, know, and actually teach" (Laird 1988, pp. 459–60).

The critical thesis

The critical thesis is, as Laird maintains, "simply an acknowledgment that all four other theses of 'woman's true profession' are critically significant" (Laird 1988, p. 460). More substantively she argues that this thesis "emphasizes the importance for teachers of both sexes to reflect upon the oppressive limitations, as well as the alternative possibilities for education, that inhere in their work's historic identification with subordinate and domesticated maternalism" (Laird 1988, p. 461).

A number of "critical" questions could be raised at this point. We will pursue one briefly. Throughout our discussion of gender and teaching there seems to be an assumed opposition between the so-called caring and nurturant dispositions of the feminine character ideal and the intellectual rigor and reasoning of the masculine character ideal. According to these ideals the feminine character is supposed to be more empathetic, intuitive, sensitive, and subjective. The male character is supposed to be less emotional and more objective, impartial, and principle oriented. In short, a feeling, caring person cannot be a rational person. Given our understanding of teaching and teacher education, this standpoint is not acceptable and needs to be examined. Viewing teaching from a perspective that accepts this opposition between reason and emotion obscures, we think, essential features of teaching. If one accepts this opposition, then the notion of teachers' work as "emotional labor" raises all sorts of problems. Teaching, within this view, cannot be "rational." Furthermore it would be difficult to justify the aim of good reason-giving for an activity that is so emotionally infused.[8]

Sara Ruddick (1989) reflects on this opposition in her work *Maternal Thinking*. As a philosopher and mother she found herself, at times, dissatisfied with the traditional separation of reason and emotion. But she notes, "However disenchanted I became with Reason, it did not occur to me that there was an intellectual life that had anything to do with mothering. I 'thought' only when I had time to myself, put my children out of my mind, and did philosophy" (Ruddick 1989, p. 11). But as she began to reflect on her maternal activities, she began to construe reason and feelings as more closely connected. She states that:

> In maternal thinking, feelings are at best complex but sturdy in-struments of work quite unlike the simple and separate hates, fears and loves that are usually put aside and put down in phil-osophical analyses. They are certainly quite unlike the simple fears and hates on which military endeavors depend. Rather than separating reason from feeling, mothering [and we would add teaching] makes reflective feeling one of the most difficult attainments of reason. In protective [and we would add, in-structional] work feeling, thinking and action are conceptually linked; feelings demand reflection, which is in turn tested by action, which is in turn tested by the feelings it provokes. (Ruddick 1989, p. 70)

Ruddick offers a clear and perceptive, but only initial and fragmentary, reflection on this issue. Our own sense is that we would benefit greatly from discarding the dichotomous opposition between reason and emo-tion. Teaching is so infused with both cognitive assessments and emotive reactions that it seems untenable to maintain the opposition between reason and emotion. In chapter 2, where we outlined the goal of reason giving for teacher education, we assumed (but did not argue explicitly) that educational deliberation entails both cognitive and emotive compo-nents. The articulation of educational beliefs and practices cannot occur in an emotional vacuum. In teaching, reflective feeling and thinking must go hand in hand. While we have not mined all the implications of this belief, it is clear to us that teacher educators, and prospective and practicing teachers, would benefit from thinking about this and other issues raised by the interpretation of teaching as a "woman's profession."

Conclusion

In this chapter we have attempted to strengthen our claim that teacher educators ought to help prospective teachers examine the social context of schooling. We have outlined substantive concerns (e.g., teachers' work, minority achievement in majority schools, and the gender dynamics of teaching) and examined specific issues (e.g., teaching as emotionally infused labor, the recognition and awareness of cultural differences, and teaching as a "woman's true profession"). A teacher education curriculum that included these sorts of issues would, we think, better prepare prospective teachers for the reality of schooling and encourage a reflective examination of their social beliefs.

In the previous chapter (chapter 3), we highlighted ways in which prospective teachers could examine their educational actions in a field or practicum setting. In many ways we have outlined two separate strategies, one for fieldwork and the other for course work, to encourage prospective teachers to reflect on their own social and political beliefs and the social context of schooling. This division, while analytically helpful and reflective of most teacher education programs, needs to be rethought. It seems there are more fruitful ways to combine programmatically the "practical" and the "academic" components of teacher education. In chapter 6 we discuss ways in which this integration has been accomplished by practicing teacher educators along with other programmatic efforts consistent with our social-reconstructionist reform agenda.

In this chapter we have also attempted to integrate, or at least combine, individual, institutional, and societal analyses. We have highlighted what we believe are, in many respects, exemplary research efforts. Unfortunately this sort of interconnected analysis—connecting the individual, institutional, and societal—is not plentiful in educational research. In fact, it is fair to say that there is not a great deal of research focused on the social context of schooling that facilitates prospective teachers' examination of the social context in an educationally or instrumentally valuable way. In the next chapter (chapter 5) we sketch, with broad strokes, a research agenda that could enhance this sort of examination. Given the noted gap between educational research and teachers' practices, and our concern for a further understanding of the social context of teaching that would benefit teachers, we think a focus on particular research issues is certainly in order.

5

Research for Teaching and
Teacher Education

Introduction

We do not know of any easy way to illuminate how larger societal
structures, cultural beliefs, and institutional dynamics affect individual
teachers, or how teachers might affect these structures and institutions.
Teacher education programs and educational research tend to emphasize
the individual level of analysis and tend to ignore more holistic and
structural examinations.[1] This focus on the individual level detracts from
examining larger societal or structural issues, and from understanding
how these two levels (individualist and holist levels) of analysis might
intertwine. In teacher education, it seems, we need an approach to
research capable of mining the ways in which larger societal structures
and institutional conditions create obstacles and opportunities for teachers and teacher educators. This framework could point to richer and
more illuminating views of teaching, and the institutional structures and
social contexts of schooling and teacher education. But even if such an
approach were available, a host of other problems would remain. One
in particular stands out, and can be posed in the following way: Given
the acclaimed gap between research efforts and teachers' classroom
practices, can we expect any research endeavor to produce something
of significant value? Educational research is not known for its ability to
help practitioners solve their conundrums.[2] Yet throughout this work we
have maintained that some of these conundrums might be illuminated
and more fully explored by examining the social context of schooling.
If educational research has had such a poor track record when addressing
teachers' classroom problems, should we expect it to offer anything

substantial when focused on the social context of schooling? We think our expectations are not unreasonable. Given our social-reconstructionist reform agenda it seems that we need to examine the tensions between holist and individualist analyses and the acclaimed gap between educational research and educational practice.

Lacking a universal solvent guaranteed to dissolve the tension between holist and individualist accounts and doubtful that we can eliminate the gap between researchers and teachers, we offer the following. First, we propose a conceptual framework of teaching as a situated practice. This framework seems capable of illuminating how teachers are both constrained and enabled by the social context of schooling. It addresses the holist-individualist problem. Second, we present a brief and pointed analysis of educational research, teachers, and teacher education. In this section we lend support to the idea that the gap between the knowledge production and use of educational researchers and teachers, although based in part on their distinct activities, may not need to be as wide as it is today. As a result of this analysis we suggest that teacher educators might profit from reexamining the past, especially as it relates to the role of educational research and teacher education within schools of education. We also identify what, we believe, is reasonable to expect from educational research. Following these two sections, we formulate a set of guidelines for research efforts focused on teacher education and the social context of schooling. These guidelines are based, in part, on the previous analyses. Finally we illustrate these guidelines further by examining three exemplary research endeavors: Shirley Brice Heath's (1982 and 1983) ethnographic research, Susan Laird's (1988) conceptual analysis of educational slogans, and Barbara Schneider's (1987) analysis of the social conditions of teacher education. We believe that our approach could enhance future inquiry into the social context of schooling and teacher education.[3]

The focus in this chapter is on educational research that is conducted by college and university academics that is intended to be of some value to teacher education students and faculty and to public school staff. Although we have chosen to focus in this book on this one aspect of educational research, we strongly agree with Cochran-Smith's and Lytle's (1990) position that it would be a mistake to limit the knowledge base for teaching and teacher education to what academics in higher education have chosen to study and write about, even if these researchers make efforts to be responsive to the questions and concerns that practitioners (of teaching and teacher education) have about their work and follow all the guidelines for educational research outlined later in this chapter.

We believe that there needs to be a greater acknowledgment within the educational research community of the significant contributions that inquiries conducted by teachers and teacher educators can make to the university-based research community and to the communities of K–12 educators and college and university teacher educators. Whether this occurs through greater collaboration between university-based researchers and researchers of their own practices in teaching and teacher education, or through greater support for and recognition of practitioner-conducted research that has no university connection, it is clear that we have barely begun to tap the potential available in what teachers and teacher educators can contribute to the creation of new knowledge about teaching, learning, and learning to teach.[4]

Individualism and holism in educational research

An individualistic, psychological perspective has dominated educational research for quite some time. But within the last decade, sociological, anthropological, historical, political, and cultural analyses have begun to flourish. While most of this recent educational research is not psychologically reductionistic, much of it tends to offer either individualist or holist examinations. Characterizing and noting the pervasiveness of holist and individualist approaches in the social sciences, Susan James (1984) writes that:

> Holists . . . aim to show why social phenomena would be as they are even if particular individuals possessed properties other than those they actually have. And the explanations they offer go back to the social wholes which form and constrain individual people. In a quite different vein, individualists who look to the properties of individuals to explain social affairs are inspired by a belief in a conception of autonomy. (James 1984, p. 156)

In many ways this seems a fair characterization not only of much of academic social science but also of educational research. James concludes, and we agree, that as mutually exclusive accounts neither holist nor individualist approaches seem satisfactory.[5] The holist approach gives too much explanatory weight to the power of the social whole, while the individualist account tends to be much too narrowly circumscribed.

In contrast to many other segments of the educational research community, writers in the radical tradition have focused explicitly on the social, political, and cultural contexts of schooling. And within the radical approach one finds not only holist and individualist analyses but also various "synthetic," or, as some call them, dialectical formulations. As holists, radicals frequently describe and explain schools as the outcome of historical and structural forces much larger than the individual. Samuel Bowles and Herbert Gintiss' (1976) *Schooling in Capitalist America* and Louis Althusser's (1971) work on schools in "Ideology and Ideological State Apparatuses" stress the all-determining force of social structures at the expense of individual action and initiative. In contrast to the more structural approach, the individualist analyses of radical "motivational" theorists (e.g., Henry Giroux) tend to highlight the individual's ability to resist and alter structures of domination and exploitation.[6] Other theorists, like Michael Apple (1982 and 1986) and Martin Carnoy and Henry Levin (1985) utilize both holist and individualist analyses, and in effect offer synthetic approaches. Apple (1986) highlights the volitional quality of teachers' and students' lives while, at the same time, he recognizes the constraining features of the dynamics of class, race, and gender. Carnoy and Levin (1985) formulate a "dialectic" between the inegalitarian imperatives of capitalism and the egalitarian dynamics of democracy. In short, the radical tradition offers: (1) holist and structuralist analyses that view individuals as significantly constrained (sometimes determined) by larger social forces; (2) individualist frameworks that endow agents or groups of actors with, at times, unrealistic transformative capacities; or (3) some variant of a "synthetic approach" that highlights the interaction between structural forces and social actors.

We doubt we will progress very far in understanding how societal and institutional forces constrain and enable teachers and teacher educators and how these educators affect their institutional context if we continue to utilize exclusively either the individualist or holist orientations. Alone, neither orientation seems capable of illuminating how teachers' actions, the institutional context, and the larger societal conditions combine to create a situation that facilitates or obstructs teachers from accomplishing their educational ends. The synthetic or "dialectical" solutions seem to offer the most promising route. What we have to offer is certainly a variant of a synthetic approach. Without elaborating fully the strengths and weaknesses of other synthetic approaches, we offer a potentially profitable, but certainly not magical, approach to the holist-individualist tension. Our suggestions rely heavily on the notion that teachers can profitably be construed as engaged in situated practices, or as some prefer, teachers can be viewed as situational decision makers. In drawing attention to this perspective, we borrow heavily from the educational analyses of Louis Smith and William Geoffrey (1968), Larry Cuban (1984), Sara Lightfoot (1978), and Arthur Bolster (1983), and from Anthony Giddens's (1979) and Derek Layder's (1981 and 1985) work in social theory.[7]

Basically the notion of teaching as a situated practice is a view of teachers as social actors engaged in practices within a particular context. Teachers, as Cuban (1984), Bolster (1983), and Smith and Geoffrey (1968) have argued, are continually faced with decisions about what to do. Those decisions and their resulting actions and practices are influenced and shaped by their particular contexts, their situations. When teaching is examined as a situated practice, teachers' actions and practices are said to occur (are situated within) institutional and social contexts, and produce both intended and unintended outcomes. In its most general formulation we want to propose that university initiated educational research intended for prospective and practicing teachers could profitably examine teaching as a situated practice and thereby highlight the unacknowledged institutional and social contexts of this practice as well as its intended and unintended outcomes. An example will illustrate further the meaning of our proposal regarding teaching as a situated practice.

In a historical analysis of teachers' pedagogical practices Larry Cuban (1984) attempts to explain why "the dominant form of instruction continued to be teacher-centered since the late nineteenth century and why hybrids of teacher-centered progressivism and informal education developed in elementary but less in high school classrooms" (Cuban 1984, p. 239). His answer relies on what he calls an argument of "situationally-constrained choice" (Cuban 1984, p. 251). He states that:

> The school and classroom structures, I believe, established the
> boundaries within which individual teacher beliefs and an occu-

pational ethos worked their influences in shaping a practical pedagogy. . . . The constraints, pressures, and channeling that the school and classroom contexts generate is the invisible, encompassing environment that few recognize potentially shapes what teachers do daily in classrooms. (Cuban 1984, p. 250)

He adds that:

For public schools, chairs in rows, recitations, whole group instruction, worksheets, and textbook assignments need to be viewed as a series of successful solutions invented by teachers to solve daily problems of managing a score or more of students while they also acquired information and values. Coping with these structures, teachers constructed workable pedagogical solutions that have proved useful in personally maintaining control while carrying out instruction. (Cuban 1984, p. 250)

Why particular veteran elementary teachers were able to alter the traditional pedagogical procedures, creating and maintaining more student-centered practices, is explained (by Cuban) by the fact that these teachers held different educational beliefs (about what constituted a "good" learning environment for children) and by the fact that the organizational pressures of the elementary school were not as constraining as those of the high school. Elementary instruction, in contrast to secondary, had larger time slots available and focused on skill rather than content instruction. According to Cuban, these two features, along with their different educational beliefs, enabled particular teachers to change educational practices.

Cuban's analysis illustrates how construing teaching as a situated practice provides a view of teachers as being both constrained and enabled by their institutional context. Other work could also be cited. Louis Smith and William Geoffrey (1968) examined the "complexities of an urban classroom" and found that scheduling within the classroom, particular pupils, teachers' reference groups, school organization, and "extra classroom events" had a large effect on the teachers' deliberations (Smith and Geoffrey 1968, p. 233). Arthur Bolster (1983) has argued that a more effective model of research on teaching should mesh better with teachers' perspectives. In order to accomplish that, he argues, it would be wise to recognize that teachers function as "situational decision makers" (Bolster 1983, p. 296). Anthony Giddens (1979) maintains that most individual actions can be profitably construed as "situated practices." All these individuals propose that some important purchase can be had by viewing teaching as a situated practice.

While we essentially agree with all the researchers cited above, we also sense significant limitations in their approaches. Examining Cuban's (1984), and Smith and Geoffrey's (1968) empirical studies and the proposals of Bolster (1983) and Giddens (1979) one gets the sense that their view of the teacher's "situation" tends to be too narrowly circumscribed.[8] The class, cultural, and gender backgrounds of children and teachers are rarely highlighted. Teaching is not frequently viewed as work, and racial dynamics are not given much prominence. This is not to say that all these features must be included in every analysis, but it is to say that we might benefit from looking at these domains and dynamics. Cuban considers, then discounts, many extra-classroom constraints in his examination of how teachers taught. We think it would be wise to see how these dynamics significantly constrain the educational process. A wider rather than narrower examination is in order. It seems important to look at the dynamics of class, gender, and race focusing on how they significantly constrain students' futures, teachers' work, and the local community's involvement in their public schools (Arfedson 1979).

One way to approach an examination of these dynamics is to construe the constraints as emanating from biographical, institutional, and larger societal sources. In our curricular program (outlined in chapter 4), we framed our curricular analysis of constraints in this manner. We examined teachers' work (essentially a class analysis) at both biographical and institutional levels, and we highlighted the biographical, institutional, and larger societal contexts of both gender and racial dynamics. In our curricular examination of the dynamics of race, we noted that personal reactions, institutional practices, and sociohistorical factors (utilizing Vivian Gussin Paley's [1989], Shirley Brice Heath's [1982 and 1983] and John Ogbu's [1987] work respectively) constrain African-American children's futures. This framework seems to have an intuitive appeal for both prospective teachers and teacher educators. It also provides a helpful first approximation of the source of potential constraints. We also sense that once the "level" of the source is identified, some purchase can be had on potential transformations. Obviously constraints emanating from biographical, institutional, or societal sources entail different remedies. For example, at a biographical level it is possible, though not simple, to change one's mistaken notions about another culture through an alteration of personal beliefs. Institutional remedies generally, but not always, require a collective effort. The alteration of societal policies and practices further removed from the school would take more concerted and more organized political action. The biographical-institutional-societal analysis seems to be a useful way to frame the analysis of gender, race, and class dynamics when teaching is construed as a situated practice.[9]

The notion of teaching as a situated practice, one that occurs amid contextual constraints, is our preferred approach to an analysis of teaching and the social context of schooling. It seems to offer the potential of diminishing the tension between the holist-individualist approach. But even with this perspective in hand, it should be clear that our research agenda is far from adequately elaborated. So as to elaborate it further, we now examine conceptions of and practices associated with the production and use of research knowledge in colleges and universities. Specifically, we think it would be helpful to examine why educational research has tended to neglect teachers' practical concerns, and to scrutinize what we can reasonably expect from research efforts focused on the social context of schooling. Once we have examined these issues we will be better able to identify directions for future research in teacher education.

Knowledge production for knowledge use

At times it appears commonplace to differentiate and accept a wide chasm between knowledge production and knowledge use. It is frequently held that university researchers produce knowledge that is context free, generalizable to many situations, neutral with respect to social and educational values, and utilized by practitioners within the schools.[10] In this way of thinking there is a sharp distinction between knowledge production and knowledge use, and also between the respective roles of producers and users. Generally it is held that researchers produce knowledge which teachers and school administrators can then use. On the other hand, there is an alternative view that practitioners produce useful knowledge which is context dependent, particularistic, and always tied to specific social, personal, and educational values. From this perspective useful knowledge is almost always knowledge gleaned from practical action and reflection on that practical action.[11]

Between these two polar views are a number of interesting variations.

Denis Phillips (1980) maintains that all too often researchers' and practitioners' interests are quite unrelated. University researchers are concerned with knowledge production within the confines of disciplinary endeavors, and teachers are concerned with satisfying the practical demands of the classroom. According to Phillips, it would be wise not to expect these distinct interests to coincide. Taking a different approach, Joseph Schwab (1978) differentiates between theoretical (research-based) and practical (practitioner-employed) reasoning. He expounds a view of the practical, quasi-practical, and eclectic arts as bridges between the "theoretical" reasoning of university researchers and the "practical" reasoning of teachers, curriculum developers, and administrators. From another perspective, Margret Buchmann (1984) has criticized the research-oriented view of knowledge for its strictly utilitarian evaluation of knowledge. She argues that the purpose of practical knowledge is to enable wise action and that the utility orientation of many researchers misconstrues the role of knowledge in informing wise action. For Buchmann, research-produced knowledge is but one factor (and perhaps an insignificant one) in considerations of what to do. Another view is provided by Freema Elbaz (1983) and Michael Connelly and Jean Clandinin (1988), who maintain that teachers' personal and practical knowledge is the key to understanding teachers' reasons for their educational actions and a basis for understanding the (asserted) "dialectical" relationship between knowing and doing.

Amidst this array of views, we think it important to make two specific claims. With respect to the distinction between knowledge production and knowledge use we would agree with Jere Confrey (1987) when she writes that

> . . . it is more helpful to conceive of knowledge production and knowledge use as a continuum by which different types of intellectual "activities" can be described, not as characteristic of different "occupations" of researcher and teacher. Both teacher and researcher engage in knowledge production and knowledge use. (Confrey 1987, p. 388)

While we agree with Confrey that knowledge use and knowledge production should be construed along a continuum, and with her view that both the teacher and the researcher engage in knowledge production and use, we also sense that teachers' and researchers' intellectual activities, their knowledge production and use, differ in important ways. Essentially we maintain that teachers' intellectual conundrums are concerned more with "solving" practical problems that they personally confront. Researchers, on the other hand, seem to be influenced less by the practical and immediately felt constraints of teaching and instead tend to be influenced and impelled by the discipline-oriented inquiries and practices of fellow researchers. In effect, we sense that although both teachers and researchers engage in knowledge production and use, they do so with different purposes in mind and within different social and institutional contexts.

It also seems reasonable to argue that although the outcomes of knowledge production come in many types and forms and can serve a variety of purposes, they cannot independently and authoritatively sanction educational practices. Generalizable knowledge about schools as institutions, about teachers's work, children's learning, and about the relationship between community and school can and has been produced. For example, it is accurate to say that public schools in the United States have become bureaucratic institutions, which teachers frequently find to be stressful places, and where children's learning is focused on basic, minimal skills. This type of knowledge can inform prospective teachers' educational plans and actions, their instructional and curricular views, and their social and political action in and around the schools. More specific and context-sensitive knowledge about particular children's linguistic backgrounds, past community-school relationships, and individual children's interest in and previous understanding of particular curricular knowledge can also be generated. As we related in the last chapter, Shirley Brice Heath's (1983) study uncovered a wealth of knowledge about one particular working-class community, its children's linguistic habits, and the way in which these habits and the linguistic norms of the public schools constrained the working-class black and white children's educational futures. This knowledge certainly can (and in the case of Heath's study did) inform teachers' educational actions. While we highlight the importance of recognizing that knowledge about schools comes in many forms, we want to stress, along with Charles Lindblom and David Cohen (1979), that research cannot deliver independent, authoritative knowledge. But the fact that it cannot deliver authoritative knowledge does not diminish the importance of research. It does not mean that social inquiry has nothing to offer. Instead we think it has a great deal to offer and we will outline potential contributions. In the remainder of this section we look first at historical accounts for why the gap between researchers' and teachers' (and teacher educators') knowledge production and knowledge use exists. We then move on to consider the potential role for university-initiated research that examines the social conditions of schooling and teacher education.

A historical glimpse

In answering the question "Why has basic research on teaching had so little influence on practice?" Arthur Bolster (1983) argues that it is because researchers utilize a theoretical perspective that is incompatible with the one teachers use. Researchers and teachers "adopt radically different sets of assumptions about how to conceptualize the teaching process" (Bolster 1983, p. 259). According to Bolster, teachers' knowledge is

> idiographic in origin and therefore particularistic in character; that is, this knowledge derives from the need to comprehend the complexity of a particular context with sufficient accuracy to be able to act efficaciously in it. (Bolster 1983, p. 298)

In contrast, university researchers' knowledge is

> nomothetic in aim and universalistic in character; that is social scientists seek to establish general principles about classes of human objects. Their aim is not to explain a particular situation in as much depth as possible, but rather to define and demonstrate the systematic operation of principles across like situations. (Bolster 1983, p. 301)

While this seems a generally fair depiction of (some) researcher and teacher approaches to knowledge production and use, we think it important to examine how the research orientation came to be *the* valued orientation in schools of education. One would think that the purpose of educational research would be to facilitate sound and desirable educational practices. However, as Bolster argues, it simply has not had that effect. One could maintain that it is wishful thinking to expect anything more from this ill-matched union. Teachers and researchers will continue to think and do as they do. But we have reason to expect that some change is possible. In the history of teacher education and educational research, we find grounds for questioning the breadth of the gap between teachers' and researchers' knowledge production and use.

Recent accounts of the formative years of prominent schools of education produce at least three notable generalizations. Relying on the research of Woodie T. White (1982), Geraldine Clifford and James Guthrie (1988), and Arthur Powell (1980), we have found that the following trends characterize research and teacher education in many schools of education during this century.

1. Schools and departments of education in prominent universities, compensating for their lack of status within the university, focused on their doctoral training function (rather than teacher education) and pursued a "scientific" research path. This meant that the problems of elementary and secondary schooling were frequently overlooked. Research tended to focus not on school issues but rather on "academic problems." That is, researchers examined "some lacuna or ambiguity in the data or interpretations of a worldwide discipline," or a problem instigated by "a question asked by colleagues who are other academics in one's field" (Clifford and Guthrie 1988, p. 88). Woodie White (1982) writes that one result of all this was that "In their search for professional respectability professors of education often ignored important teaching and learning issues" (White 1982, p. 145).

2. The faculty in schools of education tended to divide into two groups: "those who profess allegiance to scientific and disciplinary methods and those bound to the field by the mandates of professional training . . ." (Clifford and Guthrie 1988, p. 87). Higher status and prestige were attached to those who pursued research rather than those involved in professional training.

3. The emphasis on research and the lack of attention to teachers' practical problems was further fueled by many schoolmen's belief that teaching was an "activity of low prestige, suitable chiefly for women" (Clifford and Guthrie 1988, p. 116). As Clifford and Guthrie relate, "In the minds of influential schoolmen the understandable repudiation of normal schools and their preoccupation with direct practice was extended to teachers in general, to pedagogy, and to the women with whom normal schools were associated" (Clifford and Guthrie 1988, p. 116). In fact, Powell claims that Henry Holmes, Dean of the Harvard School of Education (1919–1940), believed that the school's "reputation and success within Harvard was directly proportional to its dominance by males" (Powell 1980, p. 154). Women students could come to Harvard

"so long as they did not exceed an intuitive critical mass" (p. 154). Utilizing Susan Laird's (1988) theses (see chapter 4), it seems plausible to assert initially that two beliefs were prominent at the time: (1) Public school teaching was perceived as woman's work because it was said to correspond to women's nature; (2) it was believed that women's presence would tarnish the future of the education professoriate. White's (1982), Clifford and Guthrie's (1988), and Powell's (1980) historical analyses indicate that these beliefs affected the direction of educational research, the development of teaching, and the prominence of teacher education.

White summarizes his study of the University of Chicago's School of Education in a way that captures the relationship that has developed between educational research and teacher education. By 1933

> the University of Chicago study of education had become a fragmented, highly specialized study that seemed more concerned with creating a respectable body of research, establishing specialized roles, and exerting control over mobility in the education profession than in developing a course of study where theory and practice could meet. . . . Judd and his men reinforced the notion that teaching was an endeavor unworthy of a white man's life work. They sought to achieve professional and academic status by emphasizing scientific training for roles above and beyond the classroom and by discriminating against population groups [women, African-Americans, and Asians] that detracted from the dignity of the education profession. The American classroom was no longer the central place of action for the education professional. Now there were other arenas for the development of new—and some thought more important—careers. (White 1982, p. 171)

If these characterizations capture aspects of the relationship between educational research, schooling, and teacher education in this century, we have reason to reconsider why educational research has had so little effect on teaching. While this information certainly does not establish any definitive historical factors that created the gap between teachers' and researchers' knowledge production and use, it does raise the distinct possibility that individual, institutional, and larger societal forces might have played a significant role. Given this historical glimpse, we believe that arguments maintaining an inevitable and natural gap between research efforts and teaching activities are weakened. It now seems reasonable to examine, discuss, and possibly pursue arrangements establishing a closer working relationship between university researchers and teachers. In the next major section of this chapter we will take this bit of history, along with our concern for the social conditions of schooling, into account when we suggest guidelines for university research focused on teacher education and the social contexts of schooling. But before we outline the guidelines, we need to clarify the types of research endeavors we think are reasonable to expect from educational research focused on these areas.

Potential contributions of research

One of the motivating forces behind the early schoolmen's drive toward "scientific research" seemed to be a desire for "firm" and authoritative answers. Today there are still those in the education profession who believe that educational research can provide authoritative answers to educational conundrums, while others belittle the value of most research.[12] If we are calling for further educational research on the social contexts of schooling and teacher education, then it seems we need to outline our expectations for what it can and cannot produce. Generally we maintain that educational research, or (as Lindblom and Cohen [1979] call it) professional social inquiry (PSI), has not and cannot offer independent authoritative knowledge. Educational research alone cannot produce knowledge capable of directing educational policy or practice. It cannot do so for two central reasons. First, it lacks the basis for deciding normative issues and therefore cannot secure the much-needed consensus for educational policy and practice. Second, educational research tends to raise additional problems rather than simply solve questions already posed. It usually highlights rather than diminishes the perceived complexity of the social world. As Denis Phillips argues, "The bottom line is that social scientists have not been able to discover generalizations that are reliable enough and about which there is enough professional consensus, to form the basis for social policy" (Phillips 1980, p. 17). Phillips's argument can be illustrated by the following example. Many researchers have found that tracking (and ability grouping) harms most those in the lower tracks.[13] Other researchers have found that tracking further disadvantages those students who are already at a social and economic disadvantage.[14] While these empirical claims appear fairly secure, we have not yet come up with a basis for altering the educational policy of grouping by assessed ability. As we noted in chapter 3, some critics of tracking argue that all we need is some fine tuning; tracking, in and of itself, is not the problem. Other critics argue that the entire practice needs to be dismantled. It seems a more accurate assessment of the causal connections between tracking and its effects, and between the social context of schooling, tracking and its effects are needed. Another obstacle to change seems to be the distinct and complicated political and social values associated with the practice of tracking. This example should illustrate, if only at a surface level, how difficult it is to come up with generalizations that are capable of affecting institutional change. Phillips's (1980) argument about the inability of social science to affect social action is endorsed in various ways by Lee Cronbach (1982), Alasdair MacIntyre (1984), and Charles Lindblom and David Cohen (1979). We will not repeat all the arguments here. We believe the claim that educational research cannot produce independent authoritative knowledge to be fairly secure. Instead we will raise the following question: If educational research cannot produce independent authoritative knowledge, what can it accomplish?

It can, we believe, accomplish a great deal. Just because educational research has not and cannot produce knowledge that provides independent and authoritative answers to our educational conundrums does not mean it is incapable of producing knowledge that can inform, frame, and guide educational policy and practice. The goal cannot be universal, nomothetic-knowledge claims that guarantee policy options or classroom practices. But the goals could include warranted-knowledge claims that add further evidence to arguments about the social conditions of schooling, and coherent conceptual frameworks that illuminate aspects of the social context of schooling (see Fenstermacher, 1980). More specifically, it seems that research could attempt to: (1) engage in "partisan" research focused on particular problems; (2) discover and convey journalistic reportings about the social context of schooling; or (3) elaborate conceptual frameworks that enable people to see the social contexts of schooling and teacher education in new or unexpected ways. These are three distinct directions for professional research. A single research endeavor could not satisfy all three agendas. A "partisan" research effort could not, at the same time, be characterized as a journalistic reporting of the social context of schooling. But since we sense that research efforts in all three directions might make for more effective connections between professional research and educational action, we briefly outline them below.

Partisan research efforts

In their book *Usable Knowledge,* Lindblom and Cohen (1979) propose the partisan agenda and maintain that

> even if the PSI [professional social inquiry] is itself as objective or disinterested as possible, [the] uses of it are partisan in that they serve to advance the interests of persons who, playing roles in an interactive process, are necessarily partisan. . . . To adapt PSI to interactive problem solving—and our hypothesis is that it has to be so adapted to be effective—is thus to run contrary to a widespread belief that PSI should serve non-partisan purposes. (Lindblom and Cohen 1979, p. 62)

Arguing further, they maintain that an acceptance of the partisan agenda entails that

> some common canons for some forms of PSI—those guiding academic social science, for example—will have to be amended, among them those that govern relations between pPSI [practitioners of professional social inquiry] and desired audience. It would not follow that a pPSI should bias his results to suit an audience, but it would seem to follow that in performing any given research he could usefully work for one of a variety of possible audiences and take his orientation not from an implicitly postulated "the" public interest, as is common, but from one of various explicitly recognized partisan interests each playing its role in the resolution of policy conflict. (Lindblom and Cohen 1979, p. 65)

An example of a partisan but unbiased research endeavor might help here. One of us (Liston) has argued in previous work (1988a and 1988b) that many radical explanatory theories of schooling lack substantial evidential warrant. He maintains that it is personally, professionally, and politically important to pursue a radical research agenda that is framed and informed by radical concerns, values, and conceptual frameworks. But, he also maintains that it is important to scrutinize the empirical and causal claims advanced by radicals to explain why schools are as they are. Liston's research agenda is partisan in the sense that it accepts key radical values and utilizes central radical concepts. In this way it highlights and underscores an important degree of shared normative concerns and utilizes similar conceptual categories. But the proposed research agenda is not biased since it constitutes an attempt to examine the accuracy of radical explanations of schooling. It is an example of a partisan, but not biased, research agenda.

In the domain of teacher education this policy of partisan research could take a variety of forms. At its most basic level, it would simply mean that researchers identify and elaborate their basic educational beliefs and values (that is, the educational tradition out of which they are working), and explain how their research addresses either issues within a particular research paradigm or problems faced by teachers who share similar normative commitments.[15] Now it might be argued that researchers do not ply their trade within particular educational research traditions—their work is much broader than that. While that may be the case for some research issues, we think the social, political, and cultural obstacles facing teachers are illuminated best when researchers consciously identify their educational commitments. In order for university research to have some impact, to influence educational change, we think it will have to operate within the boundaries of a degree of normative consensus. It will have to address the meanings and beliefs of practitioners, and focus on problems that both researcher and teacher feel are notable ones.

Journalistic efforts

We also sense that what Lindblom and Cohen (1979) simply call "reporting" is integral to further research in teacher education. In studies of teacher education, efforts similar to the Research About Teacher Education (RATE)[16] project of the American Association of Colleges for Teacher Education would be illuminating. In that project, researchers are attempting to provide basic data and information on program descriptions and faculty and student profiles. It seems we could also benefit from an enhanced understanding of which children benefit from school, which schools and school districts are relatively rich and which ones are poor, a knowledge of the racial, ethnic, and class diversity of school populations, the curriculum adoption procedures in various schools and states, and much much more. Little, if any, of this information entails the formulation of lawlike generalizations. Instead, it entails descriptive glimpses of life in and around public schools and schools of education. Future teachers and teacher educators would benefit greatly, we think, from more "journalistic" accounts of the social contexts of schooling and teacher education.

Conceptual frameworks

Certainly one of the most important contributions of research is the creation of key concepts and conceptual frameworks that enable people to see the world differently. These research efforts are potentially the most provocative and enlightening. Examining teaching and the social context of schools through various conceptual frameworks, one begins to see new issues, reformulate old issues, question one's accepted image of society and the social order, and look at oneself in a new light. The radical tradition has offered a number of illuminating lenses utilizing both neo-Marxist and feminist conceptual frameworks.[17] The "use" of these lenses does not amount to a "technical application" of a theory or conceptual framework, but rather has the effect of altering our ordinary way of understanding by calling into question the conceptual categories we utilize and the ends we think we want to achieve.[18] Others, notably Lindblom and Cohen (1979), and Cronbach (1982) agree. Lindblom and Cohen note that

> when one casts about for examples of PSI's contribution to so-
> cial problem solving, the most obvious examples are not the
> social engineering studies . . . but seem to be the more funda-
> mental enlightenment of thought achieved by such pPSI as
> Adam Smith, Marx, Freud, and Dewey. (Lindblom and Cohen
> 1979, p. 73)

Lee Cronbach states that the social scientist's

135

main stock in trade is not prescriptions, or laws or definitive assessments of proposed actions; we supply concepts, and these alter perceptions. Fresh perceptions suggest new paths for action and alter the criteria for assessment. . . . Concepts contribute to pluralistic decision making by helping participants examine their situations and values. (Cronbach 1982, pp. 71–72)

Whether the research be partisan, a simple reporting of "facts," or the elaboration of conceptual frameworks, it seems important to keep in mind that it has the potential to guide and inform practice. With these ideas in mind we move on to our final section where we elaborate our 'guidelines' for educational research focused on the social contexts of schooling and teacher education and examine three pieces of research in light of our proposed guidelines.

Educational research and the social conditions of schooling and teacher education

Given our previous discussion of the holist-individualist dichotomy in educational research, our analysis of the history of educational research and teacher education, and our examination of the possibilities of university-initiated research focused on the social context of schooling, we think the following "guidelines" could prove helpful. These guidelines touch on concerns raised in this and previous chapters and it is our sense that they will help orient future inquiry to the social and political conditions of schooling and teacher education.

1. Substantively, the research should focus on teaching as a situated practice and highlight the institutional and larger social and political contexts. Teachers and teacher educators deliberate, make decisions, and act within institutions and larger social contexts. Their deliberations may or may not take these contexts into account. Viewing teaching as a situated practice would encourage a heightened focus on the political, social, and institutional contexts of teachers' actions; it would also encourage attention to be given to the consequences of teachers' actions. As we noted earlier, many of the proposals that view teaching as a situated practice do not examine the relevant contexts. We maintain that research into this area needs to focus on a variety of types of possible contextual dynamics, and that leads us to our second guideline.

2. Research in this area needs to give special attention to the gender, race, and class dynamics of schooling and teacher education. This is obviously part of our social-reconstructionist agenda. But regardless of our own agenda, it seems that both teacher education research and the curriculum for prospective teachers have ignored an examination of these dynamics. Substantial investigations into the possibility that these dynamics affect the situated practices of teachers and teacher educators are in order. Although there has been some research in this area, it remains essentially uncharted. While these investigations seem to promise potentially rich rewards, one needs to keep in mind that recent investigations of the social and political context of schooling have, at times, tended to view teachers as simple puppets, "dupes," of larger social forces. When one begins to examine the "unacknowledged" conditions of teachers' actions, there is a tendency for researchers to assume a "privileged" vantage point. Our next guideline is offered to help curtail this sort of development.

3. The research focus should be informed directly by the concerns of school practitioners and teacher educators. Whether the research involves formal collaboration with practitioners of teaching and teacher education or not, it needs to be focused on issues that are of importance to practitioners, include the "voices" of practitioners as part of the interpretations of the meaning of the research, and reflect a commitment to the teachers, administrators, and teacher educators who participate in the research. Research that is focused on teaching and/or teacher education can be used either to enable tighter controls over the actions of practitioners (an instrumental view of the research-practice relationship) or to empower practitioners of teaching and teacher education to become more aware of and hence gain more control over their situations (an educative view of the research-practice relationship). We endorse the later position and agree with Nel Noddings when she writes that

> in educational research, fidelity to persons counsels us to
> choose our problems in such a way that the knowledge gained
> will promote individual growth and maintain the caring com-
> munity. . . . Researchers have perhaps too often made persons
> (teachers and students) the objects of research. An alternative is
> to choose problems that interests and concern researchers, stu-
> dents, and teachers. . . . Such research would be genuine re-
> search *for* teaching instead of simply research *on* teaching.
> (Noddings 1987, p. 394)

One way to realize this ethical commitment to practitioners of teaching and teacher education in university-based research is to develop formal collaborations with those whose work is the focus of study. The Interactive Research and Development projects of the late 1970s and early 1980s (Noffke 1990) as well as the more recent collaborative action research efforts initiated by Oja and Smulyan (1989) illustrate how these formal research collaborations can be developed between university-based researchers and teachers. Some of the recent work of the National Center for Research on Teacher Education (NCRTE 1988) illustrates how university researchers can develop collaborative relationships with practicing teacher educators in the study of teacher education programs. Another option is for university-based researchers to support the action research efforts initiated by practicing teachers and teacher educators (e.g., Golby 1989).[19] But irrespective of the form it takes, research *for* teaching and teacher education will have to work out of and develop a normative basis. In keeping with our arguments in chapter 2—where we maintained that the normative basis of teaching depends upon an understanding of the distinct educational traditions—we believe that research *for* teaching and teacher education also has to recognize the various and distinct conceptions of the teacher's role and of the activity of education. And that brings us to our fourth and final guideline.

4. Educational research in teacher education should become, in Lindblom and Cohen's words, partisan. Throughout this work we have argued for the value of identifying, elaborating, and articulating basic traditions of educational thought and practice. We examined the history of reform efforts in teacher education as constituted in part by the academic, social-efficiency, developmentalist, and social-reconstructionist educational traditions. We argued that teacher education programs ought to assist prospective teachers to articulate their beliefs and values utilizing philosophical conceptions of educational traditions as heuristic devices, or ideal types. Educational traditions (both the sociohistorical traditions and the more ideal-typical conception) provide a context of key normative agreements (and disagreements), shared concerns, and recognized problems and issues. An educational researcher who has as one of his/her key goals the guidance of educational practice, ought to recognize the normative nature of the educational endeavor, make clear how his/her normative commitments affect the research endeavor, and link the research to other efforts in particular traditions.[20]

We are calling, then, for research to focus on the social and political conditions of teaching and teacher education, to view teachers as engaged in situated practices, to examine the class, gender, and racial features as well as the institutional dynamics of schooling and teacher education, to take into account teachers' concerns and practical conundrums, and to become more partisan in direction and development. Finally, so as to clarify and give further substance to these guidelines, we move on to consider the ways in which three recent educational research efforts exemplify one or more of these guidelines.

Examples of research

Our guidelines are capable of informing a variety of types of inquiry. Generally we hold that there is not one research methodology or general conceptual framework that has any sort of privileged status. Structural, statistical, and explanatory approaches along with more interpretive, hermeneutic, and historical approaches seem plausible routes for these investigations. It would seem that the questions posed and the problems formulated would play a large part in determining what methodology was appropriate. But given our past comments we do think that some general types of inquiry are potentially more helpful than others. We would like to encourage more efforts at a basic journalistic reporting, collaborative empirical inquiries, action research, historical examinations of the social conditions of schooling and teacher education, and further elaborations of illuminating conceptual frameworks. Below we briefly examine the work of Shirley Brice Heath (1982 and 1983), Susan Laird (1988), and Barbara Schneider (1987). Their efforts illustrate well for university-initiated research many of the guidelines we think are crucial for future research into the social conditions of schooling and teacher education. Following this discussion of exemplary university-initiated research, we will consider the issue of practitioner-initiated research on teaching and teacher education.

Although Heath (1983) states in the prologue to *Ways with Words* that "By many standards of judgment, this book . . . cannot be considered a model piece of educational . . . research" (p. 7), by our standards it comes close. Her inquiries into children's language use at home and school illustrate well two of our guidelines. As noted in chapter 4, Heath's research focuses on the language use of working-class black and white children. Specifically she examines how these children's linguistic practices conflicted with the predominantly middle-class white public school teachers' linguistic norms and expectations. Her work demonstrates how educational research can highlight teachers' unacknowledged beliefs and lack of knowledge about working-class language use, incorporate parental and teacher concerns into the research agenda, and invite collaboration with teachers inquiring into classroom problems.

Heath began her research at the invitation of working-class black parents. Due to early desegregation efforts, their children were put into what had previously been all-white schools. The parents felt that "little meaningful interaction was occurring between the teachers and their children," and as a result they asked Heath to explain "why their children were not doing better in school" (Heath 1982, p. 106). Not only was she acquainted with many of the community members, but as an instructor at a local college she also taught and knew many of the teachers in the area. She indicates that teachers were "dissatisfied with the lack of involvement and the minimal progress of students from Trackton and similar communities" (Heath 1982, p. 124). She also notes that teachers who

> . . . participated in the study . . . initially held a variety of
> stereotypes about how black children learned language . . .
> [which indicated that they] thought black children's language
> socialization was somehow different from that of other children. Yet in their interactions with black children in the classroom, teachers invariably assumed they would respond to language routines and uses of language in building knowledge,
> skills, and dispositions just as other children did. Some teachers were aware of this paradox, but felt that since they did not
> know how language was taught in black communities and how
> it was used to make children aware of the world around them,
> they had no basis on which to rethink their views of the language socialization of black children. (Heath 1982, p. 114)

It seems that parents and teachers were dissatisfied with and needed more information about the school and the community.

Heath studied a problem that both parents and teachers found troublesome, and she was committed to utilizing her research to improve the situation. Her work with teachers was oriented toward having them become

> participant observers in their own domains and to use the
> knowledge from the ethnographies of Trackton and Roadville to

inform their motivations, practices and programs of teaching. (Heath 1983, pp. 12–13)

Her rationale, she says, was simple:

if change agents (teachers and parents) were willing and involved, knowledge about language use could proceed along a two way path, from the school to the community, and from the community to the school. (Heath 1982, p. 125)

Heath was quite successful. As a result of her own research efforts and teachers' inquiries, teachers altered their pedagogical questioning strategies in ways that would facilitate the black working-class children's involvement in classroom lessons. The teachers became acquainted with what were previously unacknowledged community processes of language use and learning, and as a result of this acquaintance (and a desire to enhance the learning experiences of the black working-class children) they altered their pedagogical processes.

It should be clear from this brief description that Heath's work illustrates well many of our four guidelines. Although she never elaborates a view of teaching as a situated practice, her research efforts seem to assume that it is. Much of her research program appears to be an effort to enhance teachers' knowledge of their particular situations—especially the manner in which the teachers' and the black children's linguistic norms and expectations were initially established and subsequently interacted. Her studies of community and school language use and teachers' own inquiries, gave teachers new information upon which to base their instructional and curricular deliberations. This information corrected teachers' previous conceptions about black language socialization and use, giving them crucial information about their particular social and community context.

Heath certainly shows how cultural differences become institutionalized and, once institutionalized, how they create obstacles for teacher and child alike. Her study capably highlights the institutional context of schooling, but it ultimately overlooks other potentially prominent dynamics. On the surface, it would seem that she explores the class and racial dynamics of the larger social context. She explicitly examines the lack of cultural congruence between black working-class and white middle-class language use. But Heath actually seems to evade important questions about class and racial dynamics. She maintains that

141

> . . . any reader who tries to explain the community contrast in
> this book on the basis of race will miss the central point of the
> focus on culture as learned behavior and on language habits as
> part of that shared learning. Children in Roadville and Trackton
> came to have different ways of communicating, because their
> communities had different social legacies and ways of behaving
> in face-to-face interactions. (Heath 1983, p. 11)

But, as Harold Rosen (1987) questions, it would seem that a significant part of the social legacy for the Trackton community would be "the experience of racism and its continued existence" (Rosen 1987, p. 447). Rosen maintains, and we would agree, that "black English is the expression and negotiation of black experience. Racism does no more than lurk in the shadows of this text [*Ways with Words*] raising questions which are not posed by Heath" (Rosen 1987, p. 447). Heath notes that the civil rights movement brought with it changes in black employment possibilities and that racial antagonisms existed in the town, but little else is noted. One wonders whether those racial antagonisms affected how and what Trackton parents thought about their children entering a white school with white teachers? Heath notes that the teachers held stereotypical views of black language development. One wonders to what degree these views were supported by or were an outgrowth of a very narrow cultural understanding on the part of the teachers? In Heath's account we rarely see adult black-and-white, student black-and-white interactions. It seems reasonable to wonder if this occurred and if racial tensions were present.

With regard to issues of class, Heath mentions the history of strikes but goes on to maintain that "the topics of their talk rarely include their work" (Heath 1983, p. 365). If it is accurate that the working adults did not talk about their jobs at home, did they talk about them while at work? Were there recent efforts to unionize workers? Were family members in previous generations involved in any strikes or workplace conflicts? Were there tensions between black and white workers? Heath does not pursue these issues. We believe, however, that if the class and racial contexts were more fully elaborated, additional unacknowledged factors might be uncovered.

Heath's research is certainly research *for* both teachers and the Trackton community. Her work was initiated by black parents concerned about their children's lack of educational progress. It involved teachers in an examination of their own and others' language use and focused on problems and issues that were crucial for both parents and teachers. In fact, in order for her work to be successful, Heath maintains that two components were necessary:

> first, teachers as inquirers and second, credible data from both the classroom and the students' communities. For teachers to be involved in the inquiring process, they had to want to know what and how they and their students learned in language socialization, and they had to take part in collecting the data to answer these questions. (Heath 1982, p. 126)

Finally, Heath's work can be characterized as effectively, but not explicitly, partisan. Heath does not describe her research as part of a particular tradition, nor does she identify with a strong normative stance. She characterizes her study as being appropriate for almost all those whose lives are touched by children: teachers interested in learning more about the educational process and themselves; parents and community members who want to find out more about children (Heath 1983, p. 13). And, as we noted earlier, she seems to evade the racial dynamics and class antagonisms among the people in her study. Although an explicit partisan stance seems absent, it is clear that her research is directed toward and is in a central sense *for* the people being studied. Her own ethnographic work and her work with parents and teachers clearly had an impact on altering teachers' perceptions of themselves, their students, and their instructional strategies. One could, we think, analyze Heath's work and identify key aspects of Heath's normative commitments. For example, she appears to accept a somewhat progressive view of the curriculum, one in which knowledge of the students plays a key role in instructional strategies and curricular programs. But, we think, partisan research should more clearly identify the normative commitments of the research endeavor so that they are more easily discerned by the reader.

That Heath's research illustrates positively some but not all of our guidelines is not terribly significant. Her work is exceptional. But since we wish to elaborate and illustrate more fully our second and fourth guidelines, we will discuss briefly Susan Laird's (1988) conceptual analysis offered in "Reforming 'Woman's True Profession': A Case for 'Feminist Pedagogy' in Teacher Education." Laird's analysis can be described as partisan and certainly as research that analyzes the contextual features (i.e. gender) of schooling.

In "Reforming 'Woman's True Profession' " Laird argues that the

143

recent teacher education reform reports (the Holmes Group report—
Tomorrow's Teachers and the Carnegie report—*A Nation Prepared:
Teachers for the 21st Century*) rely on unexamined views of the teacher
and teaching. More pointedly, she maintains that the Holmes and Carnegie reports fail to examine the "still common conception of school
teaching as "woman's true profession." In doing so, she argues, they
overlook the significance of feminist conceptions of teaching and of
feminist pedagogy for teacher education. Laird's analysis of the meaning
of "woman's true profession," utilizing her five interpretive theses, raises
significant questions about the ways in which current conceptions of
teaching and teachers are connected to or rely upon particular conceptual
constructions of gender: women as "natural" teachers, women teachers
as a central source of the educational profession's problems, and teaching
as an occupation that devalues women as professionals. One of Laird's
central claims is that the

> taken-for-granted language of the Holmes Group and the Carne-
> gie Forum . . . [their] "standard" or "ordinary" language . . .
> renders all talk and writing about feminist pedagogy anomalous
> in educational philosophy and policy studies and therefore mar-
> ginal at best in most talk and writing about teacher education
> reform as well. The "woman's true profession" slogan suggests
> that taking schoolteachers seriously means taking their gender
> seriously and asking again, with them, What does and should
> "teaching" mean? (Laird 1988, p. 462)

In effect, she is arguing for

> . . . the importance of philosophical inquiry concerning the
> meaning of feminist pedagogy, its implicit challenge to the
> dominant so-called gender-neutral concept of teaching that the
> Holmes Group and the Carnegie Forum do not challenge, and
> the as yet unimagined practical possibilities it may suggest for
> actually educating—not simply training—school teachers.
> (Laird 1988, p. 463)

Laird's work is explicitly partisan and focuses on the gendered context
of teaching. She elaborates and encourages others to pursue a feminist
analysis of teaching.

Finally, we want to highlight a piece of research that examines the social conditions of teacher education. In her article, "Tracing the Provenance of Teacher Education," Barbara Schneider (1987) maintains that in order to understand the problems of teacher education, one needs to examine the institutional context in which teacher education has developed. Schneider examines briefly the historical development of teacher education, and she focuses on the work environments of teacher educators in an effort to explain teacher educators' low prestige, power, and research productivity.

Historically she notes that when "pedagogical study was considered an integral part of philosophy, pedagogical literature received no more or less criticism than other disciplines." However, when philosophy and psychology divided into two distinct disciplines, educational psychology incorporated "didactic thinking" and philosophy took up the moral and ethical aspects of pedagogy. Neither philosophy nor psychology was concerned with questions of "how to teach," and this "left teacher education with having to grapple with the most technical aspect of pedagogy. Consequently, since teacher education's inauspicious beginnings, it has been faced with trying to define a legitimate substantive knowledge base focused on training" (p. 214).

Schneider goes on to note that while faculty members in research-oriented schools of education chose the "research mode of experimentalization, quantification and classification" (p. 216) as the way to acquire more technical knowledge, their successes have been minimal. And despite only minimal successes, educational research seemed to gain importance and status within the university. As it did so, however, "it became less and less available to teacher educators" (p. 218). Summarizing briefly her historical examination and highlighting the importance of a contextual-institutional analysis, she writes that:

Professors of teacher education have a continuous history of low status, and their subject area has repeatedly been perceived as devoid of content which has intellectual coherence. This historical context of teacher education has been somewhat neglected by researchers who have tended to trace some of the problems of the field to the characteristics of the faculty members who work in this area. By concentrating on the problems of individual faculty, some researchers have overlooked the relationships between the quality of teacher education and the institutional context in which teacher education departments were created and exist. (p. 219)

Pursuing further the institutional context of teacher education Schneider found that "the organizational structure of schools of education in research universities places teacher education faculty at a resource disadvantage. Schools of education are commonly structured so that faculty in educational psychology have more time for research, teach more graduate courses, and chair and serve on more dissertation committees than faculty in other specialization areas. Teacher educators are assigned less time for research, teach more undergraduate courses, and chair and serve on fewer dissertation committees" (p. 231). But the problem lies not only within schools of education but also with the perception and low regard that the larger university academy has for teacher education. Schneider maintains that teacher education's low status, power, and prestige within the university persists even when individual teacher education programs maintain high-quality programs and produce respectable research.

For our purposes, Schneider's analysis conveys the intellectual power to be had from examining the social context of teacher education. Her examination of the history and institutional context of teacher education is not pointedly partisan. But she does discuss the possible interpretations of teacher educators as gendered and class actors, and she views teacher educators as engaged in situated practices (e.g., more heavily involved in labor-intensive activities than many faculty members). Her analysis also capably highlights the dynamics that exist in schools of education and the larger university. As teacher educators, we must examine not only the social context of elementary and secondary teachers' work but also our own situations. We will explore further in chapter 7 the ramifications of such an analysis of teacher education, but for now we wish merely to note that our research "proposal" emphatically includes analyses of teacher education programs.

There are certainly other examples that would illustrate further the meaning of our guidelines and our sense of what is needed in research for teacher education. Emily Feistritzer's (1985) data collections as reported in *The Condition of Teaching: A State by State Analysis* (1985) convey a wealth of information about teachers and the conditions of teaching. The *National Survey of Teacher Education* (circa 1930) documented, among other things, how teacher education was supported in different parts of United States. Specifically, it highlights differences in teacher education for Caucasians and for "Negroes." Larry Cuban's (1984) historical analysis of how teachers taught, the ethnographic and historical examination of school innovation by Louis Smith et al. (1986,

1987, and 1988), and John Goodlad's (1990) historical analysis of teacher education institutions are very helpful. These historical analyses illuminate and convey some sense of the durability and the way in which the social context constrains and enables teachers and other educational actors. We also think it important for teacher educators to examine their own programs, to assess the degree to which their efforts fail to accomplish and also successfully achieve aspects of their program's goals. Our own work (Zeichner and Liston 1985, 1987, and 1988) examining the success and shortcomings of the University of Wisconsin's reflectively oriented teacher education program is one example of this sort of endeavor. It should be obvious that we are not attempting to prescribe one approach to research in this area. Additional examples could be cited that illustrate further the potential variety of orientations. In the future, however, we do think that researchers should consider these proposed guidelines and their implications for future research if university-initiated educational research is to play an educative role in relation to practice in teaching and teacher education.

Practitioner research

Thus far in this chapter we have emphasized research conducted by college and university academics on the teaching practices of others, either in primary or secondary schools or in teacher education programs. Now we will briefly discuss research that is conducted by either K–12 educators or teacher education faculty in higher education on their own practices. We use the label of "practitioner research" to refer to inquiries that are conducted into one's own practice in teaching or teacher education. Two of the most recent major compilations of research on teaching do not include a single chapter (out of a total of fifty-nine) authored by a K–12 school-based educator (Reynolds 1989; Wittrock 1986) and make little if any reference to the growing body of published accounts of the research of classroom teachers.[21] Nevertheless, there is little doubt that during the last two decades there has been a tremendous growth in the U.S. and elsewhere in the notion of teachers as researchers and in the acceptance of the potentially important contribution that teachers can make to the "knowledge base" for teaching and the improvement of schooling. Elliott (1985) accurately describes the current popularity of teacher-initiated educational-action research as international in scope:

In the educational field action research has developed into an international movement. Collaborative networks of classroom teachers, teacher educators, and educational researchers have been established in the U.K., Australia, Canada, Germany, Austria, and Iceland, and there are signs that the movement is spreading in the USA and Spain. The Classroom Action Research Network (CARN) based at the Cambridge Institute of Education in the United Kingdom was established in 1976 to disseminate ideas about the theory and practice of educational action research and keep individuals and groups in touch with each other on a regular basis. (p. 231)

In recent years there has been an emergence of a number of books that seek to provide methodological guidance to teachers in carrying out their own school-based inquiries (e.g., Hopkins 1985, Kemmis and McTaggart 1988, Walker 1985, Woods 1986); an increased emphasis in preservice teacher education programs on preparing student teachers to be conscious researchers of their own practices (e.g., Gore and Zeichner 1990, Ross 1987, Ruddick 1985); and a tremendous increase in the publication of studies conducted by K–12 educators (e.g., Goswami and Stillman, 1987; Hustler, Cassidy, and Cuff 1986; Mohr and Maclean 1987; Nixon 1981; Wood 1988) and in published accounts of collaborative research efforts involving university researchers and K–12 educators (e.g., Butt, Raymond, and Yamagishi 1988; Cole 1989; Gomez 1990; Oja and Smulyan, 1989). There has also been a growth in the organization of communities of teacher researchers both in the public schools (Philadelphia Teachers Learning Cooperative 1984) as well as within established academic research organizations such as the American Educational Research Association (Current and Hirabayashi, 1989).

Unfortunately, this movement to democratize the research process has not been as effective in teacher education as it has been in the research on teaching. Although there is less of an institutional division between those who do the work of teacher education and those who do research about teacher education than there is with regard to research on teaching (i.e., teacher education researchers are almost always employed in institutions that have teacher education programs), the actual involvement of teacher education researchers in the teacher education programs on their campuses is often minimal at best. Most of those in the 1,400 or so institutions across the U.S. who are closely involved in teacher education programs have little visibility in the recent compilation of the so called "knowledge base" of teacher education (Houston 1990), despite the fact that most teacher educators are continually engaged in some type of self-study of their practices required either by their institution or by state or national accreditation bodies. Knowledge production in teacher education that reaches national visibility in the published litera-ture is generated from only a handful of research universities that prepare very few of the teachers certified each year across the U.S. (Clark and Guba 1976).

One consequence of this separation of teacher educators from teacher education research is that the questions, concerns, and voices of teacher educators are often absent from research on teacher education. Much of the research on teacher education in the U.S. is not at all sensitive to the institutional and political realities of teacher education (see chapter 7) and is rejected as superfluous by teacher educators.[22] We have seen a growing acceptance of the contribution that teachers can make to the "knowledge base" for teaching and the improvement of schooling. But we also need to see more: a greater representation of the perspectives of teacher educators in the research conducted on teacher education, more genuinely collaborative research efforts involving external researchers and teacher educators, and greater support for and recognition of the action-research efforts of teacher educators who study their own practices and programs.

Most of the practitioner-oriented research on teaching and teacher education that has been conducted to date has been focused on the level of the classroom (either elementary, secondary, or tertiary). This focus on the classroom, while important for the contribution it can make to our understanding of teaching and teacher education under existing conditions, is limited with regard to its emancipatory potential. We agree with Martin Lawn's (1989) call for a broadening of the focus in teacher research to include the institutional conditions of schooling among what is considered to be problematic.[23] He believes that a broader view of the scope of teacher research can:

> Encourage teachers to turn their attention to those aspects of
> their work which define it so closely and create contradictions
> they have to deal with: management, supervision, job defini-
> tion, time, intra staff relations, resources, and so on. (p. 158)

Lawn's (1989) position is consistent with our earlier comments about the need for educational researchers to view teaching as a situated practice, highlighting the institutional and larger social and political contexts in which the teaching is embedded. One clear example of teacher research that fulfills this criterion and that also meets our other criteria of giving special attention to the gender, ethnic, and class dynamics of schooling, and of assuming a partisan stance is the work of the Boston Women's Teachers' Group, *The Effect of Teaching on Teachers* (Freedman, Jackson, and Boles, 1986).[24] This group of public school teachers in the Boston area had been meeting weekly as a teacher support group for three years and wished to study their own work situations, particularly their sense of isolation from one another, and how the structural conditions of their work influence their attitudes toward their work, self-esteem, and sense of efficacy over a career. In addition to understanding the conditions of teaching more fully, these teachers also wanted to assist one another in coping with the stresses of their work. They interviewed twenty-five women elementary teachers biweekly or bimonthly over a two-month period and identified a set of themes in these interviews that portrayed the culture that was shared by the teachers. For example, one of the contradictory aspects of these teachers' situations that was revealed in these interviews is that they work "in an institution which supposedly prepares its clients for adulthood, but which views those entrusted with this task as incapable of mature judgment" (Freedman, Jackson, and Boles 1983, p. 263).

The findings of this research[25] were used to combat the individualistic bias in the school-reform movement of the 1980s, which served to direct teachers' sense of frustration with and anger about their work away from a critical analysis of schools as institutions to a preoccupation with their own individual failures. This research is an exemplary case (within the category of practitioner research) of the kind of educational research that we have advocated throughout this chapter.

When we consider an example within the category of practitioner research on *teacher education* that approaches our proposed criteria for assessing research (i.e., partisan research that focuses on teacher education as a situated practice, highlights the institutional and larger social and political contexts of teacher education, and gives special attention to the gender, ethnic, and class dynamics of teacher education), the Researching Action Research Project conducted over the last five years by a group of graduate student supervisors in the elementary student teaching program at the University of Wisconsin-Madison comes to mind. Susan Noffke, formerly a university supervisor in this program, began this series of inquiries in 1986 with two systematic examinations of the "use" of action research as a vehicle for facilitating student teacher reflection about their work and about the wider situation in which that work was situated (see Noffke and Zeichner, 1987).[26] These initial studies were followed by two more studies in which Noffke, and two other supervisors, Marie Brennan and Jennifer Gore, explored various dimensions of using action research with their student teachers (Gore and Zeichner 1990, Noffke and Brennan, 1991).

In all these studies, the authors joined their student teachers in studying specific aspects of their own practices over time. The focus of these "second-order" action-research projects during the last five years has been on a number of different issues such as the influence of when and in what ways action research is introduced to student teachers; the ways in which students' research is supported in their classrooms, in the student teaching seminars, and through dialogue journals; and the degree to which students' written reports of their action-research projects reveal attention to the moral and political aspects of teaching. This research conducted by student teaching supervisors has addressed various ways in which the institutional and social/political contexts of the Wisconsin student teaching program have influenced the conduct of student teacher action research. For example, this work has involved analyses of the various ways in which both the conceptual apparatus of the program (e.g., conceptions of reflective teaching practice) and certain aspects of its institutional structure have served at times to undermine the democratic and emancipatory aspirations of supervisors. For example, Noffke & Brennan (1991) discuss the ways in which state program accreditation requirements (for documenting supervisory visits), particular program requirements, and the presence of a competitive grading system in the university have served to undermine their goals.[27] For example:

> Because the seminar is graded, the action research project becomes part of the assessment relationship of supervisor to student. Even where grades are negotiated, the compulsory aspect of the project tends to work against the impulse for free and voluntary association which we see as desirable in action research. Each student also has to receive a separate grade.
> Given a local context in which a student's cumulative grade point average plays an increasing role in the selection of job candidates, the grade supports the continuation of the students' understanding of schooling as individual and competitive, and

affects their approach to projects, papers, and sharing in discussion. . . . None of us can afford to ignore the institutionalized patterns of action that must be reconciled with our democratic intentions. (p. 24)

In the last few years, a growing number of analytic reports of the self-studies of teacher educators has appeared in the literature. Several institutions, such as Michigan State University, Ohio State University, the University of Utah, the University of Arizona, and the University of Florida, have emerged as centers of teacher education scholarship in the U.S. because of their efforts to use their teacher education programs as laboratories for the study of teacher education. Although we support this increased visibility for the efforts of teacher educators who systematically study their own practices, many of these efforts lack any emancipatory potential because they do not address the institutional and social/political context of teacher education or give attention to the gender, ethnic, and class dynamics of schooling and teacher education. Lawn's (1989) arguments cited above about the need to broaden the focus in teacher research beyond the level of the classroom are equally applicable to most of the current research that represents the self-studies of teacher educators. Practitioner research on teaching and teacher education needs to be part of the discourse among researchers, practitioners, and policymakers in teacher education and schooling. But it needs to be assessed, as does university initiated research, for its ability to contribute to the realization of a more just and humane situation in our schools and society. The criteria that we have offered in this chapter which emphasize attention to the social conditions of schooling and teacher education represent one possibility for assessing research along these lines.[28]

Conclusion

We began this chapter by calling for an integration of individualist and holist social analyses and for an examination of the gaps between educational research and educational practice. Our sense is that in order for educational research to inform the practice of teaching and teacher education, educational actors must be viewed as engaged in situated practices. Institutional contexts and the dynamics of race, class and gender need to be examined as well. Also, teachers' and teacher educators' felt problems and issues need to be taken into account, and the research needs to become more self-consciously partisan in its direction. There are a variety of methodological avenues available for this sort of endeavor. We are not issuing a narrow edict for all educational research, but instead we have formulated a broad set of concerns that we think should and could guide educational researchers, teachers, and teacher educators in their inquiries into the social context of schooling and teacher education, in studies of their own practices and the practices of others.

But a reformulated research direction is not the only route available for our social-reconstructionist reform agenda. In chapter 3 we examined the potential of models of reflective inquiry for this agenda, and in chapter 4 we suggested specific concerns and issues for university course work. In the next chapter we highlight and examine additional features of existing teacher education programs oriented toward a social-reconstructionist reform agenda, and we identify what we believe are characteristic features of a social-reconstructionist teacher education program. In the final chapter (chapter 7) we take to heart our claim that educational reformers need to examine the social context of schooling. We discuss the obstacles that confront teacher educators committed to the reforms we have outlined thus far.

6

Programmatic Implications of a Social-Reconstructionist Approach to Teacher Education

Opportunities to gain access to the most generally useful knowledge are maldistributed in most schools, with poor and minority children and youths on the short end of the distribution. This is morally wrong, whatever the arguments regarding teachable classes, teachers' comfort, parents' preferences, and even achievement. It is possible—indeed, likely—that college students will go through their general education requirements and academic majors, perhaps to the level of a masters' degree, without even thinking about these inequities in schooling. But it is intolerable for future teachers to remain ignorant and unconcerned. And so their professional education must ensure the necessary loss of innocence. (Goodlad 1990, p. 22)

As was indicated in chapter 1, teacher education programs that place at least some emphasis on social-reconstructionist ideals have been in existence throughout much of this century. Conceptualizations have been developed and programs have been implemented that have had as one of their central aims the preparation of teachers who can play a positive role in the making of a more just, equitable, and humane society.[1] Although these programs are held together by their shared commitment to the betterment of society by furthering the "common good," they have differed from one another with regard to the specific priorities upon which teacher education's role in social reconstruction should be grounded (e.g., the elimination of sexism, racism, poverty, capitalism, poor working conditions for teachers, etc.), and with regard to the means by which the reconstruction should proceed. The debates among social reconstructionists over the roles of indoctrination and experimentalism (i.e., the cultivation of critical intelligence) which were referred to in chapter 1, are an example of the segmentation that has characterized this subcommunity of teacher education for a long time. In this chapter we discuss specific examples of teacher education practices that are consistent with the general approach to teacher education that we have outlined in this book. We will discuss a variety of practices and programs that illustrate attempts to incorporate a social-reconstructionist dimension into a preservice teacher education program.[2] In presenting the specific examples we have chosen, we do not pretend to give a comprehensive account of the current work in this area. We have chosen specific examples to illustrate particular aspects of teacher education practice, and have neglected the work of others,[3] either when we had other examples of what we wanted to illustrate, or when we could not locate any examples of teacher education practices that were explicitly connected to a particular set of ideas.[4]

Reforming teacher education programs

Although most social-reconstructionist–oriented reforms in preservice teacher education have involved changes made in specific courses within program and institutional contexts that remain unchanged, there have been several recent attempts to reformulate entire teacher education programs around social-reconstructionist ideals. These efforts have only taken place on a very small scale, however, either with small teacher education programs in private liberal-arts colleges or with the establishment of experimental/alternative programs within larger institutions. We are not aware of any cases where an entire teacher education program, other than a very small one, has been reformulated along these lines.[5] One reason for the scarcity of highly visible teacher education *programs* that espouse social-reconstructionist ideals has been the fear of teacher educators that they might alienate their students who in many cases are supportive of the status quo in schooling and society (Lanier 1986). Another reason is the tensions that are produced in school-university relations by an approach that assumes an oppositional stance toward existing institutional and societal structures.[6] Tetreault and Braunger (1989, p. 79) conclude, for example, that one of the reasons they weren't straightforward with potential students and cooperating school personnel about their feminist agenda was because they didn't want to alienate program participants at the start:

Knowing that people in education are traditionally conservative, we worried we would alienate prospective partners if we explicitly espoused a feminist agenda. Thus we did not explicitly address gender issues as we sought to build partnerships with school districts and recruit mentor teachers.

This reluctance to articulate a program that might alienate students and cooperating school personnel is only a minor part of the explanation for why examples of social-reconstructionist–inspired teacher education programs have been so scarce. The general failure of these reform-minded educators to spell out the specific implications of their proposals for both teaching and teacher education (Brown 1938), resulting in part from disagreements about the definition of a social-reconstructionist position (Bowers 1969), the general political conservatism of teacher educators as a group (Rugg 1952; Lanier 1986), and teacher education's marginal status in the academy (Clifford and Guthrie 1988), are probably more important reasons for the lack of program-wide examples of the approach.

This inability to sustain a coherent normative focus at the program level is not specific, however, to the social-reconstructionist tradition. Atkin and Raths (1974) have contended that the most common pattern in U.S. preservice teacher education has been an eclectic one, where individual programs lack clarity and a distinctive focus. Goodlad (1990) reinforces this conclusion in his recent study of twenty-nine diverse teacher education institutions across the country. Fragmented and segmented programs that lack a clearly articulated set of purposes and goals seem to be the rule.[7]

One of the most notable contemporary examples of the social-reconstructionist orientation has been the work of Lanny Beyer at Knox and Cornell colleges, which focuses on restructuring teacher education programs along the lines of "teacher education as praxis." Knox and Cornell colleges each have enrollments of about 1,000 students and two full-time education faculty members. Beyer (1988) argues that the small size of these institutions and the location of the programs within nonvocationally oriented environments supportive of inquiry and reflection were advantages in his attempts to develop coherent program reforms.[8]

As was noted in chapter 1, Beyer (1988) has characterized his approach as "foundationally oriented." In addition to the introduction of previously excluded areas of the curriculum such as educational philosophy, history, sociology, and curriculum theory (where previously educational foundations was equivalent to educational psychology), Beyer and his colleagues attempted to reconstruct the rest of the educational studies components of the teacher education programs so that they would encourage a particular quality of analysis by students:

> Rather than tying educational foundations to specific areas within educational studies, and separating them from other aspects of teacher preparation, I propose that we regard as foundational any area or course of study that critically examines the underlying ideas, assumptions, and principles of that area, making them a subject for scrutiny; and that considers how the issues in that area relate to broader normative questions and possibilities. The foundations of education regard the nature of schooling, education and teacher preparation as political, moral, and ideological practice, and make such questions a focus of discussion. (Beyer 1988, pp. 186–87)

Beyer and his colleagues attempted to influence all aspects of the teacher education programs in these two institutions, including field experiences, with this foundational orientation. In fact, field experiences were seen as key sites for the realization of the program goals because they provided opportunities for students to link their reflections about issues of schooling and society with actions to study, and in some cases, to transform concrete school practices (Beyer 1984). Although social-foundations courses have been a common component in teacher education courses for many years (see chapter 1), it has not been common for teacher educators to attempt to link a "foundations perspective" on issues of schooling and society with student teachers' work in schools. It is this effort to broaden our conceptions of both clinical and academic teacher education that makes Beyer's work distinctive.[9]

A second example of an attempt to restructure a teacher education program along social-reconstructionist lines is provided by the MAT program at Lewis and Clark College. Tetreault (1987) and Tetreault and Braunger (1989) describe efforts to infuse a gender-balanced and multicultural perspective throughout this fifteen-month program for the preparation of high school teachers of language arts and social studies. Here, as was the case at Knox and Cornell, teacher educators attempted to revise existing courses and to incorporate their goals throughout the entire program, rather than by merely adding separate courses on women and gender onto an existing program. The feminist-inspired agenda of

Lewis and Clark teacher educators emphasized the development of respect for similarities and differences among individuals because of gender, race, ethnicity, and other characteristics. Through the selection of readings, lecturers, and particular ways of organizing issues for discussion, teacher educators continually and deliberately focused students' attention on issues of gender, race, and class and sought to create an environment where students would be inspired to work against discrimination in these areas when they confronted it as teachers.

> Our goal was a multifocal, relational perspective on the human experience and so we asked throughout where issues of gender were relevant and how issues of gender interacted with race, class, and linguistic experience. For example, in one of the courses that investigates public and private issues in education, interns read Jane Roland Martin's article calling for a broadening of our educational purposes to include education for both the public (productive) and private (reproductive) processes of society (Martin 1985). In one of the Graduate School's core courses, Organizational Cultures and Professional Life, questions of gender are infused through articles tracing the evolution of our thinking about women and gender (Tetreault 1987), comparing feminist theory and organizational theory (Kanter 1979), arguing for the articulation of a theory of reproduction as well as a theory of production (O'Brien 1982), and presenting a case study of elementary teachers in Boston who struggled to understand and then deal with the structural constraints imposed on them in their schools (Freedman et al. 1983).
> (Tetreault and Braunger 1989, p. 75)

In the reports of this program, Tetreault and Braunger (1989) raise an extremely critical issue with regard to social-reconstructionist teacher education reforms. Specifically, they argue that in addition to revising the content of a teacher education program, teacher educators also need to be concerned with the pedagogy and social relations of teacher education. The experiences of these teacher educators at Lewis and Clark underscore the fact that alterations in program content without corresponding changes in the way in which courses are typically taught will result in student resistance, which undermines the emancipatory intent of teacher educators. In the case in point, the teacher educators offered a seminar for mentor teachers who would be working in the program.

Because the teacher educators pursued their own agenda and failed to let the mentors' own experiences and questions guide the learning in the seminar, they did not begin to achieve their goals until they created a more collaborative and interactive classroom learning environment.

Restructuring program components

In addition to these relatively few efforts to restructure entire teacher education programs along social-reconstructionist lines or to develop small but coherent alternatives to standard program offerings, several teacher educators have focused on the development of reforms only in the specific courses and field experiences for which they are personally responsible.[10] Five examples of this work will be discussed here: (1) the work of Susan Adler and Jesse Goodman, which stresses the teaching of curriculum development skills in social-studies methods courses; (2) a restructured methods-practicum block in biosocial studies at Deakin University in Australia emphasizing the role of teachers as researchers; (3) a redesigned B.Ed. course at Oxford Polytechnic in the U.K. emphasizing collaborative and critical inquiry by student teachers; (4) a philosophy of education course at Washington University with an emphasis on distinct educational traditions; and (5) an inquiry-oriented student teaching program at the University of Wisconsin-Madison. The descriptions of these projects will be fairly brief, with the exception of that of the Wisconsin program. An elaborated description of the Wisconsin program will serve to illustrate some of the specific teaching strategies that have been employed in reconstructionist-oriented teacher education reforms.

Preparing teachers who
are curriculum developers

Susan Adler of the University of Missouri-Kansas City and Jesse Goodman of Indiana University in a series of papers (Goodman 1986a and b; Goodman, 1991; and Adler and Goodman 1986) describe their teaching of social-studies methods courses for prospective elementary and middle school teachers in a way that emphasizes the teacher's role in curriculum development. Adler and Goodman are concerned with the preparation of teachers who are actively committed to promoting social justice and democracy. They link their work with a body of "critical theory" which exposes various sorts of biases in the social-studies curriculum and in the ways in which school practices serve the interests of dominant groups in the society. Adler and Goodman place themselves on the side of underrepresented groups such as women, people of color, and the poor by using their courses in part to help prospective teachers question the ways in which existing school practices in the social studies help to reproduce existing social and economic inequalities. Their hope is that their students will be inspired toward and capable of teaching in ways that promote the interests of all in the society and not just those of certain privileged groups.

A central focus in their courses is the deskilling process which leaves teachers in the position of implementing a curriculum that they have had little part in developing (Apple 1986). Adler and Goodman's work emphasizes the teaching of curriculum development skills to prospective teachers along with exposing them to alternative resources for and methods of teaching social studies in the elementary school. The central assignment in their courses is the planning and teaching of an original and thematically organized social-studies unit that builds upon their own and their pupils' intellectual interests and that emphasizes further inquiry and reflection for both the student teachers and their pupils.

The kind of social-studies teaching that Adler and Goodman seek to promote in their work is that which contributes toward more democratic and socially just forms of life in schools and in the society. For example, after helping their students examine the ways in which the history that typically gets taught in schools represents the perspectives of only certain dominant groups in the society (as an example of how school knowledge can be socially constructed and historically situated), they ask their students to consider the idea of a "social history" that focuses on the lives and experiences of all people in the society. Along with this focus on the idea of social history, and consistent with their emphasis on knowledge as a social construction, student teachers are also encouraged to consider teaching their pupils how "to do" history rather than just learning about historical events. Goodman and Adler then spend time exposing their students to curriculum resources, teaching strategies, and political skills that will enable them to pursue the teaching of history in these alternative ways.

While the thematically oriented approach to curriculum planning that is taught to students in these courses is fairly common within "developmentalist" circles, certain aspects of this line of work place it within the reconstructionist tradition. These aspects are Adler and Goodman's stress on having their students examine the social and political implications of their units' content (e.g., in relation to issues of class, race, and gender) and their explicit attention to issues of social justice and democracy when evaluating the learning promoted by the teaching of the unit.

Preparing teachers to be researchers of their practice

The second example of an effort to incorporate a reconstructionist component into an existing teacher education program comes from Deakin University in Australia. Here in 1986, a number of staff associated with the three year B.Ed. teacher education program developed an alternative version of the biosocial-studies block of the course which emphasized the preparation of teachers to be inquirers into their own teaching practice. The biosocial-studies component consists of three curriculum courses (in science education, physical education, and social-studies education) and a concurrent practicum. The innovative aspects of the revamped course consisted of placing students in schools for practicum work in pairs (which was consistent with the view of collaborative inquiry underlying the program) and the organization of the methods courses in a way that emphasized understandings that emerged out of students' experiences in testing out propositions about the teaching of the different subjects.

In science, for example, students were given a series of tasks in the methods course that reflected a range of views about science and the teaching and learning of science. These tasks formed the substance of the methods course. Students completed the tasks in their practicum classrooms using their partners to help them collect data. The data brought to campus from the schools became the basis for the discussions about the teaching of science in the methods course.

Each task identifies a particular educational problem relating to science education, provides a sample of the relevant literature of the field, and requires student teachers undertaking the task

to research some of the claims made in respect of the identified
issue in the literature. Student teachers negotiate their own science education curriculum by completing some out of a range
of prepared tasks, and by writing and then carrying out their
own tasks designed on a matter of particular interest to themselves . . . Each task requires that the student teachers actually
try out a range of different science teaching strategies and reflect critically on their science teaching, making explicit their
own theories about science teaching, and considering their own
theories in relation to theories advanced in the literature of the
field and to their own practical teaching experiences.
(Robottom 1988, p. 109)

These tasks altered the conception of professional development embedded within the program from one that had encouraged students uncrit-
ically to "put into practice" the implications of theories derived by
academic theorists to one in which students were encouraged to view
these theories as problematic and to examine them in the classroom.
Thus the literature-of-science education was to be seen as "a source of
testable propositions about science teaching rather than as a source
of theories of, and attendant implications for, good science teaching"
(DiChiro, Robottom, Tinning 1988, p. 138). One of the most important
roles for the program staff was to facilitate the development of the
students' own "practical theories" about the teaching of science, a process that was informed by the learnings gained from students examining
propositions suggested by the literature. A key aspect of the course, and
one that situates it within the reconstructionist tradition of reform, is the
politicized view of science education that was embedded in the tasks.
Specifically, the tasks helped focus students' attention on such issues as
sexism in science and science teaching, participatory learning and the
negotiated curriculum, and the professional status of teachers.

For example, in one example of a task provided by Robottom (1988)
focusing on sexism in science teaching, students were required to: (1)
read a series of articles in the task library which addressed a number of
different aspects of sexism in science teaching; (2) prepare a brief
position paper on sexism in science teaching; (3) teach six science
lessons in which some of their own beliefs or some of the claims in the
literature about the issue were examined; and (4) prepare a written report
describing their action research and what they learned about the limits

imposed and opportunities for girls in science teaching by their own teaching and by their classroom settings.

An initial teacher education course with an emphasis on collaborative critical inquiry

The third example of the influence of a reconstructionist perspective in contemporary teacher education programs is found at Oxford Polytechnic in the U.K. Here the emphasis has been on the revision of the B.Ed. course to facilitate collaborative and critical inquiry by students. The conception of critical reflection that has guided these efforts includes two essential elements: (1) it is responsive to students' own definitions of their learning needs (i.e., is reflexive); and (2) it is contextual—that is, it stresses the need for students to be critical of existing forms of educational provision from a moral, social, and political point of view (Ashcroft and Griffiths 1989). Critical reflection is also viewed as a collaborative process that takes place in the context of a "community of inquiry."

In addition to the more typical activities of revising course content, much of the effort at Oxford Polytechnic in recent years has focused on changing the pedagogy and social relations experienced by students in the program (Isaac and Ashcroft 1988). Here the emphasis has been on creating conditions within the program supportive of critical inquiry (e.g., group work, exposure to the wider social context) and on developing students' capabilities along these lines (e.g., to work as part of a team, to engage in "relational" thinking).

One of the areas that has received the most attention in these program-redesign efforts has been the way in which students' work is assessed. Some of the most innovative features of this program have been the group assessment procedures, which have been developed for the analysis of students' collaborative action research, and the way in which the concern for critical reflection has been incorporated into the assessment criteria for school experiences (see Ashcroft and Griffiths 1989).

Encouraging educational deliberation by student teachers

The fourth example of an attempt to incorporate a reconstructionist element into an existing teacher education program is the work that one of us (Liston) has pursued in a philosophy-of-education course at Washington University. This course is part of a teacher education program with a long tradition in inquiry-based learning. In 1971, Arthur Wirth and some of his colleagues initiated the Hawthorne Teacher Education Program, a one-year alternative to the standard Washington University teacher education program. This experimental program was rooted in two key notions: (1) a Deweyian conception of inquiry; and (2) the Personal Causation Theory of Motivation developed by one of the program faculty, Richard DeCharms. According to Alan Tom's (1988) reflections about the origins of the program, the process of inquiry as understood by program developers:

> Was presumed to be cyclical, moving from experience to conceptualization, from conceptualization to practice, and from practice to an evaluation that produces the data necessary for the step back to experience, thus repeating the cycle. Through this cyclical process, students would *think their way into teaching* and thus develop, test, and improve their own personal theories of teaching. (p. 4)

The second key element in the conceptual foundation of the program was the origin-pawn concept which emerged from DeCharms's (1968) Personal Causation Theory of Motivation.

> Focusing on locus of control, the origin-pawn concept suggests that people who see themselves as being manipulated by forces beyond their control (pawns) have less motivation to achieve than people who believe that they have the capacity to set realistic goals and plan activities to meet these goals (origins). According to DeCharms (1968) . . . motivation is enhanced by feelings of personal causation and depressed by feelings of external compulsion and pressure. Thus the teacher education program ought not to make prospective teachers dependent on the prescriptions of authority figures . . . but rather ought to engender feelings of personal causation by challenging the novices to generate and test their own personal theories of teaching. (Tom, 1988, p. 5)

These two concepts, inquiry and personal causation, formed the basis of a program that evolved in many different ways over the last two decades (see Wirth, no date; Cohn 1979; Tom 1988). In addition, the faculty decided to organize students and themselves into what they referred to as "communities of inquiry," which involved the clustering of students and staff and the offering of courses and seminars in a small number of school teaching centers instead of on the university campus. These teaching centers were inspired by Shaefer's (1967) ideas about "schools of inquiry." Over the years, several innovative approaches to the supervision of students in their school experiences (Cohn 1981; Cohn and Gellman 1988) have emerged from this program. Despite the emphasis on inquiry and reflection, and on helping students develop their own "practical theories" of teaching, the program as a whole does not stress the kind of social and political critique that is characteristic of a reconstructionist-oriented approach. It is within this largely "developmental" context that Liston initiated a focus on educational deliberation in his philosophy-of-education course.

The Philosophies of Education course focuses on encouraging undergraduates and prospective teachers to think seriously, clearly, and thoughtfully about educational issues and conundrums, to talk with others about these thoughts, and to come to some sense of the appropriateness of some resolutions over others. It is organized as a seminar. Students read key works before each session and they are expected to come to class ready both to discuss their own reactions and feelings and to address questions posed by the instructor. The content of the course is organized as an introduction to three educational traditions: the conservative (e.g., Hirsch 1988 and Hirst 1965), the radical (e.g., Counts 1932, Freire 1974, and Kozol 1980), and the progressive (e.g., Dewey 1902 and Paley 1981). After reading works from each tradition, students read critiques of that tradition. For example, after examining work in the conservative tradition, students read Jane Roland Martin's (1981) critique of the "male cognitive perspective" in her "The Ideal of the Educated Person." After reading works in the progressive tradition, students read Mary Warnock's (1975) arguments against teachers being neutral in her article entitled "The Neutral Teacher." And after discussing the radical tradition, students examine Sidney Hook's (1989) critique of the radical humanities curriculum as outlined in his "Civilization and its Malcontents." In short, the course constitutes an initiation into and a conversation about three distinct educational traditions.

The course is an attempt to introduce students to diverse points of view, to see the "logic" and rationale behind the distinct educational traditions, and to develop and challenge their own beliefs and assumptions. It is an attempt to enable students to reason out loud the conflicts and issues attending particular educational decisions in a classroom environment that treats ideas and people with respect, care, and concern. Students are introduced to the distinct educational traditions, asked to see particular educational issues from very distinct and contrasting perspectives, and expected to come to some personal and professional resolution and/or awareness of particular educational issues. In discussions of the conservative tradition, students note the emphasis on received traditions and discuss the importance of initiating students into cognitive frameworks. When analyzing the radical tradition, many students situate for the first time the school experience within a larger social and political context, and they discuss questions connected to the issues of educational imposition and indoctrination. In discussions of the progressive tradition, they focus on the ways to connect the curriculum and the child and focus on Dewey's notions of experience, interest, and growth. The course, situated as it is within a developmentally oriented program, is an attempt to introduce students to distinct educational theories and to enable them to articulate their own educational perspective.

An inquiry-oriented student teaching program

As a result of studies conducted by faculty and graduate students at the University of Wisconsin-Madison in the mid-1970s, we and some of our colleagues became concerned about certain aspects of the teacher education program in elementary education. In some ways, the program seemed to be encouraging an overly technical and narrow emphasis on the part of our students where the main concern was with the mastery of teaching skills within classrooms. In fact, the students often ignored the goals toward which those skills were directed and the educational and social contexts in which the teaching was carried out.[11] For many of our students, pedagogy became separated from its moral, ethical, and political roots, and "good" teaching became the equivalent of getting the students through "lessons" on time without major disruptions (Tabachnick, Popkewitz, and Zeichner 1979).

In many ways the student teaching component of this program resembled a typical apprenticeship approach to clinical teacher education (Stones 1984), according to which it is implicitly assumed that good teaching is "caught," not taught, and that if good things happened they often happened more by accident or good fortune than by deliberate design (Feiman-Nemser and Buchmann 1985; Zeichner 1986a). Over the last decade, faculty, graduate students, and cooperating teachers have sought to develop strategies that would foster more systematic and deliberate attention to teacher learning during the practicum.

During the process of reconceptualizing the program, the term "reflective teaching" became a construct that organized our thinking about our work. "Reflective teaching" began as a slogan that represented more of a reaction against what we did not like about our program than as a clearly articulated and elaborated vision of the kind of teachers we wanted to prepare. Over the years, we gradually developed both our own notions about what "reflective teaching" means in our program and a repertoire of pedagogical strategies and curricular plans for attempting to bring it about.[12]

We began with the Deweynian distinction between "reflective action" (the active, persistent, and careful consideration of any belief in light of the grounds that support it and the consequences to which it leads) and "routine action" (that which is guided primarily by habit, external authority, and circumstance). Using Dewey's (1933) concept of reflective action as the organizing principle for the practicum curriculum, the program literature has stressed a desire to develop in student teachers those orientations (openmindedness, responsibility, and wholeheartedness) and skills (of keen observation and analysis) that are constitutative of reflective action.

In addition to this basic distinction between reflective and routine action, the program literature also distinguishes among different domains of reflection by drawing upon the work of Max Van Mannen (1977) and his conception of "levels of reflectivity."[13] First, in technical reflection, the concern is with the efficiency and effectiveness of the means used to attain ends that themselves remain unexamined. Second, in practical reflection, the task is one of explicating and clarifying the assumptions and predispositions underlying teaching activity and assessing the adequacy of the educational goals toward which the activity leads. Here every action is seen as linked to particular value commitments, and the actor considers the worth of competing educational ends as well as how well the particular learning goals that he or she is working toward are achieved by students. Finally, critical reflection incorporates moral and ethical criteria into the discourse about practical action. Here the major concern is with whether the educational goals, activities, and experiences

167

lead toward forms of life that are characterized by justice, equity, and concrete happiness for all, and whether the teaching activity and the contexts in which it is carried out serve important human needs and satisfy important human purposes. The program stresses the importance of reflective teaching, which incorporates all three of these reflective domains.

Along with specifying the particular quality of reflection that we seek to develop in our students, we have also stressed the importance of problematizing the teaching context and of seeing relationships between everyday actions within the classroom and issues and structures of schooling and society. One way that we have pursued the development of this "relational" thinking is by deliberately focusing students' attention on particular kinds of issues connected to their everyday teaching activities (e.g., those associated with gender, social class, and race). The most recent developments in the conceptual apparatus of this program have involved the elaboration of a process of moral deliberation about teaching which is very similar to the process described earlier in this book. Here the concern has been both with facilitating students' reasoned analyses about their teaching and the social contexts in which it takes place and with maintaining a commitment to compassionate and caring relationships with students.

The student teaching program is organized in terms of five curricular components. First, a *teaching component* seeks to ensure the exposure of student teachers to all aspects of the teacher's role in and out of the classroom. As in most programs, over the semester, each student is expected gradually to assume responsibility for all aspects of the classroom teacher's role (e.g., instruction, classroom management, curriculum development, pupil evaluation) and to complete a period of full responsibility for the classroom program. Although most student teaching programs often include this same notion of increasing responsibility for a classroom, the focus is frequently on instruction and classroom management and does not typically include the student teacher's responsible participation in other aspects of the teacher's role such as curriculum development and evaluation. The Wisconsin program places a particular emphasis on the student teacher's role in curriculum development and on the teacher as a user/developer of curriculum (Ben-Peretz 1984).

The emphasis here is very similar to that of Adler and Goodman in their social-studies methods courses and seeks to counteract the widespread phenomenon of the deskilling of teachers' work. Although students are generally expected to follow the curriculum guidelines of their schools and the curricular programs in their classrooms, they are also expected to: (1) be aware of and able to articulate the assumptions embedded in curriculum that is adopted with little or no modification (e.g., assumptions about learners and the teacher's role); (2) show evidence of adapting and modifying curricular plans and materials for use with specific pupils at particular times; and (3) make original contributions to the classroom program by creating new and varied instructional materials and activities beyond those specified by their cooperating teachers. There is also an underlying concern (which is indicated in the program's criteria for the evaluation of student teachers' work) that the students' instruction adequately reflect the diverse perspectives of all who live in the society and that it actively promote caring and just relations among pupils and between teachers and pupils within the classroom setting. Consistent with the "reflexive" character of the program's curriculum, all of the specific requirements within this teaching component (other than that of "lead teaching") are negotiated by the student and his or her cooperating teacher and university supervisor.

The second component of the program, an *inquiry component,* seeks to help student teachers situate schools, curriculum, and pedagogy within their sociohistorical contexts. The inquiry component also emphasizes the socially constructed nature of school knowledge and of school structures, and it seeks to develop students' capabilities for conducting inquiries about their work. This component is intended to help student teachers gain an understanding of the contemporary cultures of their classrooms and schools, and of the relationships between these educational contexts and the surrounding social, economic, and political milieu. The inquiry component also aims to help student teachers understand the historical development of the settings in which they work (i.e., how what is came to be). The goal of this component is to have the classroom and school serve as social laboratories for study rather than as merely models for practice. It seeks to reinforce the view that student teaching is a time for continued learning about teaching and schooling and for the establishment of habits of self-directed growth—rather than as is typically the case, only a time for the application and demonstration of previously acquired knowledge and skills (Turney et al. 1982; Haberman 1983). It also seeks to reinforce the view that teachers can be creators as well as consumers of educational knowledge.

There are several different types of activities in the inquiry component of the program. All students complete one or more inquiry assignment during the twenty-week student teaching semester as part of their responsibilities for student teaching and for the credit-bearing student teaching seminar. Three different kinds of inquiry learning activities are currently employed by program staff: (1) action-research projects; (2) limited ethnographic studies; and (3) curriculum analysis projects.

First, the *action research projects* completed by student teachers involve an adaptation of a framework for conducting action research developed at Deakin University (Kemmis and McTaggart 1988). Kemmis and McTaggart define action research as:

A form of collective self-reflective inquiry undertaken by participants in a social situation in order to improve the rationality and justice of their own social practices, as well as their understanding of these practices and the situations in which these practices are carried out. (p. 5)

Although we probably do not go as far in emphasizing the collaborative aspects of reflection as Kemmis and McTaggart suggest,[14] our approach to action research comes closest to the Deakin "emancipatory" approach than to any existing alternative because of our desire to focus students' inquiries both on their teaching and on the social context of schooling.[15] While we are interested in facilitating reflection about teaching practices and the elaboration of the "practical theories" of student teachers, we are also concerned with encouraging action research that contributes to the elimination of social conditions that obstruct the educative potential of schooling.

Although the methods utilized by student teachers loosely follow the self-reflective spiral of planning, acting, observing, and reflecting that is outlined by Kemmis and McTaggart, it is important to stress that in practice the process is much messier than this with the different "steps" often overlapping and occurring in different sequences.[16]

The action research that has been initiated by Wisconsin student teachers has been quite varied. Students spend a portion of their weekly seminar time discussing and reacting to one another's developing projects, and they prepare written accounts of the evolution of their projects at the end of the semester. The university supervisor and sometimes the cooperating teacher, as well, seek to facilitate the students' inquiries by reacting to them along the way, by serving as "data collectors." The university supervisor frequently structures opportunities both for student teachers to learn about and discuss various research strategies (e.g., collecting data about pupil learning) and for student teachers to support their peers' research efforts. Some of the student projects have included experimentation with different grouping procedures within the classroom to assess the effects of alternative strategies for maintaining pupil involvement, examinations of a student teacher's behavior toward high- and low-ability groups, and the careful monitoring of efforts to introduce cooperative learning into a classroom.[17]

Although it is hoped that student teachers will learn valuable lessons about teaching from their participation in action research, the value of the experience is intended to go beyond the lessons that students might gain from specific projects. The hope is that students' experiences with action research will contribute toward the development of a disposition to view inquiry about teaching and the social conditions of schooling as part of the work of teaching (Elliot 1985).

One alternative to the completion of classroom action-research projects for some students is to conduct limited ethnographic type studies in their classrooms, and schools.[18] These projects, examples of which are discussed in some detail in Zeichner and Teitelbaum (1982) and Gitlin and Teitelbaum (1983), have focused on such issues as the allocation of resources (e.g., the teacher's time) among students of varying character-istics, abilities, and backgrounds; studies of school life from a pupil's perspective; and the hidden curriculum. These projects, which involve the exploration of selected issues both in the field and on campus, enable university supervisors to develop closer links between students' experiences in schools and the material they read as part of the seminar. The data that students collect in the field illuminate the issues that they read about, and the readings inform their examinations of the specific cases in the field.

A third option for the inquiry component is to conduct *analyses of school curricula* and the processes of *curriculum development* in their school placement sites. In addition to the completion of projects that include the examination of the values and assumptions embedded in particular curriculum materials and programs (e.g., assumptions about learners, teachers, and knowledge), students have conducted local exam-inations of the history and context of curriculum development in particu-lar content areas. In so doing, they address such questions as: Who made specific decisions about the curriculum? Why were certain decisions made? and How did specific institutional and cultural factors affect the processes of curriculum development in particular instances? While our students generally have very little experience working on the develop-ment of curricula at the school-district level, we want them to have a very clear understanding of the processes of curriculum development beyond the classroom.

The various inquiry projects (action research, ethnographic studies, and curriculum analysis) are carried out in the schools by students, and they are closely linked to the third component of the program, the *student teaching seminar*. The weekly seminars are jointly planned by university supervisors and their students and focus on a variety of issues such as multicultural education, the hidden curriculum, cooperative learning, grouping, assessment, and the process of learning to teach. While this course is related to and builds upon the student teachers' school experiences, it is not limited to a focus upon strengthening students' performances in their current classroom placements. The intent is to use the current placements and students' ongoing teaching experiences as vehicles for the exploration of important educational issues that transcend individual settings. For example, for specific issues like grouping, pupil assessment, the teaching of writing, or a multicultural curriculum, students bring data from their individual classrooms to their seminars, and these data inform the group discussions. Because students are placed in classrooms that represent a variety of positions on almost every issue that is explored, and because of the deliberate selection of seminar readings that represent a variety of perspectives on particular issues, seminar discussions would ideally resemble the kind of educational deliberation described in chapter 2 and elaborated further in chapters 3 and 4.

Consistent with the program's emphasis on preparing teacher researchers, there has been an emphasis in the seminars in recent years on using the writing and research of classroom teachers as reading material. In addition to reading articles written by college- and university-based academics and independent entrepreneurs like Madeline Hunter and Lee Canter, student teachers read and discuss material from publications dominated by teachers' voices such as *Rethinking Schools* and *Democratic Education*. Some student teachers also read material produced by students from previous semesters (e.g., action-research reports) when particular issues and practices are considered. This focus on including a variety of voices in the seminars, in addition to the usual academic voices (including those of parents and children), helps ensure that in their discussions students and faculty consider different substantive positions on particular issues and practices. For example, in discussions of "Assertive Discipline" (Canter and Canter 1983)—which is a currently popular competency-based technology for managing and controlling

student behavior in Madison, Wisconsin, area schools—seminar participants have read articles written by Lee and Marlene Canter, the developers of the approach, and material written by parents, academics, and
classroom teachers who are critical of the approach for a variety of
reasons.

The fourth critical feature of the program is a *writing component*.[19]
Student teachers keep a journal related to their development as teachers
during the student teaching semester and are given guidance in their
efforts by the university supervisors. These journals are shared on a
regular basis with the supervisors, and the supervisors respond in writing
to the students' entries. The journals are valuable in that they stimulate
student teacher reflections about their teaching, the social context of their
teaching, and their development as teachers over time. Furthermore, the
journals are intended to provide supervisors with more information about
the ways in which the students think about their teaching and particular
school, classroom, and community contexts so that the supervision
provided is sensitive to each student teacher's unique reality. The journals are viewed as an integral part of the supervision process.

Another dimension of the writing component is the use of autobiography by some supervisors as a strategy for helping students examine the
assumptions underlying and the influences on the teaching perspectives
that they bring to the student teaching experience.[20] It is very common
in the seminars for students to construct autobiographical accounts of
their own experiences as learners, including those experiences in the
teacher education program itself. Given what we know about the powerful impact of pretraining influences on teacher learning (Zeichner and
Gore 1990), we feel it is critical to focus students' attention more
consciously on the conceptions, ideas, and values that they bring with
them to their teacher education programs.[21]

Finally, although most of the writing is done alone by individual
students, there are also occasions when group writing assignments are
used in the seminars to enable a cohort of students to construct interpretations of particular experiences which were shared in the seminar. In one
seminar group, for example, several small groups of students meet for
a portion of each seminar meeting and write statements of what they
have learned as a group during particular sessions. These statements are
then shared with the other students in the large group (Maas, 1991).

The fifth and final dimension of the student teaching program is a
supervision component. The supervisory conferences that precede and
follow formal observations of student teachers are viewed as important

occasions for student teacher learning. These conferences are concerned both with the specific teaching activities that have been observed and with the more general development of student teacher perspectives over the course of the semester.[22] Although the form of supervision employed in the program resembles the "clinical supervision" model (Goldhammer 1969) in its structure and in its emphasis on the analysis and discussion of teaching activities, supervisors attempt to ensure that their analyses of teaching address the social context surrounding it and move back and forth across all three domains of reflection (technical, practical, and critical).

Also, as is the case in the seminars, supervisors deliberately focus attention during the supervisory conferences on issues related to gender, race, class, and other differences when they arise in students' teaching. In this way, questions of equity and justice are kept at the forefront of concern. For example, instead of merely being concerned with the question of whether "students" have learned what was hoped for by the student teacher, the focus is directed to the opportunities for learning subject matter that are made available to particular students and groups of students and to what they have learned as a result. Instead of merely looking at whether undesirable pupil behaviors have disappeared through the use of a competency-based classroom management system such as Assertive Discipline, the focus is also directed to the quality of human relationships through which particular "outcomes" were generated. While none of these things is explicitly excluded from clinical supervision as it is described in the literature today,[23] the commitment in clinical supervision to reflection about teaching "in general" is an inadequate basis, by itself, for an approach to the kind of student teacher supervision that encourages the development of socially conscious and ethically responsible teachers.[24] In addition to benefiting from the supervision provided by individual university staff and cooperating teachers, some students are involved in a peer-supervision program where they observe and confer with other student teachers about particular instances of teaching (Miller 1989).

Key aspects of social reconstructionist practices in teacher education

There are several important aspects of social-reconstructionist practices in teacher education that are implicit in the preceding descriptions of program and course innovations. These features, while not necessarily descriptive of the current realities of the individual projects described above, represent the ideals toward which reconstructionist teacher education projects aspire. We will now summarize these elements before moving on to an assessment of the successes of recent reform efforts. The first critical element in social-reconstructionist–oriented reforms in teacher education is related to the scope of the changes that are attempted. It should be evident from the examples provided above that individual efforts within this group of reforms have focused to varying degrees upon changes in course content, the pedagogy and social relations within courses, and the structure and organization of programs. It is very clear from the experiences of these teacher educators that changing course content, pedagogy, or program structure by itself is insufficient for helping students develop the dispositions, knowledge, and skills that are valued within this tradition. While there may be a variety of organizational patterns that would lend themselves to the realization of the democratic aspirations of reconstructionist teacher education projects,[25] at the very least, the scope of these reforms must address both the content and pedagogy of teacher education courses.

Ideally, these projects would establish a consistency and coherence between the course content and pedagogy, and create a situation where that which teacher educators seek to have their students learn is modeled in all aspects of the course or program (Noddings 1987). For example, if teacher educators want their students to teach in a way that involves the integration of material and ideas across content area boundaries, the curriculum of the teacher education program would itself represent an integrated curricular approach. If teacher educators want their students to foster cooperative and collaborative learning within their classrooms, classes in the college and university component of the teacher education program would be infused with cooperative learning structures. Finally, if teacher educators want their students to be reflective about their teaching and the social conditions of schooling, the students must see teacher educators who are reflective about the work and social conditions of teacher education and must experience teacher education programs that are undergoing continual revision and critique.

These projects must avoid situations where commitment to a particular ideology leads to a neglect of the vulnerable condition of student teachers (Lucas 1988), where teacher educators aim straight at their goals "over the heads" of those whom they teach (Noddings 1986). We need to recognize clearly that student teachers and beginning teachers are often in the least powerful positions to create changes and that they often undergo a great deal of stress and put their careers at risk when offering challenges to some of the unjust and inhumane practices they find around them.[26]

It goes without saying that changes in the contextual elements of teacher education programs (e.g., in funding patterns, in work responsibilities) are often necessary for the realization of desired changes in curriculum and pedagogy. In the next chapter we will discuss the problems teacher educators have had in achieving the ideal of educating teachers to assume reconstruction-oriented roles in both schools and society, when in many cases students are disposed toward the maintenance of the status quo. Achieving a social-reconstructionist agenda in U.S. teacher education in these times of conservative restoration, without violating an ethic of care to students, is a most difficult issue for teacher educators who affiliate themselves with this reform tradition.

Another key element in the examples described above is the attempt to create a situation that acknowledges the interactive relationship between theory and practice. Rejecting the instrumental view that theory is something only created outside of the classroom by academic researchers, and that practice is something only engaged in by teachers within primary and secondary classrooms, these projects have attempted to address the interrelationships between thought and action within and between the school and university domains.[27] As a consequence of adopting this perspective, and in addition to the typical focus on the thoughts of university educators and the actions of primary and secondary teachers, these projects reflect a concern with the pedagogy and social relations in university-based teacher education components and with the "practical theories" of student teachers and teachers. For example, each of these projects, in seeking to help student teachers develop their "practical theories," has rejected the historically dominant social-efficiency view in teacher education where the main task has been seen as figuring out how to get students to "apply" the findings of externally conducted research.

In each of the social-reconstructionist–oriented projects described above, teaching itself is viewed as a form of inquiry and teachers are viewed as researchers of their own practices, capable of producing legitimate and worthwhile knowledge about teaching which can contribute to their own and others' professional development. Knowledge about teaching and the social conditions of schooling that is generated outside of the immediate teaching context is to be valued for its contributions to the development of teachers' understandings and capabilities. But it is not thought, as has commonly been the case in the past, that this externally derived knowledge can achieve a final or legislative relationship to teachers' actions (Winter 1987). Knowledge about teaching is believed to exist, in part, in the actions of teachers (Schon 1983).[28]

In its ideal form, the curriculum of teacher education courses is reflexive and emerges in part from the experiences of teacher education students. Student teachers' actions in schools, for example, are both informed by, and in turn inform, the consideration of issues and practices in seminars and courses that extend beyond the immediate teaching context. The pedagogy here is ideally interactive as opposed to the more common transmission mode of teaching which dominates many university classrooms. It seeks to draw on and legitimate students' experiences as contributory to the subject matter of the course (Maher and Rathbone 1985)[29] and makes every effort to integrate students' experiences on campus with those in schools.

> This goal asks teachers to situate learning in the students's cultures, their literacy, their themes, their present understandings, their aspirations, their daily lives. The goal is to integrate experimental materials with conceptual methods and academic subjects. . . . Only a situated pedagogy can bring critical study to bear on the concrete conditions of life, which critical learning may help recreate. (Shor 1987, 1977)

Two examples of this tendency to develop the interplay between student and faculty perspectives and between campus and field experiences are the action research projects at Deakin University where the curriculum of the science methods course is based on the knowledge generated by students' investigations of propositions about science education, and the limited ethnographic studies conducted by some University of Wisconsin student teachers on issues considered in campus seminars.

It is important to recognize that the ideal of interactive teaching and "dialogue" that is sought in reconstructionist teacher education projects is an oversimplification of a much more complex reality. In reality, power cannot truly be equal between teacher educators and their students; nor does it necessarily have to be to establish a learning environment that is connected to and values and builds upon the perspectives of teacher education students.

177

Dialogue in its conventional sense is impossible in the culture at large because at this historical moment, power relations between raced, classed, and gendered students and teachers are unjust. The injustice of these relations and the way in which those injustices distort communication cannot be overcome in a classroom, no matter how committed the students and teacher are to "overcoming conditions that perpetuate suffering." (Ellsworth 1989, p. 316)

A third key element of reconstructionist-oriented reforms is the belief that knowledge and school structures are, in part, socially constructed and historically embedded entities that are shaped by and in turn influence and help sustain particular aspects of the society in which they exist. One consequence of this acknowledgment of the inevitable partiality and embeddedness of curriculum knowledge and school structures is an emphasis on helping student teachers examine the relationships between what they experience in the immediate reality of the classroom and the institutional and larger social contexts in which that immediate reality is embedded.

One example of this is the focus in the projects described above on helping student teachers examine the school and local community conditions that facilitate and obstruct the realization of their goals. Reflection about teaching from this perspective is turned both inward toward the thinking and acting of individual teachers and outward toward the situations in which teachers find themselves (Kemmis 1985). Student teachers are encouraged to view curriculum and school structures as value-governed selections from a larger universe of possibilities and to imagine possibilities that exist outside of their immediate range of vision.

A fourth element of reconstructionist teacher education projects is a focus on collaborative modes of learning both in campus courses and in school experiences. Here teacher educators seek to create "communities of learning" where students and teacher educators can support and sustain each other's growth. Examples of this attempt to incorporate collaborative learning into teacher education courses include the collaborative action-research projects at Deakin University, Oxford Polytechnic, and the University of Wisconsin-Madison, the use of cooperative learning strategies in classes at Oxford Polytechnic, and the employment of peer supervision with student teachers at the University of Wisconsin-Madison.[30]

This commitment to collaborative modes of learning supports the intent to create a more interactive pedagogy in teacher education classes, and a desire on the part of teacher educators to conjoin the domain of reason with that of feeling and emotion. The establishment of collaborative learning environments makes it more likely that efforts to help students develop the capability to reason about and justify their teaching practice using the criteria of justice and equity will not come at the expense of their abilities to be compassionate and caring teachers. By making sure that collaborative modes of learning have a strong presence in the curriculum, teacher educators maintain a dual commitment to an ethic according to which both justice and equity, on the one hand, and care and compassion, on the other, are strongly valued. King and Ladson-Billings (1990) argue that the group experience in collaborative learning helps students consciously reexperience their own subjectivity when they recognize similar and different outlooks and experiences among their peers.[31]

The desire to help prospective teachers develop dispositions and skills of collaboration is also of important strategic value when we consider the potential for transforming social and institutional structures that hinder teachers from accomplishing their educational missions.[32] Specifically, it is felt that the empowerment of individual teachers *as individuals* is inadequate, and that the potential for institutional and social change is greater, if prospective teachers see their individual situations linked to those of their colleagues—and if they develop the capabilities to work along with those colleagues and others, such as parents and community activists, for changes both within the classroom in the schools and in the society.

> For both pedagogical and political reasons, it is important for students to engage in projects cooperatively, sharing ideas where appropriate and learning new possibilities from others in the cohort group . . . If a communal identity can be established early on in the program, it can be extended throughout subsequent courses and in student teaching. The process of forming such a communal identity is an important part of developing teaching as an empowering, creative, critical praxis—one in which the virtue of caring is significant. (Beyer 1988, p. 192)

Another critical element of social-reconstruction–oriented teacher education is the efforts that are made to ensure that the content of the teacher education curriculum reflects the perspectives of diverse intellectual traditions and disciplines, and of groups that are typically underrepresented in the school and university curriculum. Some examples of this include Lanny Beyer's efforts at Knox and Cornell colleges to broaden the foundations of education beyond an exclusive focus on educational psychology; the infusion of issues of gender into the curriculum at Lewis and Clark by Tetreault and Braunger; Dan Liston's work at Washington University in asking students to examine issues and practices from conservative, progressive, and radical perspectives; and Sue Adler and Jesse Goodman's work in their social-studies methods classes incorporating the notion of "social history," where the lives and stories of people other than white males, military heros, political leaders, and industrialists are studied. Another example of this attention to underrepresented perspectives in the teacher education curriculum is the incorporation of the writing of teachers into the student teaching seminars at the University of Wisconsin-Madison.[33]

The incorporation of these neglected voices into the teacher education curriculum involves much more, however, than merely adding content about women, Latinos, and Native Americans, for example, to what already exists to provide a more "balanced" approach. As Maher and Rathbone (1986) point out, once previously excluded perspectives begin to be incorporated into the curriculum, the guiding generalizations of particular fields of study are challenged and a fundamental rethinking of the curriculum becomes necessary.

A final characteristic of social-reconstructionist teacher education projects—one underlying all the other features—is the acknowledgment of the fundamentally political character of teaching and teacher education and the deliberate emphasis in courses and in the supervision of field experiences on issues and practices that bring the factors of injustice, and inequity into focus for scrutiny.[34] Social-reconstructionist–oriented teacher educators maintain a belief that teaching and teacher education can make contributions, along with other educational and political projects, to the creation of a more just and compassionate society. While not believing that educational projects by themselves can transform the social order, reconstructionist-oriented teacher educators recognize that their own actions and those of teachers are linked in important ways to the creation of a situation where *all* children are able to lead decent and rewarding lives.

Examples of this commitment to exposing the political realities of schooling to more careful analysis include focusing on such issues as the gendered nature of schooling and of teachers' work, the relationships between race and social class on the one hand and access to school knowledge and school achievement on the other, and the influence of external interests on the processes of curriculum production, as they arise in the practices of student teachers. It is very common for example, in the Wisconsin student teaching program, for student teachers' classroom situations to reflect the same social-class disparities in curriculum and in teacher-pupil relations that Anyon (1980) found in her investigations of the teaching of social studies. When these and other issues are found in student teachers' teaching practices and in the social conditions of their teaching, Wisconsin teacher educators focus students' attention upon them.

This deliberate effort to bring into focus substantive issues that highlight gender, class, race, and other differences in relation to curriculum, instruction, and the school structure and organization is fundamental to the approach. Much of the language used within the reconstructionist tradition—such as "reflective," "collaborative," "dialogical," and even "critical"—has also been used in the service of other reform traditions. We are in agreement with Calderhead (1989) who has observed that we are at a point now where the full range of beliefs within the teacher education community about teaching, learning, schooling, and the social order have now been incorporated into the discourse on reflective practice in teaching and teacher education.[35]

We strongly feel that, unless teacher educators deliberately initiate discussions that consider the ethical dimensions of issues and practices emerging out of students' work in schools, many instances of questionable ethical worth will pass by either unnoticed or will not be seriously examined by students.[36] This deliberate focus on the critical domain of reflection, one that addresses the justifications for practices and recognizes the larger social context, does not mean that the technical and practical domains of reflection are of no concern. It does mean, however, that the consideration of issues according to technical criteria, such as efficiency, must be extended into deliberations that also consider their educational value and moral worth.

For example, an issue that is confronted fairly regularly by University of Wisconsin-Madison student teachers is the disproportionate assignment of pupils of color to the lower tracks in school programs and to such remedial categories as "learning disabled." In the local area (Madison), pupils of color also have higher than average school suspension rates and lower than average high school graduation rates. Currently all this is fairly common across the U.S. (Oakes 1985). In a social-reconstructionist–oriented teacher education project, these so-called "facts" about the context of student teachers' work that highlight racial and social class differences would be made problematic and examined as part of the process of reflection about teaching. The more usual scenario is for these and other similar issues to serve as background during student teachers' deliberations.[37] Social-reconstructionist teacher education projects bring these kinds of issues into the foreground and use them to stimulate an exploration of alternative possibilities in which the painful effects of these practices are lessened.

Fortunately, the examination of specific school conditions that may be linked to inequalities among students because of their gender, race, social-class background, or other characteristics is becoming more common in the public schools. In Madison, for example, a committee appointed by the school board recently issued a comprehensive report calling for many fundamental changes in school practices throughout the district (e.g., grouping practices, teaching practices, home-school relations) to lessen racial inequalities in the district (Madison Metropolitan School District, 1989). In Milwaukee, the group of teachers that publishes *Rethinking Schools* has stimulated much discussion and debate in that district about such contextual factors as standardized testing, basal readers, and behavior-management systems like "Assertive Discipline." These teachers have also provided a rich set of resources and ideas about alternative practices that seek to overcome the significant racial, gender, and ethnic- and class-based inequities that prevent many students in Milwaukee from receiving an equal and effective education. Finally, Bastian et al. (1985) provide a lot of very useful information about citizen groups for democratic schooling across the U.S. who are also combating these same problems. In addition to the more conventional academic sources, social-reconstructionist teacher education projects ideally draw heavily on these "grassroots" movements for social-reconstructionist educational reform; for, as we will discuss in the next chapter, one of the most important tasks for those who affiliate with this tradition is to be able to help their students link up with progressive/reconstructionist forces already working in schools.

The success of social-reconstructionist teacher education projects

We must be very careful not to romanticize either the accomplishments of social-reconstructionist teacher education projects in the past or what they are likely to accomplish in the future. Educational projects, no matter how well conceived and carried out, can at best play contributory roles in transforming unjust and inhumane social structures. Ultimately these actions in the educational arena must be linked with those of progressive activists in other spheres of the society such as health care, child care, housing, affirmative action, the environment, the politics of food production and distribution, and so forth. As Ira Shor (1987, p. 190) says, "Individual classrooms cannot change an unequal social system; only political movements can transform inequality." Social-reconstructionist teacher educators must step outside of their normal state of overt political neutrality in the academy and assert their connections to the larger political projects of which their own educational work is a part.

All the teacher educators associated with the projects discussed in this chapter have candidly reported various difficulties that they have faced in implementing their reforms. Nobody involved with this group of projects has pretended that the work being done here is anything but extremely complex and difficult. These difficulties include student rejection of opportunities made available in a project to engage in critical analysis, and failures to conduct a project in ways consistent with teacher educators' intentions. An example of contradictions between course content and pedagogy is the situation mentioned earlier at Lewis and Clark. There, in a seminar for mentor teachers, and despite the emancipatory course content, university-based teacher educators at first failed to situate their teaching in the concerns and realities of the teachers. Another example of this gap between reconstructionist aspirations and the reality of their teacher education programs[38] can be found at Deakin University. There the detailed presentation of the tasks to students and the competitive assessment system used in all Australian institutions[39] undermined the intent of the lecturers to foster a critical or politicized perspective by students in relation to their practice and the social context of that practice.

> The requirement of the tasks, while justified by an interest in directing attention to the relationship of understanding, situation, and practice, in the event were seen (by students) as suggestive of an impositional directive that is contrary to the alleged responsiveness of participatory research. While espousing a paradigm of professional independence in the form of participant research, the details of the tasks requirements coupled

with the competitive assessment of the course, suggested the conventional paradigm of technical competence. (Robottom 1988, p. 112)

Another area that has caused difficulty in these projects has been the tensions between schools and universities. These tensions are intensified by the presence of a teacher education program that overtly assumes a critical and sometimes oppositional stance to much that is taken as natural in the status quo of schools and society. Although all these projects have assumed the position of trying to prepare teachers who can successfully work within the present educational system in order to change it—and have sought to form alliances with teachers, administrators, and parents who are also working to change some of the same conditions that are made problematic in the teacher education curriculum—there is no getting around the tension and conflict that is caused by questioning what is taken for granted. Lanny Beyer very clearly describes the "deep seated antipathy" which developed between the critically oriented foundational perspective embodied in the principles of the elementary teacher education programs at Knox and Cornell colleges and the work contexts of his student teachers. The pressures exerted on students in these particular schools, which were dominated by deskilled and patriarchal practices, made it harder for teacher educators to create a distance from those practices that would allow for analysis and critique. For example, students in these programs often felt pressured to implement prepackaged curricula in their practicum classrooms in a routine and mechanical fashion despite their desire in some cases to play a role in shaping the classroom curriculum. These pressures made it more difficult for these students, as well as the ones who were happy with their school situations, to imagine or implement alternatives to what they were faced with during practicums because their "success" (e.g., as measured in teaching evaluations) depended upon doing well many things that their teacher education program curriculum sought to make problematic.

Primary and secondary school sites for clinical teacher education experiences are not the only places in which resistance to social-reconstruction–oriented teacher education arises. In an earlier paper on the Wisconsin student teaching program, for example, we described a situation that is common to many institutions in the U.S. where the norms of the academy and the system for rewards and promotions undermined the efforts of teacher educators to develop a coherent teacher education program across a two-year professional course sequence (Zeichner and Liston 1987). This coherence becomes even more difficult to imagine once we consider the entire scope of the teacher education curriculum and the commitment of energy to teacher education by faculty outside of education units. These problems, stemming from teacher education's marginal status in the academy, will be more fully explored in the next and final chapter.

In addition to these and other difficulties that have been reported by those who have attempted to implement social-reconstructionist–oriented projects in teacher education programs, many instances have also been reported where teacher educators have been successful in helping students examine their teaching and the social conditions of schooling in ways suggested above. All these projects have presented at least a few cases where students' actions or statements reveal a break from unthinking submergence in the prevailing views of schooling and society (Greene 1973), the gaining of confidence and ability by students in exercising their own judgments about their teaching, and students' adoption of a healthy skepticism about educational claims and prescriptions generated by others. Despite this documentation of student teacher growth during their participation in social-reconstructionist teacher education projects, it is not altogether clear that the successes reported can be attributed to participation in the projects. In some cases of success documented in the literature, for example, there is a strong possibility that students adopted socially critical perspectives before entering a project (see Zeichner 1987). At this point there is a lot that we just do not know about the impact of these reform efforts.

One way to address this situation is to treat the teacher education project itself as a form of inquiry, or strategic action open to continual revision and critique. In a recent report of action research in the Wisconsin student teaching program (Liston and Zeichner 1989) and in an earlier report on the same student teaching program (Zeichner and Liston 1987), we describe efforts over the last decade to conduct inquiries into various aspects of the teacher education program. Apart from the substantive information that we have gained about the impact of our efforts on ourselves and on our students (which enable us continually to revise our practices), this research conducted by teacher educators into their own practices carries an important message to teacher education students about the value of the dispositions, knowledge, and skills that are emphasized in the formal curriculum of the teacher education program. For example, if student teachers can see their cooperating teachers and university supervisors engaged in an analysis of their own teaching and the social conditions of teaching and teacher education (utilizing some of the same strategies that the students are asked to use), then it is more likely that the students will be encouraged to analyze their own situations.[40]

It seems very unlikely to us that a social-reconstructionist teacher education project can have much success without this effort to model the critical and compassionate stance that it seeks to have its students adopt. We will now consider in much more detail than here the extent to which we feel it is possible to realize the social-reconstructionist agenda in teacher education during these times of conservative restoration (Shor 1987) and the strategies at several different levels which we feel are needed to move beyond what is realistically possible at the present moment.

7

Asserting the Social-Reconstructionist Agenda in Teacher Education

We will now consider the question of what we can realistically expect to achieve in the social-reconstructionist agenda for teacher education during these times of conservative restoration in the U.S. While we agree with Apple's (1986) cautions against superficial optimism, we also see some reason for hope that important gains can be won, at least under certain conditions. First, given the political orientations of most teacher educators in the 1,200 or so teacher education institutions across the U.S. (Lanier 1986), and the continued dominance of academic and social-efficiency reform traditions in the field (Clark and McNergney 1990), it is very unlikely that the social-reconstructionist reform agenda will become a dominant force in U.S. teacher education at any time in the foreseeable future—even according to the most optimistic scenario. Although it is important to continue to imagine possibilities beyond what we can now realistically achieve,[1] and continually to push the limits beyond what can be gained in our present circumstances, it is also essential that social-reconstructionist discourse begin to take more into account the culture and social conditions of teacher education. Much of the current reconstructionist rhetoric about teacher education reflects an insensitivity to the cultural and political realities faced by teacher educators in the U.S. today and to the political currents in the field. Also, despite the emphasis on such things as dialogic teaching, cross-cultural communication, and situated pedagogy in reconstructionist scholarship, there is very little evidence that many of these reformers have incorporated these notions into the way they relate their own arguments for teacher education.[2] One consequence of this insensitivity, and the failure of reconstructionist scholars of teacher education to emulate in their own scholarship the very pedagogies they propose for others, is that the arguments are largely ignored by mainstream teacher educators in the U.S. or are converted into the service of other interests through the cooptation of democratic language such as "reflective teaching" and "critical pedagogy."[3]

If we can learn from these and other errors of strategy in the past and begin to become more active forces for change within the field (as opposed to only looking in from the outside and telling others what they should do), while at the same time acting more vigorously to combat the contextual conditions of teacher education that obstruct the realization of our democratic aspirations, we see cause for genuine optimism. The essential ingredient for the establishment of a social-reconstructionist agenda as a more active force for change in U.S. teacher education is the involvement and engagement of teacher educators in several different but interrelated arenas. Social-reconstructionist teacher educators should be: (1) directly involved in a teacher education program in some capacity (e.g., as a teacher or administrator); (2) engaged in political work within colleges and universities; (3) actively supportive of efforts within the public schools to create more democratic work and learning environments; (4) engaged in political work within professional associations and in relation to state educational agencies; and (5) working for democratic changes aimed at achieving greater social justice in other societal and political areas.

Following a discussion of each of these arenas of action, we will assess the relationships between social-reconstructionist impulses for change in teacher education today and the dominant social-efficiency and academic-oriented impulses in several of the most publicized "reports" of the day. Then we will consider the relation of all these tendencies to the amelioration of the crisis of inequality in our schools and society: the concern with which we began. In doing so, we will argue for new efforts to build bridges across reform traditions and for the breaking down of the ideological insularity that currently plagues our field. Although it is important to articulate clearly and defend vigorously an agenda for democratic social and educational reform, we should not needlessly alienate potential allies among teacher educators whose primary allegiance may be to other reform traditions.[4] One of the most important tasks that lies ahead is the building of new bridges across reform traditions that can help to focus everyone's attention on creating more democratic schools; there must be a shift in the nearly exclusive focus that now exists on academic competence.

Direct involvement in teacher education

Despite the important need for conceptual elaborations that challenge our present limited horizons, we feel that it is also essential for more of us who espouse elements of a social-reconstructionist platform for teacher education to become directly involved in some aspect of the practice of teacher education. This call for direct involvement in "doing" teacher education should be very broadly construed to include instructional work with teacher education students either inside or outside education units (e.g., as a professor of an education or liberal arts course with teacher education students, or as a school- or university-based practicum supervisor) or in some administrative capacity in a teacher education program. Whatever specific role in teacher education is involved, it is critical that this commitment be for the long haul and not just for the short run. Given the difficulty of the work to be done and the likelihood of a long road ahead, we should not tolerate those who are "in the game" primarily for the academic mileage that they can accrue for themselves while remaining personally detached from the consequences of their proposals for the preparation of teachers.

More of us who espouse social-reconstructionist goals for teacher education must begin to move beyond telling *others* what to do and begin to develop concrete proposals for programs that are sensitive to the cultural and social realities of teacher education. Otherwise, the scholarship from this tradition will continue to be dismissed as it is now by many of those who identify themselves with and engage in the practice of teacher education in the U.S. today, including those who are sympathetic with our goals.[5] There is a certain elitism and arrogance associated with this tradition in the minds of many teacher educators, one that will always be present as long as we remain personally detached from the consequences of our proposals. Teacher education cannot be reformed from the outside looking in.

Furthermore as Apple (1986) has pointed out, reconstructionist proposals for education in general have frequently been cast in mystical and arcane language which is inaccessible to many whose sphere of practice is outside of a small segment of the academy. Again, while there is an important place for unrestrained conceptual work that "interrupts" existing norms and pushes us beyond our current limited horizons (Lather 1989), the undemocratic character of much reconstructionist discourse in teacher education today visibly contradicts the substance of the reform proposals and needs to be addressed if we are seriously concerned about influencing those who conduct teacher education:

> The way we talk to others in education and the language we use to describe and criticize the workings of educational institutions constitute our audience as subjects. The language we use embodies a politics in and of itself. . . . It has a vision of the reader already built in, a set of social relationships between author and reader. And too often that relationship is a bit too elitist. (Apple 1986, p. 199)

This detachment of would-be reformers of teacher education from the actual practice of the work of teacher education is a problem that is not uniquely owned by social-reconstructionist–oriented reformers. As Sarason et al. (1986) point out:

> As a group, educational researchers have nothing to do with the preparation of teachers . . . in our prestigious universities, those who are calling most articulately for upgrading programs for the preparation of teachers and for eliminating programs substandard by their criteria, spend no part of their days in the nitty gritty of teacher training. (p. xix)

The direct involvement of reconstructionist reformers in the practice of teacher education, whatever its specific manifestation, must aim to reflect the same qualities (e.g., of dialogue and collaboration) that we seek to have student teachers adopt as the basis for their work. Recent research has very clearly shown the important influence that the pedagogy of teacher education plays in the socialization of teachers. Some have even gone so far as to argue that this aspect of so called "hidden curriculum" of teacher education programs—the ways in which we act with our students and they with one another—stands at the core of teacher socialization (Ginsburg and Clift 1990).[6] Noddings (1987) expresses very well our sentiments about this issue in her discussions of an ethic of care and the importance of maintaining fidelity to persons in teacher education:

> It is tempting to suppose that, if caring is central to teaching, we must strive to produce caring teachers and then, of course, prove that we have done so. It should, indeed, be our goal in

all of education to produce caring, moral persons, but we cannot accomplish this purpose by setting an objective and heading straight toward it. Rather, we approach our goal by living with those whom we teach in a caring community, through modeling, dialogue, practice, and confirmation. . . . The best way to ensure that they will treat children as we want them to be treated is to demonstrate, in our own teaching, how teachers convey their caring. Thus modeling is central in teacher education. (pp. 390–91)

The necessity for coherence between the rhetoric and the pedagogy of social-reconstructionist–oriented teacher education projects creates certain difficulties for the realization of our democratic aspirations, given the characteristics and dispositions of many of the students who enroll in teacher education programs and the influence that these features exert on the process of teacher learning. First, the empirical evidence from studies conducted in the last decade very clearly demonstrates that the perspectives, conceptions, and dispositions that students bring to teacher education programs are very influential in determining what students will learn in those programs.[7] As case studies of students moving through teacher education programs have begun to accumulate in recent years, we have seen more and more examples of students interpreting the messages of teacher education courses in ways that reinforce the perspectives and dispositions that they bring to the program—even when these interpretations involve a distortion of the intended messages of teacher educators. One very striking example of this process can be found in Feiman-Nemser and Buchmann's (1986) case study of Janice. In this example, Janice, a student in one of Michigan State's alternative teacher education programs, construed a critique posed in one of her course readings of the unequal distribution of knowledge according to pupils' social class backgrounds as an argument for the way things ought to be. In this case, the emancipatory message of Janice's teacher educators was missed entirely.

It should not be surprising that students' entering conceptions and expectations about teaching, learning, schooling, teacher education, and society play an important role in determining what they learn and that teacher education students are active constructors of meaning rather than mere consumers of knowledge. An enormous amount of work from cognitive science (Reilly 1989), from sociologically oriented literature on social and cultural production and reproduction (Weiler 1988), and from literature on teacher socialization itself (Zeichner and Gore 1990) has convincingly demonstrated the validity of this interactive view of learning to teach. When we consider the expectations, beliefs, and dispositions that many teacher education students bring to their teacher education programs, a serious dilemma arises for social-reconstructionist teacher educators.

Apart from the important issue of the intellectual competence of teacher education students (about which there currently is much disagreement[8]), there is a fair degree of consensus among teacher education scholars today about the politically conformist orientations and cultural insularity of many teacher education students. Despite the presence of at least some "counter identifiers" (Lortie 1975) who come into teacher education programs already somewhat critical of the status quo in schooling and society, it is very clear that the vast majority of prospective teachers do not come into teacher education programs with dispositions to reconstruct schooling and society in a manner that challenges the institutional structures within which their work takes place (Lanier 1986; Ginsburg 1988). Nor, for that matter, do students come expecting to learn very much of anything about teaching from their university course work (Book, Byers, and Freeman 1983).

A recent national study of teacher education across the U.S. has described teacher education students as largely white and female, monolingual, from rural (small town) or suburban communities, who prefer to teach in traditional classroom settings with middle-income children of average (not gifted or handicapped) ability. Only 15 percent of this group would like to teach in urban areas where cultural diversity and inequalities are most visible (Zimpher 1989). Thus, teacher education students as a group are very homogeneous and are oriented toward working in schools with students very much like themselves. As Zimpher (1989) points out, this is in sharp contrast to the current and future demographic profiles that show that our public schools are increasingly serving pupils of color who come from backgrounds of poverty.[9]

Given the apparent homogeneity and the tendencies toward political conservatism among teacher education students, and their desire deliberately to avoid teaching in schools where inequalities are most visible, social-reconstructionist–oriented teacher educators are faced with a serious dilemma. If, given our current student population, we try to be truly responsive to our students and build the teacher education curriculum from the ground up, so to speak, solely on the basis of our students' experiences and concerns, then it is unlikely that issues of inequality based on race, class, ethnicity, and gender will surface for discussion and analysis.[10] If, on the other hand, we seek to impose a critical perspective on schooling and society through methods that approach deliberate indoctrination, then we will also not accomplish very much because students will tend either to reject messages with overtly political ramifications or restructure the messages so as to reinforce their own entering perspectives. In many cases, these entering perspectives implicitly reinforce the status quo by not acknowledging their political nature (Feiman-Nemser and Buchmann 1986; Ginsburg 1988).

What we tried to do in the previous chapters (2, 3, 4, and 6), in outlining what we consider to be the central features of social-reconstruction–oriented teacher education practices, is to articulate a middle-ground position between the two extremes of indoctrination and total responsiveness that are implicit in many current reform efforts.[11] We have presented a framework for a pedagogy of teacher education that is situated in students' realities and responsive to their concerns but, at the same time, takes them beyond their current horizons to consider perspectives and issues that they would not normally entertain.[12] In this framework teacher educators are supposed to enable prospective teachers to articulate defensible justifications for their educational actions, to take into account the institutional and larger social contexts of schooling, and to examine their own implicit social, cultural, and political beliefs. Teacher educators should provide deliberate direction by including certain kinds of issues and perspectives in the teacher education curriculum (e.g., teachers' work, inequalities in access to knowledge according to students' social-class backgrounds, race, and gender. See chapter 4) and by insisting upon an analysis of those issues that addresses the moral and political implications of particular practices and institutional structures.[13] Although we cannot be assured that students will adopt the socially critical positions we might personally prefer, we can aim to ensure that they are at the very least aware of the moral implications of particular practices and school structures. We also can try to ensure, as Adler & Goodman (1986) argue, that students are aware of and develop capabilities to implement alternatives to practices they find questionable or objectionable. One key to the success of this pedagogy, as we tried to point out earlier, is the ability of teacher educators to maintain an integration of theory and practice by focusing attention on issues of equity and justice when they arise out of the students' experiences in schools.

This tension between a responsive orientation toward students and a focused examination of critical social issues has been part of the social-reconstructionist reform tradition in teacher education throughout the twentieth century and, in its more general form, a part of "progressive"-oriented reforms aimed at all segments of the educational sector.[14] Apart from our particular proposals for resolving this tension, it should be kept in mind that we are also making a more general claim that nothing of lasting importance will be achieved by social reconstructionist reformers of teacher education if they remain on the outside looking in. We feel that the current detachment from the practice of teacher education of many reformers within this tradition is responsible for some of the cultural insensitivity in some social-reconstructionist reform proposals. While we may not be able realistically to create a situation where teacher education students are as a group at the vanguard of efforts to restructure the society, we can make important progress toward such a restructuring if we offer our proposals in a way that is sensitive to the political and structural conditions faced by teacher educators in their daily work. Direct involvement and cultural responsiveness are not necessarily synonymous—and, of course, are not guarantees that our proposals will succeed. But it seems that the marginalization of the social-reconstructionist perspective by many of those who work in the field will persist unless efforts are made to speak to people in the field in more responsive ways.

Working within the college and university context

The second major arena for action for social-reconstructionist teacher educators is the college and university environments in which most teacher education programs are located.[15] It is no secret that teacher education programs are low-prestige and low-cost endeavors in most of the 1,200 or so institutions of higher education across the U.S. that offer teacher education options to their students (Clark and Marker 1975; Zeichner 1986b). Recent work has convincingly shown that this low status and prestige of teacher education in the academy has been a problem throughout the twentieth century and that institutions have sought to gain status and recognition by emphasizing areas more prestigious than teacher education (Powell 1976; Judge 1982; Kerr 1983; Schneider 1987; Clifford and Guthrie 1988; Herbst 1989). This has been especially true, as Clifford and Guthrie have shown, in our most prestigious research universities:

Early on and in their own ways, then, the prestige schools of education either eliminated teacher education or confined it to a limited and peripheral role in their increasingly graduate-oriented organizations. Education schools focused professionalism on those who were *leaving* teaching, rather than those entering the classroom. (p. 115)[16]

As early as 1933, in the report of the first National Survey of Teacher Education in the U.S. sponsored by the U.S. Office of Education, the lack of faculty commitment to the enterprise of teacher education was evident:

The faculty of any institution the graduates of which are recognized for certification should possess a high degree of contagious enthusiasm for teaching and a sincere interest in the students as prospective teachers in the public schools. Survey data would indicate that a majority of the staff members of many such institutions are not primarily or even seriously interested in the professional problems of educating teachers for different types of positions. (National Survey-Volume 6, 1933, p. 180)[17]

Since then, it has been abundantly clear that the closer one is associated with the preparation of teachers, the more difficult it is to gain status within academe. In many teacher education institutions throughout the U.S., individual faculty gain status and prestige by demonstrating their ability to produce research and secure extramural funding. Demonstration of their ability to conceive of and implement high-quality teacher education programs is not rewarded in most cases and might even serve to lower their status in the academy:

There is an inverse relationship between professorial prestige and the intensity of involvement with the formal education of teachers . . . It is common knowledge that professors in the arts and sciences risk the loss of academic respect, including promotion and tenure, if they assume clear interest in the responsibility for teacher education. Professors holding academic rank in education units are even in greater jeopardy of losing the respect of their academic counterparts in the university, because their close proximity makes association with teacher education more possible. And finally, those education professors who actually supervise prospective or practicing teachers in elementary or secondary schools are indeed at the bottom of the stratification ladder. (Lanier 1986, p. 530)

There are several very visible consequences of this low status and prestige of teacher education in higher education that pose serious obstacles to the reform of teacher education programs. One consequence of low status has been the chronic underfunding of teacher education programs in relation to other occupational preparation programs on U.S. campuses (Bush 1987). Peseau and Orr's (1979, 1980, and 1981) longitudinal studies of funding patterns in sixty-three institutions in thirty-seven states has convincingly documented what they refer to as an "outrageous underfunding" of teacher education where, as Peseau (1982) concluded, the average direct cost of instruction per year for the preparation of an undergraduate student in teacher education is only 50 percent as much as the average spent to educate undergraduates in all university disciplines. With regard to clinical teacher education in particular, the Study Commission on Undergraduate Education and the Education of Teachers (1976), sponsored by the U.S. Office of Education, concluded that at most institutions field-based or practicum courses in teacher education are less well supported than are practicum courses in most other fields with clinical components, such as nursing, engineering, and social work.[18]

Various explanations have been offered for this meager financial investment in teacher education. Some have criticized state funding formulas and internal college and university policies that treat teacher education programs as any other undergraduate program taking no account of the need to support complex and demanding clinical studies (Kerr 1983; Palmer 1985). Others have argued that the limited allocation of funds to teacher education mirrors conditions in the larger society which tend to undervalue anything, like the occupation of teaching, associated with women and children (Clifford and Guthrie 1988; Goodman 1988)[19], or that it is a reflection of a lack of confidence in the knowledge base underlying teacher education (Lanier 1986). Although there is much debate about the specific causes of current funding patterns, there is little dispute that the rhetoric regarding the importance of teacher education in higher education is rarely supported in practice by the commitment of financial resources that would support specific proposals.[20]

Another consequence of the low status of teacher education in higher education is that those faculty who identify with and are most closely associated with teacher education programs are faced both with greater demands on their time for teaching and the supervision of students in schools and with having less time for scholarly pursuits, including research and development activities related to their teacher education programs (Schneider 1987). The excessive teaching loads of teacher education faculty have long been recognized as serious structural impediments to enhancing the quality of teacher education programs even by some of the harshest critics of the field who have placed most of their emphasis on the deficiencies of individuals (e.g., Koerner 1963). The demands associated with supervising teacher education students, in practicums in particular, are unparalled in any other type of professional school (Fuller and Bown 1975). And this supervision is relegated primarily to junior faculty and graduate students in many institutions (Lazerson 1989). Furthermore, relatively little financial support is available to support teacher education research, even if faculty were given more time to conduct it and were inclined to do so (Koehler 1985).

The low status of teacher education in the academy is also partly responsible for the fragmented nature of the curriculum in many U.S. teacher education programs and for the lack of distinctiveness and coherence in programs. In an earlier paper which analyzed various aspects of the elementary student teaching program at the University of Wisconsin-Madison (Zeichner and Liston 1987), we described a situation that is still quite typical in the U.S., except in those institutions having small teacher education programs with just a few faculty (Goodlad 1990). In this situation, each component of the professional education portion of a teacher education program is under the control of different faculty who are also affiliated with one or more disciplinary areas (e.g., math education, social studies education). Although faculty are engaged in the teacher education program in a limited way within their own area (e.g., a methods course in math education), very few faculty think about the program as a whole, affiliating primarily with their discipline and not with teacher education:

> Identifying primarily with their disciplines, the professors
> teaching foundations courses to prospective teachers (e.g., the
> psychology, sociology, history, or philosophy of education)

tend to deny their teacher education role and identify those who teach methods courses and supervise practice teaching as the real teacher educators. But most professors of teaching methods courses would disagree. Identifying with the school subjects of their expertise, they tend to consider themselves science educators, mathematics educators, or reading educators and point to those who coordinate and supervise student teachers as the real teacher educators. Those who supervise fieldwork in the schools are probably the only faculty, as a group, who publicly identify themselves as teacher educators. (Lanier 1986, p. 8)

Under such conditions, it becomes very difficult to engage faculty in program development efforts that move them outside of their own disciplinary areas and that would contribute to overall program coherence. The reluctance of faculty to spend a lot of time working to develop the best teacher education programs they are capable of mounting is quite understandable given the reward systems in institutions, which either value teaching (in the case of small liberal arts colleges and some universities), or primarily value scholarship and grantsmanship (as in a growing number of universities). The result is a very fragmented teacher education curriculum which is poorly articulated and coordinated across subject areas and over time.

Unless teacher educators begin to confront more adequately the immediate structural context of their work, there will continue to be very severe limitations on the changes in teacher education programs that are possible. Innovations in teacher education will continue to be assimilated into current arrangements and lend credibility to the very practices they seek to change (Popkewitz 1987). We see a need for vigorous action on the part of teacher educators to secure more adequate funding for teacher education programs, especially their clinical elements. This entails a more openly politicized and activist stance on the part of faculty than we are used to assuming. Strengthening the position of teacher education in the college and university also requires, as many have stressed, changes in the reward structures of colleges and universities that will value, more than is now the case, efforts to do exemplary work in teacher education (Clifford and Guthrie 1988).

Although there are some who now say that adequate support for teacher preparation can only occur by moving teacher education programs from the undergraduate context to the graduate level (e.g., Kerr 1983), or by establishing an autonomous professional school of education outside of the sphere of universities and colleges (Hedges 1989), we feel that equity questions still associated with such moves necessitate much more debate about the specific institutional patterns that should be supported.[21] Given the current college and university context for teacher education and short of moving programs to the graduate level or into a separate professional school, there are important reforms that can be accomplished until we have a more adequate debate over organizational forms.

One thing that needs to happen is for teacher education faculty to become more involved in college and university politics, serving on key university committees and generally becoming more active participants in the making of the policies by which higher institutions are governed. Generally, this is not the case now for education faculty as a whole, especially in large research universities:

> Generally, schools, colleges, and departments of education are politically impotent. Most of their faculty are marginal figures in institutional politics, and naive about institutional processes. (Clifford and Guthrie 1988, p. 40)

This greater involvement in institutional politics[22] is only one of the ways we can work to secure more adequate resources for supporting high-quality teacher education programs. Also needed is more interaction between arts and science and education faculties in terms of both teacher education and undergraduate education in general.[23] It has been repeatedly pointed out by teacher educators, in part because policymakers act as if they were unaware of the fact that teacher education students spend the bulk of the time in preparation for teaching with arts and sciences faculty. In most places in the U.S. today, the problems of teacher education are in essence problems of undergraduate education as a whole. The same problems that were discussed above in relation to teacher education (e.g., a fragmented overspecialized curriculum) have also been identified as campus-wide problems in recent reports on undergraduate education in the U.S. (e.g., Boyer 1987).

Another way to combat the low regard that is given to educational studies and teacher education in many institutions is to make selected education courses more available to students who do not enroll in teacher education programs—through the use of such mechanisms as joint appointments, the cross-listing of courses, and interdisciplinary majors and minors. There is no reason to assume, as has been pointed out for many years (Borrowman 1956), that educational studies need necessarily be technical or vocational in the narrowest sense. It has been demonstrated that these courses, when they are well taught, can be just as liberalizing as arts-and-sciences courses that are similarly well taught (see Beyer 1988; Travers and Sacks 1987). The greater involvement of elementary teacher education students in arts-and-sciences courses, which is a part of most contemporary reform proposals, needs to be complemented by more involvement of non–teacher education students in educational studies courses. Currently, only about 36 percent of higher-education institutions in the U.S. offer any education-related courses for general education credit (Johnston et al. 1989).

There is another issue within the college and university context that needs to be addressed if we are serious about making our social-reconstructionist perspective a more active force for change in teacher education. Specifically, if we are concerned with preparing socially conscious teachers who will be capable of working against the antidemocratic features in schooling and society, we need to examine the very composition of our own teacher education community. Recent analyses of preservice teacher education in the U.S. have shown that gender relations between faculty and students, and among faculty in teacher education, mirror the patriarchal relations in schools between administrators and teachers. Ducharme and Agne (1989) summarize some of these findings as follows:

> Surveys of the education professorate consistently find that most teacher educators are men. The education professorate which represents a variety of disciplines within teacher education is approximately 65% male, 35% female. In 1986, the American Association of Colleges of Teacher Education (AACTE) conducted a study of the secondary education programs of nearly ninety member institutions and found that the faculty was 70% male and 30% female (AACTE, 1987). The 1987 Research About Teacher Education survey (RATE), which gathered data on faculty teaching the introductory foundations courses, found 72% male and 28% female. In brief, survey after survey shows the education professorate to be more than 65% male, a condition contrasting sharply with the population of teacher education students which is approximately 70% female. . . . There are clear differences in gender distribution across professorial ranks. For example, while women ac-

count for 30% of the secondary education professorate in the RATE study, they form only 16% of the full professor rank. Our study of the professorate found a similar pattern; 14% of the full professors were female and 86% were male. At the assistant professor level, there was a more even distribution with 46% female and 54% male. This more balanced representation offers some hope for change for there is a larger pool of women entering the professorate than previously. . . . Despite this positive trend, a note of caution must be raised. Other data in our study suggest, that women enter the professorate later, teach more and publish less. (pp. 74–75)

When we consider the racial dimensions of the teacher educator group, the problem is even more severe. Ducharme and Agne (1989) summarize some of these data as follows:

Minorities are much less represented in the education professorate than are women. In the RATE study, 2.9% of the full professors are minority; 6.4% at the associate level; and 9.9% at the assistant professor level. The representation of minorities appears to be growing, but the growth may be short lived inasmuch as these institutions showed a total of only 8% minority in doctoral programs. (p. 75)[24]

These problems are complemented by the well-publicized problem of an imbalance between the numbers of minorities entering teacher education programs and general population demographics. Although it is projected by some that, by the year 2000, one out of every three people in the U.S. may be nonwhite (Hodgkinson 1985), the number of minority students enrolled in teacher education programs across the U.S. is pathetically low and declining. According to national data from 1985 (The Condition of Education, 1988), 88.3 percent of teacher education students were white, 6.2 percent African-American, 2.9 percent Hispanic, and 1.4 percent Asian/Native American. Although there is some variation in these percentages by geographical area of the country, by field of study, and by institutional type, the situation is bad and getting worse just about everywhere. In addition to the low numbers of minority teaching candidates overall, there is an extreme concentration of those minority students who do choose teacher education in relatively few institutions. This concentration of minority students in relatively few teacher education institutions makes it very difficult to deal with the problem of underrepresentation in teacher education institutions across the country. Although historically black schools, colleges, and departments of education constitute 4 percent of the institutions with teacher education programs, they enroll more than 30 percent of African-American students in teacher education programs (AACTE, 1988). Many current reform policies such as competency testing for prospective teachers are helping to make this bleak situation even worse (e.g., Witty 1982; Smith, Miller, and Joy 1988).

Although the white-male dominance of the faculty of colleges of education and the white domination of the prospective teacher group is not unique to teacher education (Howey and Zimpher 1990), it should not be tolerated by the field much longer. Numerous proposals for the recruitment of minority students into teacher education programs have emerged in the past few years in most of the teacher education "reports," and in the actions of state education agencies, colleges and universities, and independent groups such as the Teacher Corps alumni network.[25] The white-male dominance of education faculties has received far less attention in the literature and has mainly been addressed by the affirmative-action plans of individual institutions. Social-reconstructionist teacher educators need to work actively and visibly in support of these efforts to diversify the teacher education community. A more gender- and racially balanced faculty as well as a more visible presence of students of color in teacher education institutions is critical to the success of the reconstructionist pedagogy for teacher education that we have described in this book. One of the most effective ways to expose teacher education students to diverse perspectives on educational issues and to sensitize them to issues of equity and human dignity is to have our teacher education programs reflect the racial and ethnic character of the society, as well as the gender equity that we seek to have them promote in the elementary and secondary schools of the nation.[26] It is very hard to imagine that we could be very successful in getting our students to assume activist roles in the public schools working on behalf of social justice and human dignity unless we get our own house in order. We must continually remember that the hidden curriculum of our teacher education programs often speaks much louder than our rhetoric (Ginsburg and Clift 1990). We strongly support the Holmes Group consortium (1990) when they argue that

We must bring into both university and public school teaching more faculty from America's rainbow of nations and peoples.

To do so would help to diminish the powerful negative messages about justice, fairness, and about authority and power, about inclusion and participation, that are implicit in the prevailing monochrome of our nation's teaching cadre. To do so will allow different voices to be heard and different outlooks to be shared. . . . The current situation calls for radical action by universities, colleges of education, and school systems. (p. 40)

Supporting efforts to democratize schools

In the preceding discussion of the college and university context of teacher education, the fragmented curriculum of U.S. teacher education programs was identified as a serious problem. One particular area where the lack of coordination and coherence has been the greatest is between the campus and field-based components of teacher education programs. In addition to the marginal status of teacher education in colleges and universities discussed above, teacher education is rarely a priority in the primary and secondary schools which serve as sites for clinical teacher education courses. This is the case even for the "good" schools where practices are consistent with those advocated by college and university faculty. Cooperating teachers who work with teacher education students are often unaware of what students are exposed to in their university course work and of university expectations for the practicum (e.g., Griffin et al., 1983), are given only token payments of around fifty dollars for a full semester's work with a student, and most often assume the role of teacher educator with minimal preparation and in addition to their full-time responsibilities for teaching pupils (Guyton and McIntyre 1990). In most cases, no provisions whatsoever are made in the structures of teachers' jobs for their work as teacher educators.[27]

The overall improvement of school and university relations has been highlighted in the current wave of educational reform (Sirotnik and Goodlad 1988). Many of the current reports on U.S. teacher education discuss the benefits for teacher education programs that will come from an overall improvement in school and university relations.[28] Apart from the current focus on school-university partnerships, which covers a lot of areas in addition to teacher education, significant progress has been made in recent years in school and university relations specifically within the sphere of teacher education. For example, public school personnel are now involved much more than before in the planning and evaluation

203

of teacher education programs. Practicum and teacher education advisory committees composed primarily of elementary and secondary teachers and administrators are now commonplace (Zeichner 1986a).[29] Although much of this collaborative activity has given public school personnel a greater voice in colleges' and universities' efforts in teacher education, it has also left them in many cases on less than equal footing with their university colleagues in terms of formal power. Advisory committees give advice. It has been rare that they are actually able to implement directly their advice or that school voices carry as much weight as academic voices when it comes to decisions about polices and programs (Ervay 1985). However, in recent years school personnel have gained ground in their ability to influence college and university teacher education in other ways such as through their influence on state standards for the accreditation of teacher education programs, and state certification standards.[30]

The question of school and university relations is an especially difficult one for social-reconstructionist–oriented teacher educators who, by definition, assume a skeptical if not an oppositional stance toward much of what is accepted as part of the settled context in public schools. Under these conditions, one key element with regard to "improving school and university relations" for social-reconstructionist teacher educators must be the development of better linkages with those individuals within the public schools who are working for the kinds of democratic changes that would give more people a greater voice in the determination of school policies and more students access to a better education.

The opportunities for developing these relationships with progressive forces for change in the public schools have increased in recent years as external policies and the overall climate have shifted somewhat toward the decentralization of school decision-making and toward fewer controls over what and how teachers teach (Darling-Hammond and Berry 1988).[31] "Restructuring" has become the new buzzword in U.S. education (Fiske 1990). This is not to deny the influence of the processes of deskilling and intensification of teachers' work which continue to undermine school democratization efforts (Apple 1986, Densmore 1987).[32] It is our belief, though, that despite continued efforts to centralize control and standardize practice within the schools, the current legitimacy of "school restructuring," provided in part by the analyses of powerful groups such as Carnegie and the National Governors' Association,[33] has enabled more and more forces for democratic change to emerge in the public schools. These efforts should receive the active and vigorous support of social-reconstructionist teacher educators.[34]

As we stated in chapter 6, in our comments about the curriculum and instructional practices in teacher education programs, we think it essential that teachers and administrators (such as the ones who are involved in the Institute for Democratic Education and Rethinking Schools)[35] be given a more prominent place in teacher education programs either through their direct participation in programs (e.g., as clinical supervisors) or through the use of their writing in teacher education courses. Although we should not limit ourselves to interacting only with like-minded teachers and administrators, individuals working for the democratization of schooling within the system are especially important for the success of social-reconstructionist teacher education projects. It is critical, for example, for our students to be able to make connections with these alternative voices within the system so that they are aware of the diversity of perspectives among teachers and administrators, and do not think that progressive pedagogy and democratic organizational practices are things that exists only in the minds of university scholars or in private schools for the professional class.

In addition to developing these connections between progressive educators in the public schools and our teacher education programs, we need to support actively the efforts for democratic change themselves. All over the U.S. teachers, administrators, and parents are working in many different ways at the grass-roots level both to combat such things as the centralization of school curriculums, standardized testing, poor working conditions for teachers, and to promote such things as the development of a gender-balanced and multicultural curriculum and more responsive teaching practices, such as whole language instruction. While these efforts do not often directly address the systemic roots of problems in the society itself, they are compatible with a reconstructionist agenda and need to be supported.[36]

One example of the supportive role that social-reconstructionist teacher educators need to play in relation to democratic school-based reforms can be found in a recent experience that one of us (Zeichner) recently had with teachers in a local school district. From 1988 to 1990, elementary teachers in the Madison Metropolitan School District sought to obtain from their school board more "planning" time during the school day to enable them to do a variety of things, including meeting with one another to engage in cooperative staff development activities. What they sought was additional planning time that would put them on a par with teachers in the same district at the middle-school level. As part of their strategy, they wanted to be able to document how teachers currently spent their time. A principal and a group of teachers approached Ken

Zeichner and asked him to help them document the nature of elementary teachers' work throughout the district. For two semesters, Zeichner coordinated efforts of several faculty and graduate students as well as many undergraduate students in the elementary teacher education program to "shadow" teachers and keep track of the time that they spent in various kinds of activities in and out of school.[37] Zeichner and a group of teachers jointly developed a set of categories to be used for the analysis. These data were then compiled and used in presentations to the school board and in contract negotiations. Zeichner was also called upon to help the teachers devise alternative strategies for structuring the teachers' day at the elementary level to accommodate the extra planning time, and to help build a case for the extra time, which would be used in presentations to the district.

Although the contract settlement in January 1990 brought the teachers only one extra hour of "planning" time each week, what was won was a step in the right direction and helped bring the elementary teachers together as a group in an effort to better the conditions of their work.[38] It also helped make school board members much more aware of all of the different kinds of demands that elementary teachers face on a daily basis. The important thing about this case for our purposes here is that it illustrates the way in which university teacher educators can play a supportive role in teachers' and administrators' efforts to create more democratic and humane conditions within our public schools. This kind of activity requires that university teacher educators step outside of their usual roles as highly visible and well-paid expert consultants. It is important that school personnel be in charge of these efforts and that the use of any expertise that university faculty might offer be directed by the teachers and administrators.

In addition to these efforts in support of those who are already working for democratic changes within schools social-reconstructionist teacher educators must actively work against those forces within the public schools that obstruct democratic education. One example of that which needs to be countered is the widespread utilization of the "hucksters of school improvement and staff development" by school districts. These independent agents, many of whom are former university academics, market prepackaged "solutions" to schools' problems such as "Assertive Discipline," "Project T.E.A.C.H." and "Instructional Theory into Practice."[39] All these programs absorb a tremendous amount of public resources that could otherwise be spent to support the school restructuring efforts that have been placed on the agenda by almost every recent proposal for school reform.[40] This "What Works" mentality[41] and the packaged solutions to schools' problems that flow from it generally support the further deskilling of the staff who must implement any reforms. These "solutions" take the process of defining the nature of the problems to be solved and the nature of the appropriate solutions out of the hands of local school personnel. Expertise about problems of teaching in these problems is located in the external consultants. This reliance on external experts, rather than on the expertise within a staff, is often justified in terms of cost effectiveness. For example, Performance Learning Systems (1986) asserts:

> There is no need for the district to spend time and money creating their own comprehensive training designs. Performance Learning Systems has already created proven, sophisticated programs. Performance Learning System training designs took 28 person-years of research, development, and field testing. The entire 180 hour program of training and coaching is guaranteed to deliver effective mastery of the classroom. (p. 8)

We should have learned by now from the failures of the recent past that this essentially top-down strategy of school reform ultimately fails everyone, except those who profit from the sale of these educational solutions (Sarason 1971). In addition to fact that there is very little systematic evaluation of the numerous fads that move in and out of school districts in predictable cycles,[42] the selling of educational solutions is big business. For example, the first published article evaluating Madeline Hunter's "Instructional Theory into Practice" (ITIP), one of the most controversial of the current fads, appeared sixteen years after the program was established in many schools and, then, only assessed the model in one school in Napa, California (Stallings 1985). Slavin (1989) summarizes the only three significant evaluations conducted on this program since its inception and concludes that:

> The case of ITIP provides a vivid example of the educational pendulum in action. It is particularly instructive because of the breadth of adoption of the ITIP model, the lack of evaluative evidence until very recently, and the unambiguous failure of the program to affect the only variable that it is designed to affect: student achievement. (p. 755)[43]

While it is difficult to obtain very precise figures on the extent to which programs like the ITIP are adopted and the amount of resources that are consumed, there is no question that these programs have been widely adopted by school districts. Render et al. (1989) comment about the Assertive Discipline program, for example:

> The technique seems to have experienced meteoric growth. According to advertising materials from Canter and Associates, more than 500,000 teachers have been trained in Assertive Discipline techniques in countless workshops in thousands of schools. Assertive Discipline has expanded beyond the classroom and training is now available for paraprofessionals, including playground and cafeteria personnel, teacher aides, and school bus drivers. Materials are also available for parents. (p. 607)

Advertising materials from Performance Learning Systems, marketers of a number of teaching skills training programs including Project T.E.A.C.H. (Performance Learning Systems, 1986), claim that over 160,000 teachers have been trained in their programs. It is estimated that hundreds of school districts and tens of thousands of educators have been involved with the so-called "Hunter model" (Goldberg 1990). School districts who hire one of these companies have been willing to pay up to $3,000 a day for the services of well-known consultants and speakers like Madeline Hunter (Stover 1988). According to Stover, the basic one-day workshop for the Assertive Discipline costs a minimum of $1500 for fifty participants. Performance Learning Systems also charges $1500 plus expenses for their basic one-day workshop. Their initial forty-five-hour course, "Project T.E.A.C.H.," costs a district from $4,000 to $4,500, plus expenses for an instructor.

Apart from specific criticisms of the substance of these programs which have begun to appear in the literature only recently,[44] there is little question about the exaggerated nature of the claims that are made by the advocates of these programs, both about their basis in research and their impact upon teachers. For example, in *We Can Show You the Secrets of Creating a Championship Teaching Staff*, the promotional booklet from Performance Learning Systems, it is asserted that:

> Performance Learning Systems offers a complete comprehensive series of teacher training courses which provide the per-

forming moves to make every teacher on your staff a champion. Performance Learning Systems has spent 15 years investigating what elegant teachers do in the classroom that makes them champions. More than a quarter century of person-hours has been devoted to shaping our findings into concrete skills that can be passed on to all teachers . . . We analyze the practices of exemplary teachers . . . those whose students learn and who deal successfully with critical incidents and learning problems. By identifying their skills, strategies, and decision-making protocols, we are able to isolate techniques and practices and design them into a format from which other teachers can learn. Ours is a pragmatic practitioner model that is 100% congruent with the findings of educational research. (pp. 4, 18)

Few of those who have been centrally involved in conducting research on effective teaching behaviors over the past twenty-five years, such as Jere Brophy, Tom Good, David Berliner, or Jane Stallings, would probably endorse such exaggerated claims as these. While the presentations in these workshops are very slick and polished (Stover 1988) and while there is no shortage of testimonials in the promotional literature to the wonders produced by these programs, the analysis of Hunter's programs by Slavin (1989) and of the data on Assertive Discipline by Render et al. (1989) leave little doubt that these programs fail to produce the effects they promise. It should be kept in mind that hucksters of school improvement represent only one example of the kinds of antidemocratic tendencies in the schools that should be opposed by social-reconstructionist teacher educators.

Working with state educational agencies and in professional organizations

Everywhere in the U.S., state governments have authority for all education within their borders, including teacher education. Throughout the history of formal teacher education in the U.S., the state has gradually increased its influence on teacher education programs and acted as a standardizing force in the field (Cremin 1953). This influence has been exerted through the promulgation of state standards for teacher certification and the accreditation of teacher education programs. During the twentieth century, state requirements have been largely responsible for increasingly rigorous requirements for entering teaching at a beginning level.[45]

Despite the important role that the states have played in raising the status of teaching by developing more rigorous standards for entry into practice, the role of the states in teacher education has been a frequent target of criticisms from within and outside of the teacher education community. During the late 1950s and 1960s the states were accused by many from outside the teacher education community (e.g., Lynd 1953 and Koerner 1963) of being part of an interlocking directorate with groups like the National Education Association, American Association of Colleges for Teacher Education (AACTE), and National Council for the Accreditation of Teacher Education (NCATE), all of whom were thought to be conspiring to protect the interests of education courses in the teacher education curriculum and to keep people out of teaching who had not completed a full quota of these courses. James Conant (1963), in his study of the role of sixteen state educational agencies, repudiated these theories about a conspiracy of educationists. He found a much looser association among these various organizations than was alleged by many, as well as significant variations in teacher education policies in the sixteen states. Conant's (1963) analysis has been supported by many others who challenge the notion that cooperative self-serving relationships exist among all the various organizations having some role in teacher education (Clark and Marker 1975, Lanier 1986).

From the 1970s onward, as states have significantly enlarged their control over teacher education programs throughout the U.S. (Atkin and Raths 1974, Drummond and Andrews 1980, Cronin 1983, Tate 1988, Clark and McNergney 1990), criticisms of the role of state educational agencies in teacher education have come increasingly from within the teacher education community. There is little question about the way in which the states have become increasingly more aggressive in recent years by promulgating more specific and detailed standards for the approval of teacher education programs.[46] These standards have required more stringent qualifications for entering and completing programs such as higher grade point averages and competency tests, the reflection of particular "competencies" in the teacher education curriculum, and a longer stay for students in programs as a result of increased requirements (Leatherman 1988). These increased requirements are rarely followed by additional state resources to support them.[47] The growth in state intervention into teacher education has been swift and substantial. With regard to state-mandated teacher competency tests, for example, in 1979 only six states required some type of competency test to enter or complete a program or for teacher certification. By 1986, however, forty-six states had mandated teacher competency tests in basic skills, subject matter, or professional knowledge (Sandefur 1986).

Although most states have adopted a more aggressive role in the regulation of teacher education, there is still much variation in specific policies among states (Coley 1985). For example, in some states like Wisconsin, recent policies have substantially increased course work in professional courses offered by schools, colleges, and departments of education and in academic course work (Prestine 1989). In other states, such as Texas, recent policies have increased academic requirements at the expense of course work in education units (Simms and Miller 1988).[48] Despite this variation, the overall emphasis has been on increasing academic requirements at the expense of education course work:

> If there has been an identifiable conceptual theme in the chang-
> ing programmatic requirements for teachers in recent years, it
> would be one of mastering content. Competence in teaching,
> particularly at the high school level is being defined first by the
> acquisition of knowledge in one's discipline. This is being re-
> flected in program accreditation procedures at the state level by
> increasing the emphasis on studies in the liberal arts and sci-
> ences and decreasing the emphasis on professional education.
> (Clark and McNergney 1990, p. 104).

Although specific aspects of these recent state regulations have sought to address long-neglected problems in teacher education such as providing more assistance to beginning teachers, and have tried to ensure that all prospective teachers in a state are exposed to course material related to certain critical issues such as tribal treaty rights, the protection of the environment, and diverse cultures, there are many aspects of the recent intervention of the state into teacher education that should be vigorously opposed by social-reconstructionist and other teacher educators.[49]

One specific aspect of recent policies that should be actively opposed is their sometimes elitist quality. It has been clearly documented that recent policies such as competency tests and longer programs undermine efforts to create a more diverse teaching force.[50] While few would support policies that permit people to enter teaching who have not attained certain minimal academic capabilities, some policies, like stringent test score minimums for entry into teacher education, are overly restrictive because they do not even permit teacher education institutions to work with students who come to them disadvantaged by their public school education. Recent policies that place exclusive emphasis on the intellectual competence of teachers ignore the moral dimensions of teacher education and many of the qualities needed by teachers to enable them to provide an education that can be characterized by both equity and excellence (Sirotnik 1990).[51] Finally, as Apple (1987) points out, extending teacher education programs beyond four years, as has become more common in recent years, will simply have elitist effects unless large sums of money are made available to enable less economically advantaged individuals to become teachers.

Another negative consequence of the recent state onslaught upon teacher education is the way in which state mandates have contributed to the fragmentation of the teacher education curriculum and have undermined efforts to develop more coherent programs. The typical scenario is for state officials, in response to the arguments of various interest groups, to make determinations about additional areas that should be incorporated into the teacher education curriculum. It is the rare case in which a state department has mandated the removal of something from programs. As Cronin (1983) has pointed out, these mandates have led over the years to an overcrowded curriculum in which choices and options for students have been eroded. In addition to eliminating many electives for students, these increasingly specific and detailed state mandates for the teacher education curriculum have stifled the process of innovation in program development efforts. As campus- and school-based teacher educators have contemplated the creation of new and creative teacher education programs, they have often been hampered by the need to include numerous required topics in the curriculum or not to exceed a certain number of credits for particular kinds of courses.

This increased intervention of state education agencies into the curriculum and organization of teacher education programs is not entirely a result of the actions of state educational officials. To describe this state of affairs as a "we-versus-them" issue would be a gross oversimplification. For example, as Levin (1990) points out, it has been university teacher educators in many cases, as appointed or invited representatives of various state committees, who have proposed the controversial regulations in the first place. In Wisconsin, for example, many of the people who testified in support of the recently implemented state teacher accreditation standards were university-based teacher educators from campuses other than Madison (Prestine 1989). Additionally, at least some of the people who work in these agencies, especially at the lower levels, have sometimes advocated progressive proposals for teacher education such as mentoring programs for beginning teachers, programs to attract more people of color into teaching, and programs to help student teachers become more sensitive to cultural traditions other than their own.[52] There is at least some potential available for forming alliances with state education agency personnel in support of those specific policies and programs that are aimed at promoting more humane and just school environments.

To influence state policymaking in teacher education, though, teacher educators will have to go beyond efforts to support those state policies that address questions of social justice. Reconstructionist-oriented teacher educators will need to become more involved than most are now in the political arena of teacher education, lobbying to place progressive faculty on key state committees in which policies are crafted, and lobbying state legislators in behalf of particular programs. When state officials ask for advice on particular programs or offer opportunities for public testimony on particular policies and programs, it is important that social reconstructionist perspectives be represented in the discourse. We are not so naive to believe that current problems stemming from the states' intervention into teacher education curriculum can be solved through the strength of reason, logic, and evidence in arguments to state officials. The game is political and not an academic one. We do feel, though, that it is important to keep the moral implications of state policies visible to both elected public officials and to the general public. When states like Wisconsin, for example, implement program accreditation standards and testing policies that make it more difficult (despite rhetoric to the contrary) for students of color to gain entry to and then complete teacher education programs, these consequences need to be publicized widely.

There are many signs that the politicization of teacher educators has increased in intensity in recent years. A usually publicly apolitical Don Cruickshank of Ohio State University recently issued a call for increased lobbying of the two professional organizations in the U.S. representing state education departments.[53] In 1987, the Dean of the School of Education at the University of Wisconsin-Madison assigned faculty to lobby specific state legislators who would be voting on proposed accreditation standards for teacher education programs. The Association of Teacher Educators (ATE) sponsored a seminar on Effective Communication with

Elected Officials in July 1989. Hendrick Gideonse filed a petition with the National Council of Accreditation in Teacher Education challenging the accreditation of teacher education institutions in the state of Texas given the recent gutting of the professional education component in Senate Bill 994 (Imig 1988). As these political maneuverings are played out in the face of the likely continuation of aggressive state intervention into teacher education, it is important that social-reconstructionist voices be heard from within the teacher education community.

So, too, is it important that social-reconstructionist perspectives are raised and argued in the professional associations attended by those who do the work of teacher education, such as the national and state affiliates of the Association of Colleges for Teacher Education, and the Association of Teacher Educators, and the teacher education groups within the various subject matter and/or specialty associations such as the National Council of Teachers of English, and Mathematics, the National Council for the Education of Young Children, or the Council for Exceptional Children.[54] While it is important that reconstructionist analyses of issues in teacher education have become more visible in recent years at meetings of the American Educational Research Association (AERA), many of those who identify themselves as teacher educators (Lanier 1986), especially those associated primarily with clinical teacher education, do not attend AERA meetings or read its journals. Attending annual meetings of AACTE or ATE, the two major organizations in the U.S. devoted exclusively to teacher education, and/or publishing in their journals (*Action in Teacher Education,* the *Journal of Teacher Education*) serve a particularly important political purpose. On the one hand, progressive forces already present in these organizations (such as the equity and multicultural education committees within AACTE), would receive more support. It does not make much sense in our view to say that one is for the achievement of social justice and equity and then fail to support those forces already within the system working in these directions. On the other hand, as in the example cited earlier regarding the writing off of a group of eighth-grade Latino students by their teacher and his supervisor (see pp. 182 n.37), issues of social justice would be raised in meetings of teacher educators that probably wouldn't be raised otherwise.[55]

Supporting progressive political movements

Although it is important for social reconstructionist teacher educators to be involved in each of the arenas we have discussed thus far (teacher education programs, schools, university and state politics, and the professional associations of teacher educators), it is also essential that we be actively involved in a wide range of political struggles in the broader society, especially those that are aimed at altering unequal economic, social, race-ethnic, and gender relations. As was pointed out at the beginning of this book, our society is in crisis. In our society large numbers of children, from the time of their birth, are now denied the opportunity of securing their basic rights as human beings to adequate shelter, decent health care, an adequate diet, access to a high-quality education, and the promise of securing a meaningful job that pays a decent wage. The gap between the wealthy and the poor in the U.S. is the largest it has been in forty years and is growing wider as we continue to experience the inadequate allocation of our nation's resources to social services of almost every kind.[56] We live in a nation where the government spends roughly 290 times more on defense research than it spends on research on education (Biddle 1989) and pours billions of dollars yearly into weapons systems, the support of dictatorships throughout the world, and "tax relief" for the rich here and abroad. The U.S. currently ranks fourteenth out of sixteen major industrialized nations in spending for precollegiate education as a proportion of national income (Mishel and Rasell, 1989). We do not give money only to dictatorships, corporations, and to military preparedness, of course, but we give enough of it to make the accomplishment of our noblest educational and social goals virtually impossible under current conditions.[57] There is just no way that we can build a public-school system and a society that will provide everyone with access to decent and rewarding lives without diverting more of our resources from such things as military preparedness and the kind of tax and economic policies that have permitted the gutting of social programs of every kind during the last decade, and that continue to permit endless obscene contrasts such as the recent building of a billion-dollar Taj Mahal gambling casino in the midst of the poverty of Atlantic City (Goldberger 1990).

Although there has been a lot of rhetoric offered in the last few years regarding the creation of "Tomorrow's Teachers" and "Tomorrow's Schools," very little has been said about "Tomorrow's Society" and the kinds of fundamental changes in societal structures and institutions that will be necessary for the realization of proposed reforms in teaching and teacher education. We cannot build tomorrow's schools in today's unequal society.[58] Whether the issue is the politics of food production, distribution, and the elimination of hunger, eradicating homelessness, working for the betterment of race relations and against gender discrimination, working for the demilitarization of the economy, supporting socially responsible businesses and investment practices, working toward the achievement of full employment, or the preservation of the environment, social-reconstructionist teacher educators need to be active in working on issues that contribute to a fundamental transformation of the economic, social, and political structures in the society, so that all of us and all of our children can have access to decent and rewarding lives.[59] Obviously each of us cannot be involved in all these arenas. We need to choose the particular issues on which we can focus our energies.

It is important to remember that these broader political struggles against such things as hunger, homelessness, unemployment, racism, sexism, ageism, homophobia are intimately connected with our work as teacher educators. It is just plain foolish or dishonest to speak of the restructuring of schools and teacher education programs and the professionalization of teaching, as many have done, without explicitly acknowledging the need and providing active support for broader social and economic transformations—the societal preconditions for realizing school reform. Much of the current reform literature in teacher education is silent, for example, about the need for any transformations beyond the walls of the school, and the empowerment of teachers to have a greater say in how schools are run. While we are supportive of the numerous efforts that have been made in recent years to enhance the dignity of teachers' work by creating more participatory and collaborative school environments, these efforts do not go far enough and even may, in some cases, result in a deepening of the divisions between schools and communities that currently contribute to school failure for thousands of children (Comer 1988).[60] This widening of the gap between school and community can come about, for example, in those cases where newly empowered teachers fail to become more responsive to the communities they serve and actually use their enhanced professionalism to further distance parents from the decision-making processes in schools (Zeichner 1990a).

There is little question that the various proposals for school restructuring that are the centerpiece of almost every contemporary report on the reform of teaching and teacher education will require substantial redistribution of our nation's resources. When we take into account the societal preconditions for school reform such as those discussed above, this need for resource redistribution becomes irrefutable. To call for the reform of schooling and teacher education while remaining silent on the need for broader social and economic changes in the society is to lend support to the view so successfully ingrained in the public consciousness in recent years (see Shor, 1986), that what is wrong currently in the larger society is largely either the fault of the schools or amenable to correction by the schools (Apple et al. 1989).[61] We reject this exportation of our economic, political, and social problems onto schools and teacher education institutions and the implication that educational reform alone can solve our societal crisis. While we are supportive of many of the proposals for school restructuring contained in recent reports, few of these proposals even begin to touch the full scope of our difficulties and what will need to be done to overcome them.

In addition to the silence of recent teacher education reports on the need for societal reforms, which we want to highlight here, many of the reports also give only minimal attention at best to problems of educational inequity. The Carnegie Report (1986) states, for example, that "America must now provide to the many the same quality of education presently reserved for the fortunate few" (p. 14). "Tomorrow's Teachers" (Holmes Group 1986) also gives token recognition to the problem when it argues that the professionally educated and certified teachers that graduate from its institutions would possess commitment to the responsibility for the learning of all children. Neither of these 1986 reports, however, develops specific proposals to show how these goals concerned with equity will be accomplished. Almost all their specific proposals are concerned with strengthening the intellectual dimensions of teaching and teacher education with little attention to the problem of making sure that all children, and not just some, benefit from the improvements. Many of the "reports" on teacher education such as the one issued by the AACTE Commission on Excellence in Teacher Education (1986) are silent on these issues. The proposals have become well known—tougher standards for entering and graduating from teacher education programs, more liberal arts and sciences course work for prospective elementary teachers, a greater use of research on teaching in the teacher education curriculum—all aimed, as "Tomorrow's Teachers" states, toward making the education of teachers intellectually more solid. The only place where equity is addressed in many contemporary teacher education reports is in proposals to bring more people of color into the teaching force.

While we are supportive of many of the specific proposals contained in these reports, including those aimed at diversifying the teaching force and enhancing the intellectual competence of teachers, we strongly object to the almost complete absence in some of the reports to proposals to enhance the moral consciousness, social and political commitment,

217

and capability of teachers to work toward the elimination of social, educational, economic, and political inequalities. We must begin to change the current situation in which so few of our prospective teachers desire to work with children of color and of poor economic circumstances. We must also alter the circumstances, both internal and external to the school, that are connected to the pervasiveness of inequalities based on class, race, ethnicity, and gender. Otherwise, all our alleged reforms in teacher education will have accomplished little.

Teacher education in the United States has a long history of implementing various reforms that primarily benefit those students who are already relatively well off (Keppel 1986, Zeichner 1987).[62] As we have repeatedly pointed out in this book, the education of the urban and rural poor has not been a visible concern in the field. Unless we begin to prioritize the development of a system of teacher education in the United States according to which the very best of what we have to give is focused on those whose basic human needs are not currently being met in the society, both our public-school system and our nation are indeed truly at risk. It is not so much our failure to compete with other nations at the higher ranges of academic achievement or in science and mathematics that has put our nation in this position, as some have suggested,[63] as it is our failure as a people to provide for the basic human needs of all of our citizens. This is not to say that we are opposed to changes that seek to counter the drill, drudgery, and bureaucratic superficialities that are endured by so many of our teachers and their students even in public schools for the relatively advantaged. The conditions for teaching and learning in all our public schools are in great need of improvement (Moore-Johnson 1990). We should provide better subject matter preparation for our teachers, and take advantage of knowledge about learning and teaching that has been generated by recent research, as has been suggested in recent reports. We are not opposed to these efforts. We must realize, however, that "the cognitive revolution" and "the knowledge base" do not by themselves provide the basis for our work as teacher educators. We agree with Ken Sirotnik (1990) when he argues that teacher education is more a process of moral development than a process of building a knowledge base, skills, and expertise. What we need most of all in these times in the United States is a corps of teachers passionately committed to work in and outside of schools for a more decent, humane, and just society, and for the creation of conditions in schools and society that will support their efforts. We also agree with Constance Clayton (1989), superintendent of schools in Philadelphia, who has argued that the future of our public schools depends less on the development of a new pedagogy through further research and development than on the emergence of a new politics. She argues, reiterating the position of the late Ron Edmonds, that we already know much more than we need to teach all children successfully. The central question continues to be whether we as a society are seriously committed to creating the conditions that will enable us to eliminate permanently the underclass we have created.[64]

Obviously teacher education and schooling cannot, by themselves, solve problems that are rooted in the very fabric of our society. But they can each do their part.

> The concern of teacher educators must remain normative, critical and even political. Neither the teachers' colleges nor the schools can change the social order. Neither colleges nor schools can legislate democracy. But something can be done to empower teachers to reflect upon their own life situations, to speak out in their own ways about the lacks that must be repaired; the possibilities to be acted upon in the name of what they deem decent, humane, and just. (Greene 1979, p. 71)

The time has come for those of us who are involved in the education of teachers in the United States to give explicit emphasis in our scholarship and in our numerous professional activities to the social, economic, and political changes that must occur beyond the school if we are ever to realize the noble platitudes about excellence and equity to which we all affirm allegiance in the arena of the school. Unless we do this, and unless the political dimensions of our work are explicit, we help to sustain the very oppressions and injustices that we say outrage us.

Postscript

In this book we have argued for a more visible presence of social-reconstructionist perspectives within the community of teacher educators in the United States and have presented a number of specific proposals of our own and of like-minded colleagues that would contribute, along with efforts in other spheres of activity, to the realization of a more just and humane society. Although we are passionately committed to the program of work laid out in this book, we do not wish our proposals to further the ideological insularity that plagues our field. This insularity continues to be one of the most serious impediments to the improvement of teacher education in the U.S. The common pattern continues to be for various subcommunities of teacher educators to operate relatively independently of one another. There is little substantive cross-fertilization of ideas across traditions of practice. Members of the various subcommunities typically read, discuss, debate, and cite only work within a particular tradition and dismiss or ignore everything else. In offering our social-reconstructionist–inspired proposals for teacher education in the United States, we hope to facilitate dialogue across as well as within the particular traditions of reform that we have described in this book. This is not to say that we should aim for some eclectic combination of ideas and practices that seeks to accommodate everyone and offend no one. Ideological evenhandedness and moral relativism do not do justice to any tradition. We should all have morally justifiable passions and commitments for which we are willing to work. In doing so, however, we shouldn't be so close-minded as to lose sight of the limitations of our own particular perspective, whatever it may be. The costs of failure are too great for us to become preoccupied with disputes over academic turf. The social-reconstructionist agenda in teacher education must be pursued vigorously, but in a manner that attempts to appeal to the noblest impulses in all of us.

Notes

Series Editor's Introduction

1. See Michael W. Apple, *Ideology and Curriculum,* 2nd edition (New York and London: Routledge, 1990).
2. See Michael W. Apple, *Teachers and Texts: A Political Economy of Class and Gender Relations in Education* (New York and London: Routledge, 1988) and Michael W. Apple, "Redefining Equality," *Teachers College Record* 90(Winter 1988), pp. 167–184.
3. Stephen Ball, "Staff Relations During the Teachers' Industrial Action," *British Journal of Sociology of Education* 9(number 3 1988), p. 290.
4. Michael W. Apple, *Education and Power* (New York and London: Routledge, 1985) and Apple, *Teachers and Texts.*
5. See, for example, Michael W. Apple, "Will the Social Context Allow a Tomorrow for *Tomorrow's Teachers?*" in Jonis Soltis, ed. *Reforming Teacher Education* (New York: Teachers College Press, 1987).
6. R. W. Connell, *Teachers' Work* (Boston: George Allen and Unwin, 1985), p. 83.
7. John Rury, "Who Became Teachers? The Social Characteristics of Teachers in American History," in Donald Warren, ed. *American Teachers: Histories of a Profession at Work* (New York: Macmillan, 1989), p. 10. For more detailed analysis of how and why teaching became "women's paid work" and what the effects of this were, see Apple, *Teachers and Texts.*
8. James W. Fraser, "Agents of Democracy: Urban Elementary-School Teachers and the Conditions of Teaching," in Warren, ed. *American Teachers,* p. 127.
9. Apple, *Education and Power* and Apple, *Teachers and Texts.*
10. Connell, *Teachers' Work,* p. 116.
11. Ibid, p. 121.
12. Ibid.
13. Ibid, p. 124.
14. Ibid, p. 153.

Preface

1. According to Ornstein and Levine (1989), estimates of dropout rates in some of our largest cities are 40 to 60 percent. Comer (1988) and Cuban (1989) both estimate dropout rates in our cities to be at about 50 percent. It is in those schools that serve mostly underclass students that the dropout rates approach 75 to 80 percent (Hahn, Danzerger, and Lefkowitz 1987). Across the nation, the high school completion rate is at about 75 percent (Cuban 1989). According to figures for 1985, the completion rate for whites was 76.7 percent; for blacks 62.8 percent, and for Hispanics 59.8 percent.

2. Of the 98,000 pupils in the Milwaukee, Wisconsin, public schools, for example, about 70 percent are minority members and about 60 percent live at or near the poverty level (Goldberg 1990). The city of Milwaukee is composed of about 64 percent whites, 24 percent blacks, 10 percent Hispanics, and 2 percent Asians and other groups, according to school officials (Personal communication, February 1990).

3. One clear example of the unequal allocation of resources to schools that serve children of the poor is the existence of teacher shortages in the poorest neighborhoods of our urban areas (see Berger 1990). There are also inequities in the allocation of funds to school systems. For example, while about 80 percent of the bilingual children and more than half of the poorest children in Illinois attend the Chicago Public Schools, Chicago schools are forced to operate on 15 percent less money per pupil than the average surrounding districts (Ayers 1989, p. 7).

4. "Children are educationally disadvantaged if they cannot take advantage of available educational opportunities or if the educational resources available to them are inherently unequal" (Committee for Economic Development 1987, p. 5).

5. Edelman (1989) estimates that "nearly half of black children, almost two-fifths of Hispanic children, and nearly one-seventh of white children in the United States are poor" (p. 23).

6. Although Lortie (1975) concluded that there are few "counter identifiers" among teacher education students who are critical of the status quo, certain programs like the Teacher Corps (Smith 1980) and Ellner and Barnes's (1977) experimental program at Clarmount College seem to have been dominated by such students (see Tabachnick 1981).

7. In the recent study of a representative sample of teacher education programs in the U.S. ("The Study of the Education of Educators") Edmundson (1990) reports that only 2 percent of the faculty and 3 percent of the students felt that societal inequities and the need for transforming the social order received significant attention in their teacher education programs.

8. Here we are alluding to our general support for the idea of professional

development schools (Holmes Group 1990), or clinical schools (Carnegie 1986). These public schools with diverse student populations would be given special resources to carry out their roles in preservice teacher education and, if adopted on a wide scale, would involve substantial changes in practices in clinical teacher education.

9. As Rhoades (1985) points out, there is a mythology across the U.S. about the supposed dominance of educational studies in a teacher's education. In reality, most of a prospective teacher's college or university career (including most prospective elementary teachers) is spent in courses offered outside of schools, departments, and colleges of education.

10. By academic we are referring to the general education, major, and minor courses in students' education. We are deliberately avoiding the use of "liberal studies" components because of its implied message that educational studies courses cannot be liberalizing in their effects upon students (Borrowman 1956).

1 Traditions of Reform in U.S. Teacher Education

1. A rapidly growing literature has emerged in the past few years that focuses primarily on the analysis of the various reports (e.g., see Association of Teacher Educators 1986, Popkewitz 1987a; and Soltis 1987).

2. This is ironic because many of the key actors in contemporary teacher education reports were participants in many of these reform initiatives.

3. In a recent national meeting of the Holmes Group, Paul Olson, a key participant in the TTT program, reflected about the ways in which this "Grand Experiment" from 1968 to 1973 can help us think about the reform of teacher education in the present. For example, it was reported that Olson said that "TTT's short life serves as a negative model to Holmes . . . because it attempted to transform higher education from the margins of the university rather than at its center. This meant that the reform ignored the central forces that create and govern higher education—such as the accreditation, budget, and faculty assessment procedures—and this was a primary reason for its failure" (Devaney, 1989). This type of reflective statement about how past teacher education reform efforts can help us think more intelligently in the present is the exception rather than the rule.

4. Although there is some resemblance between our notion of reform traditions and abstract philosophical categories such as Brameld's (1955, 1962) classification scheme of essentialist, perennialist, progressive, and reconstructionist philosophies of education, it is important to emphasize that reform traditions are historically based in the actions of real people who have shared certain ideological commitments about education and who have acted on those commitments. For a further discussion of "educational traditions," see chapter 2.

5. See Cohen (1976) for a discussion of this debate within the field of history.
6. See Coley and Thorpe (1986), Elisberg (1981), and Zeichner (1988b) for an analysis of these programs and their impact on teaching and teacher education.
7. According to Shulman (1987), pedagogical content knowledge represents "the blending of content and pedagogy into an understanding of how particular topics, problems, or issues are organized, represented, and adapted to the diverse interests and abilities of learners and presented for instruction" (p. 8).
8. According to the reform traditions that we have identified, we would consider the feminist and multicultural critiques as emerging out of the social-reconstructionist tradition and the cognitively oriented subject matter knowledge critique as part of the developmentalist tradition.
9. Gage and Winne (1975, p. 148) address the different meanings associated with the terms "performance-based" and "competency-based" teacher education. "For some writers, competency refers to cognitive knowledge only, for others teacher competency entails effects on students' learning. In contrast, performance falls between these conceptions, denoting the ability to perform according to a model of teaching." Gage and Winne go on to argue that all three elements—knowledge, effects, and performance—are needed in an adequate definition of the approach. C/PBTE will be used here to indicate reference to the approach in its broadest sense.
10. C/PBTE also received enthusiastic support from several state education departments and from the American Association of Colleges for Teacher Education (AACTE) (see Sykes 1984, Joyce 1975).
11. Protocol materials and simulations are records of events that occur naturally in classrooms. After a protocol or simulation is presented to preservice teachers, they are guided in analyzing it in terms of either the educational concepts it illustrates (Cruickshank 1974) or as a specific case that is to be illuminated by the application of educational concepts from the disciplines (e.g., Smith 1969). Cruickshank (1984, pp. 87–88) discusses a simulation program that is typical of those used in teacher education programs in the 1960s and 1970s: "This simulation ("Classroom Simulation") uses a specially constructed mock classroom facility in which an elementary education student teacher, following an orientation to a hypothetical school and sixth-grade classroom, is shown up to sixty filmed classroom problems. After each problem is presented, the student teacher is asked to act out or talk out a response. An experimenter sitting nearby considers the student teacher's response and decides how the class or a student therein probably would react. The experimenter then projects a film segment of the class or student reaction for the student teacher to see. The intention of the simulation is to shape a student teacher's behavior in ways that juries of master teachers feel are optimal."
12. In addition to the criticisms discussed above, the high cost of developing,

implementating, and evaluating these programs was thought to be a major reason for the lack of implementation. See Gage and Winne (1975, pp. 162–64) for a discussion of this issue.

13. For example, *Tomorrow's Teachers* argues that "within the last twenty years . . . the science of education promised by Dewey, Thorndike, and others at the turn of the century has become more tangible" (Holmes Group 1986, p. 52).

14. Cowley (1934) discusses two segments of the progressive education movement that existed in the early part of the century: the Bohemian segment, which involved a revolt of individuals against puritan restraint, and a radical element, which involved a social revolt against the evils of capitalism. Cremin's (1961) discussion of sentimentalists and radicals in the progressive movement is also relevant to this discussion.

15. The title of Margaret Pollitzer's (1931) article in *Progressive Education,* "Growing Teachers for our Schools," is very descriptive of this emphasis on student-centered teacher education.

16. Also quoted in Perrone (1989, p. 135). The Cooperative School for Student Teachers was a joint venture between the Bureau of Educational Experiments (forerunner to Bank Street College) and eight progressive schools. The teacher education curriculum included practicum work in the progressive schools and seminar, field, and studio work in New York City.

17. In addition to Lucy Sprague Mitchell's Cooperative School for Student Teachers in New York City, many of the most prominent independent schools across the county (e.g., Beaver Country Day School, Shady Hill School) ran formal apprenticeship systems. One of the few reported efforts to prepare child-centered progressive teachers that involved a public school system was in Oakland, California where the Peralta School was staffed entirely by student teachers from San Francisco State Teachers College who worked under the guidance of an Oakland public school principal and four teachers (Beatty, 1933).

18. See Zeichner and Teitelbaum (1982) and Feiman-Nemser and Floden (1980) for a critique of this position.

19. Bowers (1969) summarizes the economic conditions within the U.S. in the early 1930s at the time when the social reconstructionists began to gain influence within the Progressive Education Association: "There were an estimated four million Americans unemployed in 1930; by the fall of 1931 the ranks of the unemployed had increased to eight million. Those who were fortunate enough to retain jobs found their hours cut and wages reduced. . . . Even those who had savings in the bank were not immune to the misery that engulfed millions of lives; a total of 3,643 banks failed between 1930 and 1931, rendering penniless hundreds of thousands who thought they had some security against the economic storm" (p. 12).

20. Social radicalism in education was not confined to this relatively small group of professors at Teachers College. Support for the social-reconstruc-

tionist call for political leadership by teachers was given, for example, by the Progressive Education Association in its establishment of an Economics and Sociology section in 1932, by the National Educational Association board of directors' establishment of a committee on Social and Economic Problems in 1931, and by the American Historical Association. Although these actions certainly did not represent the support of the entire memberships of these organizations, they do indicate some support for this position across the U.S. (Bowers 1969, Cohen 1976).

21. This is now the National Society for the Study of Education.

22. The reconstructionist position in education was articulated earlier by Dewey in his seminal work, *Democracy in Education,* in 1916 and in the writings of Adams, Veblen, Sinclair, Lippmann, and Counts. The focus here begins with the 1930s because this is when the reconstructionists began explicitly to address the problem of teacher education. For discussion of these earlier educational reconstructionists see Cremin (1961, pp. 224–27), and Cremin (1988, pp. 172–88). For a detailed history of social-reconstructionist thought in education until the early 1960s see Bowers (1969).

23. Also cited in Cremin (1961, pp. 229–30).

24. Rugg (1952, p. 6) concluded regarding teacher educators of that time that "not a platoon in an army of them is concerned with either the theory or practice of reconstruction."

25. During the 1930s it was estimated that Teachers College Columbia graduates held 20 percent of the instructional and administrative positions in the nation's teacher education institutions (Cremin, Shannon, and Townsend 1954).

26. The Teacher Corps, which involved the expenditure of over one-half billion dollars in its fifteen-year life, has been the largest single effort ever made in U.S. teacher education to try to overcome the effects of poverty on education (Bush 1987).

27. This is not to say that individual teacher education programs or reform proposals represent "pure" examples of any one tradition. With the exception of a few small thematic teacher education programs that exist in various parts of the country, teacher education programs represent some mixture of the reform traditions. See Zeichner and Tabachnick (1991) for an analysis of the slogan "reflective teaching" in relation to the four reform traditions.

2   The Aims of Teacher Education

1. For a historical examination of the institutional context of teacher education see Clifford and Guthrie (1988), and Powell (1980).

2. We also want to acknowledge and rectify the lack of attention in the work of early social-reconstructionists to the dynamics of gender.

3. In the past we have not been as explicit as perhaps we should have been. An earlier attempt to identify the perspective and commitments underlying our own approach can be found in Zeichner and Liston (1987a).

4. While other approaches in a "reflective" vein may encourage prospective teachers to examine their reasons and purposes, only the social-reconstructionist reform agenda gives adequate attention to the inspection of reasons and purposes *and* the institutional, social, and political context.

5. Some critics might claim that the aim of reason giving divorces reason from emotion, and thought from feeling. We do not accept the dichotomous opposition between reason and emotion. For a further elaboration see chapter 4.

6. It is probably somewhat inaccurate to characterize individual educators as either conservative, progressive, or radical. Most educators, most teachers, hold beliefs that are a composite of these three educational traditions. But, for many educators, an overriding tendency can be identified. We find these three characterizations (conservative, progressive, and radical) to represent useful heuristics. We elaborate further below.

7. One of us, Liston, has utilized the tradition-articulation approach in a course for prospective teachers and interested undergraduate and masters students (Philosophies of Education 1985–1990, Washington University in St. Louis). References to students' reactions are taken from that course.

8. Students read Dewey's (1902) *The Child and the Curriculum* along with Herbert Kliebard's (1986) account of the curriculum of the Dewey School, and Vivian Gussin Paley's (1981) account of children's views of the world around them.

9. Sirotnik (1990) attempts to create a nonrelativistic and "universal" moral basis for teaching and teacher education through a commitment to inquiry, knowledge, competence, caring, and social justice. Although all three of our noted traditions recognize each of these "moral commitments," we would argue that the traditions offer distinct interpretations for each commitment and give distinct assessments of the comparative value of one commitment over another. (For example, clearly, the radical tradition interprets social justice in a manner that tends to be unacceptable to most members of the conservative tradition. Furthermore, radicals, in contrast to conservatives, emphasize the achievement of their view of social justice.)

10. The aim of articulation is not to attempt to legitimate a radical over a conservative, or a progressive over a radical, orientation. It does, however, maintain that reason giving is an essential educational aim.

11. We accept, for the development and elaboration of our position, the traditional separation between university course work and field experiences. However, we maintain, in chapter 6, that this separation needs to be reexamined.

3 Teacher's Knowledge, Models of Inquiry, and the Social Context of Schooling

1. In Connelly and Clandinin (1988) reference is made to the larger social context when discussing Phil's sets of images, but this discussion is very narrowly construed.
2. We do need a better empirical understanding of teachers' social beliefs and how these social beliefs affect teachers' educational actions. Sara Lightfoot's work is helpful in this regard. For a review of the literature on teacher socialization, see Zeichner and Gore (1990).
3. Sarason, Davidson, and Blatt (1962) made this same point almost thirty years ago.
4. These three views are rough elaborations of frameworks that have appeared in the social-scientific literature. We do not intend to offer these three views as accurate characterizations of people's beliefs. They do, however, capture important aspects of belief systems that prospective teachers and the general public hold.
5. See Tom (1984).
6. See, for example, Belenky, Clinchy, Goldberger, and Tarule (1986).
7. For criticisms along this line, see Confrey (1987) and Buchmann (1987). For an example of a work that attempts to recognize the complex and, at times, contradictory nature of teachers' deliberation, see Berlak and Berlak (1981).
8. This aspect is also noted by Feiman-Nemser and Buchmann (1985).

4 Bringing the Social Context of Schooling into Teacher Education

1. Urban (1982) argues that "economic issues dominated early organizational activities" (p. 173). But it also seems clear that teachers' organizations also focused on issues of educational quality and equality, and social reform (Eaton 1975). For a review of recent work on teachers' organizations see Urban (1989).
2. What follows is taken from an article by Lynn Olson entitled "Work Conditions in Some Schools Said 'Intolerable.' " *Education Week* 8(4), July 28, 1988, 1, 21.
3. It is important to note that teachers' work conditions vary. In some situations it seems they are "intolerable," in others perhaps "tolerable." But in most situations they do not seem to be conducive to the tasks of teaching. Metz (1989) shows that teachers' work conditions differ in schools that serve different social classes.
4. Connell (1985) describes this characteristic as a valuable disposition for teachers and one that should be encouraged by teacher educators (Connell 1985, pp. 152–53).

5. In this section we focus on the relationship between white teachers and African-American students for two reasons: African-Americans constitute the largest minority population taught by our student teachers; and we have found significant cultural differences between most of our prospective teachers and many black children. Our focus on African-Americans as a minority is not intended to exclude a discussion of other minority groups. Instead it illustrates the types of concerns we think are important to raise when prospective teachers begin to think about cultural differences.

6. Williams notes this tendency of teachers to deny cultural differences. See Williams (1989, p. 31).

7. For more on this issue see Hochschild and Machung (1989).

8. See chapter 2, where we develop the position that an essential aim of teacher education ought to be the enabling of prospective teachers to give good reasons for their educational actions.

5 Research for Teaching and Teacher Education

1. Both holist and structuralist accounts of social phenomena emphasize the existence of larger societal structures and forces that constrain individuals' actions. But holist and structural accounts are not, strictly speaking, identical. A holist orientation tends to view society as an integrated entity with an existence and character of its own, while a structural view tends to portray society as an ordered, independent, but loosely integrated set of roles, norms, practices, and structures. For our purposes, we will use the two terms interchangeably to denote a mode of analysis that assumes the existence of larger societal structures and forces.

2. For examples of discussions of the relationship between educational research and practice see Phillips (1980) and Schwab (1978).

3. In chapters 3 and 4 we focused on the import of the social context of schooling for prospective teachers. In this and subsequent chapters our focus on the social context of schooling is enlarged to include the social context of teacher education. Teacher educators, we argue, could become more knowledgeable and reflective about the social and political context of teacher education.

4. We also need to note, however, that while we are supportive of efforts to create conditions of greater respect for the role of school-based educators and university-based teacher educators in the creation of a "knowledge base" for teaching and teacher education, we recognize that there is a danger involved in this stance of romanticizing practitioner research. Not all forms of practitioner research have an emancipatory intent and are consistent with our social-reconstructionist perspective on teacher education and schooling. In some cases, for example, practitioner research (e.g.,

action research) has been used as a form of social control to "engineer" teachers to change (Elliott 1990 and Noffke 1990). The democratization of the research process (as is the case with the professionalization of teaching) can, but does not necessarily, lead toward more just and humane environments in schools and society (Zeichner, 1990). While we are supportive of practitioner research, we feel that it needs to be subjected to the same kinds of normative criteria for assessing its worth that we offer later in this chapter for assessing the worth of university-based research.

5. James supports a view that she terms "concessive holism." For a further elaboration of her view see James (1984).

6. Richard Brosio (1990) aptly characterizes a segment of radical theorists as "motivational" theorists.

7. Anthony Giddens (1979) argues for the need to view social actors as engaged in situated practices. His work, however, does not seem able to capture how societal structures and forces constrain those actors. Layder's (1981 and 1985) and Stinchcombe's (1986) critiques provide helpful correctives to Giddens's basic direction. For further elaboration of this issue, see Clegg (1989).

8. While all the authors cited propose a framework of viewing teachers and/ or social actors as engaged in situated practices, they tend to circumscribe much too narrowly the relevant situation. The reasons for this narrow orientation vary by author, and we will not examine them here. Our view is that the situation needs to be more broadly construed and that one needs to be able to theorize adequately the strength and source of societal structures and dynamics.

9. In formulating our ideas about viewing teaching as situated practice, we have been greatly influenced by much of the recent British work on teachers—"coping strategies" (e.g., Woods 1980, Pollard 1982).

10. This view has been criticized by a number of writers. For examples, see Bernstein (1978) and Feinberg (1983).

11. This alternative view is symbolized by the rise of the teacher-as-researcher movement since the 1960s (Elliott 1990) and by the recent popularity of Schon's ideas about reflection-in-action (Schon 1983).

12. For a review of current positions and a "prediction" of the future course of events, see Gage (1989).

13. Hallinan (1984).

14. Oakes (1985).

15. Our central concern is that researchers identify their pertinent normative commitments and relate how these commitments affect their research endeavor. There does not exist a correspondence between the individual traditions of educational thought and practice (either our sociohistorical accounts of teacher education or the more conceptual elaboration of educational traditions) *and* separate and distinct research paradigms. But this lack of correspondence does not detract from our claim that researchers should engage in an articulation of their own normative values.

16. For examples, see Galluzzo and Arends (1989), and Howey (1989), and Zimpher (1989).
17. See, for example, Apple (1979) and Martin (1985).
18. For a further elaboration, see Greene (1989).
19. The distinction between collaborative research projects like the Interactive Research and Development projects and the action research-efforts of practitioners is in terms of the degree to which the practitioners own and control the research. In action research, the practitioners are typically more in control of the research process than they are when they join collaborative-research projects initiated by university-based researchers.
20. See note 15.
21. As Cochran-Smith and Lytle (1990) point out, however, these sources do focus on such topics as teacher thinking, teacher knowledge, and teacher cultures, a stance that recognizes the purposefulness and intentionality in teachers' work. This situation is unlike the stance assumed in earlier comprehensive reviews (e.g., Travers 1973), which emphasized the examination of teacher behavior.
22. It is also the case that some of the scholarship in teacher education that is produced by practicing teacher educators is also insensitive to the institutional and political realities faced by teacher educators. Some of these accounts are, in our view, nothing more than celebratory testimonials that claim to have solved the enduring problems of teacher education through the implementation of some magical structural, instructional, or curricular innovation.
23. This same position has also recently been expressed by Pollard (1988) and by Hitchcock and Hughes (1989).
24. It is assumed that our other criterion (that the research be directly informed by the concerns of school practitioners and teacher educators) is not a central concern in practitioner research because of who initiates and conducts the research.
25. The Boston Women's Teachers' Group produced a thirty-minute slide-tape show based on the interviews and sponsored workshops for teachers across the U.S.
26. All these teacher educators have argued not only for the "use" of action research with student teachers but also for the "doing" of action research *with* students.
27. Noffke and Brennan's (1991) action research work also led to a critique of the notion of "levels of reflectivity" which had at one time been used within the program to delineate different kinds of reflection. Another "second-order" action research project conducted at Deakin University in Australia (DiChiro, Robottom, and Tinning 1988 and Robottom 1988) also focused on the ways in which a competitive assessment scheme served to undermine their desire to promote collaborative action research by student teachers. This Deakin University experience will be discussed in chapter 6.

28. For other examples of practitioner research on teacher education that fulfills our criteria for assessing research see the self-studies reported in Tabachnick and Zeichner (1991).

6 Programmatic Implications of a Social Reconstructionist Approach to Teacher Education

1. Throughout the 1980s, the term "inquiry-oriented" teacher education has been used in the U.S. to refer to teacher education programs that place some emphasis on social-reconstructionist ideas. This label, as well as the label of "research-based teacher education" which has been used in the U.K. and Australia, is no longer adequate for this purpose. This is true because of the way in which teacher educators who represent various reform traditions have used these terms to describe forms of inquiry and reflection that lack a reconstructionist intent or democratic impulse. As we discuss in Zeichner and Tabachnick (1991) and Zeichner and Liston (1990), each tradition of teacher education reform now has articulated its own version of inquiry and reflection to the point where these labels have become almost meaningless.

2. This focus on programs that are explicit about their role in preparing teachers who will act in ways that contribute to the alleviation of poverty, inequality, sexism, racism, and so forth, does not imply that we think teacher educators whose priorities would place them within other reform traditions are unconcerned with these societal ills. We do think, however, that the explicit affiliation of teacher educators with social critique and societal reconstruction is an important step in combating these ills and is a distinctive characteristic of the programs to be described in this chapter.

3. Some of the ongoing social-reconstructionist work in teacher education that has not been discussed in detail here includes the feminist-oriented program at Wheaton college (Maher, 1991), the efforts of Bill Ayers at the University of Illinois at Chicago (Ayers 1989), of Jim Henderson at Roosevelt University (Henderson 1989), of Bill Armaline and Randy Hoover at Youngstown State (Armaline and Hoover 1989), and of Joyce King and Gloria Ladson-Billings (1990) at Santa Clara State University. Similar work has also been going on at Bristol Polytechnic in the U.K. (Personal correspondence with Geoff Witty, June, 1990).

4. For example, although we see much in common between our own proposals for teacher education and those of Giroux and McLaren (1987), Ginsburg (1988), and Shor (1987), we could not identify examples of current work in teacher education programs that explicitly refer to their ideas.

5. The major efforts in this century to address problems of poverty and inequality through teacher education were the federally funded programs

Teacher Corps and TTT (Trainers of Teacher Trainers). Although millions of dollars were spent in support of these large-scale efforts, within individual teacher education institutions these programs represented experimental alternatives to the standard programs that enrolled most students. The long-term impact of these experimental programs on the standard programs has been minimal (Sykes 1984).

6. The conditions involved in furthering the goals of social reconstruction in teacher education are thus far different from those faced by educators who have attempted to pursue critical and feminist teaching strategies with groups of students who have already assumed an oppositional stance to the structures of schooling and society (see Ellsworth 1989).

7. There are some notable exceptions to this pattern of eclectic and fragmented teacher education programs. One example of these is the "alternative programs" which have existed since at least the early 1950s at a limited number of institutions as either alternatives to standard teacher preparation programs within an institution, or as part of an array of small distinct program options that represent the totality of teacher education at an institution. Atkin and Raths (1974) discuss the distinct alternative programs that existed at UCLA, Indiana University, and at the University of Massachusetts in the early 1960s. Probably the most publicized contemporary example of this trend can be found at Michigan State University (Book 1983).

8. Although Beyer identifies the advantages of situating teacher education programs in a liberal arts environment where pressures on teacher education to become merely technical vocational training are not as strong as in the university, he is careful to point out that his proposals do not represent an embracing of liberal studies as they are normally conceived. Beyer explicitly rejects elite conceptions of liberal studies that would have students value allegedly objective, value-free, rational, and decontextualized inquiry. Instead he develops a view of liberal inquiry grounded in the Aristotelian notion of "phronesis," or practical wisdom. In so doing, Beyer rejects the dichotomization between liberal and applied study (i.e., theory and practice) and locates his unified conception of liberal inquiry at the core of his proposals for teacher education. See Travers and Sacks (1987) for a general discussion of the strengths of locating teacher education programs in small liberal arts colleges.

9. Beyer's efforts to link course work and fieldwork extend beyond the school into the community. He has developed a human-service project option for the basic school and society course taken by all students who are interested in either elementary or secondary teacher certification at Knox College. The purpose of this option is to enable prospective teachers, many of whom have led lives that have kept them distant from poverty, to come to grips with the realities of social inequality in a way that cannot be accomplished by readings alone. In addition to reading about social and

233

economic inequalities in schooling and society, students who elect this option work in various social-service agencies in the immediate Knox community or in some more informal, socially or economically disadvantaged setting such as the home of a local person or family (see Beyer, 1991, for a discussion of this course component and for three examples of students' work).

10. The distinction between reforming entire teacher education programs and changing program components is not as sharp in reality as it appears in this chapter. In several of the programs that are discussed here where the focus is on efforts to reform a particular course component (Wisconsin and Oxford Polytechnic), changes have also been initiated in other course components. It also needs to be noted that the reforms that are discussed in this chapter reflect those that were reported in the sources that are cited. In some cases (e.g., Deakin University, Oxford Polytechnic), the reforms that are described here no longer exist to the same extent (Deakin University) or are currently being undermined by external governmental policies (Oxford Polytechnic).

11. Zeichner has been the co-director of this program since 1976. Liston worked in the program as a student teaching supervisor and administrative assistant from 1980 to 1985.

12. See Kennedy and Zeichner (1989) for a discussion of the history of this program.

13. Van Mannen (1977) presents three *levels* of reflection. The hierarchical implications of the notion of levels conveys the mistaken impression, however, of a developmental framework where technical and practical reflection are eventually transcended and critical reflection prevails. This devalues technical skill and the reality of teachers. The theoretical stance taken in the Wisconsin student teaching program is that "reflective teaching" involves reflection in all three domains (technical, practical, and critical). From this perspective, technical issues are not transcended but become linked to discussions of the nature and justification for educational ends and goals.

14. We and our students work collaboratively in groups but on our own individual projects.

15. See Grundy (1982) and Carr and Kemmis (1986) for a discussion of three different modes of action research: technical, practical, and emancipatory.

16. See Elliot (1990) for a discussion of this issue.

17. More detailed information about action research in the Wisconsin elementary student teaching program including details about students' projects, can be found in Noffke and Zeichner (1987); Noffke and Brennan (1991); Liston and Zeichner (1989); and Gore and Zeichner (1990).

18. See Smith and Sachs (1988) and Beyer (1991) for discussions of ethnographic work by student teachers that extends beyond the school into the surrounding community. Also see Teitelbaum and Britzman (1991) for a discussion of the use of ethnographic studies in teacher education programs

at Syracuse University and the State University of New York at Bing-hamton.

19. See Maas (1991) for a detailed discussion of one Wisconsin university supervisor's use of writing with his student teachers.

20. See Maher (1991) and Bullough (1990) for a discussion of the use of autobiography with student teachers.

21. This increased attention to influences on the process of learning to teach can also be accomplished through attention to the experiences of other teachers. See Broudy (1990), and Richert (1991) for discussions of the use of case studies in teacher education programs.

22. Student teachers are observed by their university supervisors approximately once every other week. Recently, in part as a result of the influence of the work of Handal and Lauvus (1987), the learning potential of the supervisory preconference has been increasingly emphasized.

23. See Zeichner and Liston (1987) for a discussion of this issue.

24. Even in examples of so called "critical" approaches to clinical supervision (Smyth 1984), the focus tends to be upon a very narrow range of classroom behaviors. See Zeichner (1990b) for a discussion of the limitations of generic approaches to teacher reflection which do not make an explicit commitment to analyses of teaching that involve all three domains of reflection.

25. The focus in this chapter is on the content and pedagogy of teacher education programs and not on issues related to their structure and organization. While such issues as the length of programs, whether they are located at the graduate or undergraduate level, and their procedures for entry and exit have important consequences for issues related to equity (e.g., the numbers of minorities who are willing and able to pursue teaching as a career), we feel that too often the focus has been on the structural characteristics of programs to the neglect of the prior questions of curriculum and instruction. In chapter 7, we will discuss the structural and institutional contexts of teacher education as we consider strategies for accomplishing the social-reconstructionist agenda in teacher education.

26. See Beyer (1988), pp. 219–24, for two specific examples of cases where student teachers become more vulnerable by acting on insights that were gained through critical reflection.

27. See Fay's (1987) discussion of the difference between an educative and instrumental view of the theory and practice relationship for an elaboration of this point of view. Also see Carr and Kemmis (1986).

28. This does not mean that anything is to be valued merely because it is expressed by a teacher, and devalued just because it is expressed by a university-based academic. The point is that the epistemology of social-reconstructionist teacher education projects, unlike conventional teacher education projects, includes the voices of both school- and university-based practitioners.

29. The description of "connected teaching" in Belenky et al. (1986) is one

example of this more interactive pedagogy from a feminist perspective. Freire's (1973) notion of "dialogic teaching" is probably the best-known example from a critical theory perspective. See Gore (1990) for a discussion of other examples contained in the literatures on critical and feminist pedagogy.

30. Also see Comeaux (1991) for a discussion of an attempt to make collaborative learning an integral part of an educational foundations course at Gustavus Adolphus College in Minnesota.

31. See Sikes and Troyna (1990) for several specific examples of student teachers who gain insights (e.g., that schools are stratified to some degree by the social-class composition of their surrounding communities) during this participation in collaborative life history exercises in their preservice teacher education program at the University of Warwick in the U.K.

32. This educational mission is not considered fulfilled unless the practice can be characterized by certain specific standards of justice (e.g., equal access to knowledge) and care (e.g., the maintenance of fidelity to pupils).

33. Recently several campuses such as the University of Wisconsin-Madison, and the University of California-Berkeley have incorporated an "ethnic studies" requirement into their general education curriculum in an effort to ensure that all students are exposed to underrepresented perspectives. In Wisconsin, the state education department has also required prospective teachers to complete course work in Non Western History or Contemporary Culture and teacher educators to include content about Native American Treaty Rights in the teacher education curriculum. Also, in Wisconsin, University of Wisconsin-Madison faculty have recently decided to designate additional credits of the course work that elementary education students take in general education and for their minor to courses that emphasize the perspectives of underrepresented groups.

34. Recent evidence suggests that this focus is not now common in teacher education programs across the U.S. See Grant and Secada (1990) and Sadker and Sadker (1985).

35. There is a great deal of difference, for example, between the academically oriented proposals for reflection by those like Shulman (1987), the developmentalist proposals of those like Duckworth (1987), the social-efficiency–oriented proposals of those like Berliner (1985), and the reconstructionist proposals of someone like Beyer (1988). Each of these lines of work directs teachers' reflections to particular aspects of teaching practice (e.g., to the representations of subject matter, children's thinking, the social context, or to particular teaching strategies suggested by research on teaching). Each of these views of reflective practice establishes certain priorities about schooling and society that emerge out of a particular educational and social philosophy. Given these diverse affiliations to reflective practice in teacher education, the term "reflection" becomes almost meaningless without further elaboration.

36. See Zeichner (1990b) for examples of this neglect of ethically questionable issues in supervisory conferences.

37. One of us (Zeichner) recently had an experience in which he was one of four teacher educators who was asked to react at a national meeting of teacher educators to written transcripts of three supervisory conferences. The focus in this exercise was on what the beginning teachers and student teachers were being taught by their supervisors. One of the three cases contained some very disturbing comments about a group of eighth-grade, mostly Latino students who were being taught in a remedial-English class by a beginning teacher. The supervisor at this conference promoted and actively reinforced a deficit orientation toward the home backgrounds and families of the pupils, and very limited expectations about what they could be expected to accomplish. For example, at various times the beginning teacher was told such things by his supervisor as "I don't think that in a group like this you can expect too much," and "At home, someone is always yelling at them." The supervisor also reinforced the teacher's comments that the parents of these Latino students are all illiterate, even though this alleged illiteracy was probably limited in some cases to English. The main concern at this conference was to find ways to keep this group of students busy and happy. This deficit-oriented view of these children and their families, in which no effort is made to think about adapting the school to the culture that the students bring with them, is highly questionable in terms of any reasonable moral and ethical standards (see Zeichner 1990b for a more complete analysis of this case).

    Each of the four teacher educators was asked to give a fifteen-minute presentation of the analysis of the three cases. What is truly amazing about this experience is that not one of the teacher educators, with the exception of Zeichner, *even mentioned* the questions of equity that are involved in this case. One reason why questions of social justice so often pass by students in U.S. teacher education programs is because they pass by their teacher educators.

38. This gap between the rhetoric and reality of teacher education programs is an inevitable consequence of the complexity and inherent uncertainty of human affairs (Tabachnick 1981). In these times of ascendancy for educational entrepreneurs who have successfully marketed "solutions" to schools and universities in the form of prepackaged curriculum programs, competency-based behavior management, and teacher evaluation systems, it is especially important to keep this fact in mind.

39. In Australia, teachers are hired by state educational authorities and not by local school districts. In the state of Victoria, for example, where Deakin University is located, all graduates from teacher education institutions in the state are given a numerical score at the time of graduation based on their grades in the teacher education program. Teaching positions are allocated to students on the basis of their standing on this list. One can

easily see how this external situation can undermine teacher educators' attempts within institutions like Deakin to emphasize collaborative modes of learning.

40. It is common practice now for university supervisors in the Wisconsin student teaching program to conduct action research into their supervisory practices. Ken Zeichner now encourages this in the graduate-level supervision course completed by most university supervisors in the program (see Liston and Zeichner 1989).

7 Asserting the Social-Reconstructionist Agenda in Teacher Education

1. Giroux and McLaren's (1987) proposals for construing teacher education as cultural politics and Shor's (1987) proposals for an egalitarian teacher education are examples of the kind of work that is important to help keep our sights set beyond our present limits. Although both of these programs for teacher education consider and take into account the conservative restoration in the larger society, neither one deals in any significant way with the realities of teacher education in the U.S. today, its students, faculty, and its marginal status in the academy, and its susceptibility to state control.

2. See Gore (1990) for a discussion of this view of pedagogy in which how one teaches is inseparable from what is being taught and how one learns.

3. See Zeichner and Liston (1990) for a discussion of the way in which "reflective teaching" has been adopted by teacher educators of different reform traditions.

4. It has been fairly common within reconstructionist circles, for example, to summarily dismiss anything and anyone that can be associated with the social-efficiency reform tradition in teacher education. This position is mistaken for at least two reasons: (1) The assumptions made about the motives and sentiments of teacher educators who espouse social-efficiency—oriented reforms are that they are unconcerned with ameliorating the inequities and injustices that exist in schooling and society. While some of them may indeed be focused solely on personal gain and be unconcerned about the larger social good, it is unfair to assume that this characterizes all whose reforms can be categorized as social efficiency. (See Gage, 1989.) (2) A blanket rejection of and/or ignorance about social-efficiency–oriented proposals for reform in teaching and teacher education prevent one from utilizing the tremendous potential in the research like that which has been conducted on teacher expectations (Good 1987) or the allocation of content (Berliner 1984) for helping students become more sensitive to the injustices and inhumanities that exist in schooling.

5. This dismissal of the reconstructionist reform tradition is evidenced in part

by the absence of reconstructionist voices in the two major associations devoted exclusively to teacher education in the U.S., the Association of Teacher Educators (formerly the Association of Student Teaching) and the American Association of Colleges for Teacher Education (AACTE). While there are more voices from this tradition present at the annual meetings of the American Educational Research Association, relatively few of those who do the work of teacher education in the U.S. today belong to AERA.

6. Ginsburg and Clift (1990) provide a very thorough discussion of the "hidden curriculum" of teacher education programs. In addition to the relations between faculty and students and among students, they also discuss the ways in which certain biases in the content of teacher education courses influence prospective teachers. Also see Bartholomew, (1976), Dale (1977), and Popkewitz (1987b) for discussions of the hidden curriculum of teacher education.

7. This does not mean that these entering dispositions cannot be altered as some scenarios of teacher socialization suggest (see Zeichner and Tabachnick 1981).

8. Kerr (1983) summarizes data supporting the view that teacher education students as a group are unacceptably incompetent in terms of traditional academic criteria. Lanier (1986) examines these and other similar data with a critical eye and raises several serious questions about the way in which they have been interpreted. While not challenging Kerr's overall conclusions about the academic weakness of many teacher education students, Lanier does point out that the large number of teacher education students makes the academically weaker students more visible than they would be otherwise. This fact is responsible for much overgeneralization on this issue. She also discusses the great variation that exists among students in different institutions. Also see Zeichner (1988a) for a discussion of some of the problematic aspects of the commonly held view that teacher education students are intellectually inferior in relation to students in other fields.

9. One example of the growing gap between teachers and their students is the essentially monolingual nature of the teaching force under conditions where increasing numbers of students have limited proficiency in English (LaFontaine, 1988). The recent national surveys of teacher education sponsored by AACTE found that approximately two-thirds of teacher education students spoke only English and of the one-third who claimed some familiarity with another language, fewer than 15 percent considered themselves fluent in that language (Zimpher 1989). These findings are not surprising given that, in 1988, it was still possible to graduate from nearly 80 percent of four-year institutions in the U.S. without a course in a foreign language (Johnston et al. 1989). See Eubanks (1988) for a detailed analysis of socioeconomic trends in the teaching force and student population.

10. Two examples of this neglect of issues related to equity in teacher education

as it is normally conducted can be found in Zeichner (1989) and Zeichner (1990b). The first case discusses methods class instruction which does not explicitly address questions related to the differential distribution of knowledge about writing to elementary school pupils according to their social-class backgrounds. As a consequence, student teachers develop perspectives about the teaching of writing that serve to reinforce social-class inequalities. In the second case, which was discussed in chapter 6, a mentor teacher in an alternative route teacher education program reinforces low expectations for Latino students by accepting the culturally deficient view of Latinos articulated by an intern teacher. This neglect of equity issues is probably less true for issues related to gender. As McCarthy (1986) shows, teacher education students in elementary education, most of whom are women, are sensitive to the issue of gender inequality in schooling, in part, because they themselves have been victims of that inequality.

11. Ellsworth (1989) shows that even in situations where students are all oriented toward a radical position on issues of race, class, and gender, "total responsiveness" is not possible because of the multiple subjectivities of individual students in the group. In reality, where all students in any learning situation are directly connected through their own lives to various forms of oppression and domination as both the oppressor and the oppressed, it is not even possible to conceive of what "total responsiveness" would mean.

12. There are other ways to think about addressing this problem beyond considerations of the pedagogy of teacher education. One example of other needed changes is the alteration of program admission polices in a way that would enable the recruitment of a different pool of teacher education students. Currently, most institutions (even taking into account recent changes stimulated by the Holmes Group and other reform efforts) use only traditional academic criteria to admit students to teacher education programs (Clark and McNergney 1990). If, on the other hand, we begin to heed the advice of those like Haberman (1987) and incorporate criteria into the policies for admitting students to programs that account for elements of social consciousness (as well as intellectual competence), we might be able to alter the composition of the teacher education student group to a degree where there would be a more noticeable presence of those students who are concerned from the beginning with equity issues. Given the huge size of teacher education in the U.S., we can not realistically hope that these reconstructionist-oriented students will ever dominate our programs, but we think that their visible presence will make a difference (e.g., see Ellner and Barnes 1977).

A related issue concerns the ethnic and racial composition of the teacher education student group. One way to counteract what Zimpher (1989) has termed the cultural insularity of the current student group is to make deliberate efforts to have our programs consist of students from different cultures and races. Although many of the current polices of state education departments, and colleges and universities, continue to make this multicultural reality harder to achieve (e.g. Smith 1987), this is an area that deserves vigorous attention by reconstructionist-oriented teacher educators.

13. We also need to help our mostly white middle-class students see the numerous ways in which their own lives and the privileges they enjoy are bound up in issues of race, class, gender, and ethnicity, how the benefits that they frequently enjoy (e.g., in their diets, wardrobes, places of residence, and leisure activities) frequently help maintain the very oppressions that they often say offend them. They need to see how injustices and inhumanities in schooling and society are not something "out there" to be fixed, but at the very center of their own experience. We thank Kathleen Densmore for reminding us of this important task of teacher educators in helping our students see their own personal connections to inequalities in schooling and society, wherever they teach. Despite the relatively privileged status of teacher education students, however, they are also likely to be on the receiving end of particular forms of oppression as a result, for example, of being female in a male-dominated society. Focusing students' attention on both aspects of their contradictory roles, as both the "oppressor" and the "oppressed," is an important part of mobilizing their commitment to working for the elimination of these oppressions.

14. By "progressive," we are referring to what we have labeled developmentalist and social reconstructionist. This tension is, for example, one of the main issues addressed in Dewey's (1938) classic *Experience and Education*. See Apple (1986) for a discussion of this tension from a radical perspective and, in a more general sense, beyond issues related to teacher education per se.

15. We say "most," of course, because of the growing presence of alternate route programs, some of which do not directly involve college and universities at all (Uhler 1987).

16. This purposeful distancing of individual faculty and schools and departments of education from teacher education was not limited to these prestigious research universities. In fact, as Herbst (1989) has documented, even the normal schools of the nineteenth century were guilty of this "betrayal of the teacher" through expansion beyond their original mission as teacher preparation institutions. The situation was more complex however, than one of enthusiastic abandonment of teacher education. Herbst (1989) describes the reaction of early-twentieth-century normal school and single-purpose teacher college faculty to the transformation of their institutions into multipurpose ones as ambivalent: "Normal educators were ambivalent in their reactions. They resisted this trend if it meant yielding institutional influence to colleagues in other parts of their college or university. They welcomed it if they could now devote their energies to educa-

tional research, inservice training and consultancies, and to the training of curricular and professional specialists, administrators and faculty members of schools and colleges of education. For the majority of teacher educators the professional prestige to be gained by exchanging the education of classroom teachers for the opportunity to move into graduate and professional instruction was irresistible. For them professionalization came to mean the relegation of teacher education to the least-valued assignment in departments and colleges of education" (p. 161).

17. Another national survey of college and university faculty carried out by the Study Commission on Undergraduate Education (1976) came to similar conclusions: "Unfortunately, many college professors see the teaching of undergraduates as of trivial consequence, and most college of education professors see teaching teachers to teach as a second-level priority both for themselves and for their colleges."

18. Guyton and MacIntyre (1990), in a recent review of the practicum in teacher education, conclude that the situation has become even worse in recent years with the expansion of clinical courses in response to state department mandates and a reduction in program budgets, when inflation is taken into account.

19. Schwebel (1989) takes the argument regarding the different constituencies served by teacher education and other areas within the academy in a different direction by incorporating the dimension of social class: "Within a university, the various components do not all serve the same constituencies in the national population . . . the arts and sciences faculties and the education faculty have different constituencies. The student body of arts and science faculties, and of some professional faculties as well, is composed of future leaders and managers in business and government. The research of those faculties is attuned to the needs of government and the economy. Education faculty, by contrast, have as the bulk of their students those who will serve as teachers to the multitudes who will become factory workers, word processor operators, or unemployment statistics. Educational research is presumably directed toward the problems of educating students who will educate the broad mass of young people" (pp. 61–62). Although his description of an elite/nonelite division within universities and between public and private schools is somewhat oversimplified, Schwebel (1989) makes a very strong case for the view that one of the reasons for teacher education's marginal status in the university is because it primarily serves a particular population of children in the public schools, many of whom the society has not made a serious commitment to educating. Schwebel (1982) has argued elsewhere that this is an especially difficult issue to address because of the fact that the real commitment in the society to an education for leadership takes place in the private sector in an elite group of private and independent schools.

20. It has also been argued that economic and social-class differences between education faculty and those in other areas of the university are responsible

for some of the status problems of teacher education in the academy. Fuller and Brown (1975) observed: "Teacher educators have, by and large, humble social-class origins and low status in comparison with their academic colleagues. They more often hold paying jobs while working toward a degree, enter the faculty later, perhaps with the EdD., and so are less likely to have acquired the scholarly credentials valued by academicians" (p. 29). Since then, other studies have confirmed and elaborated these observations about the relatively lower social-class origins of teacher educators. See Ducharme and Agne (1989) for a summary of this literature. These social-class differences among faculty are complemented by the relatively low salaries of education faculty compared to those in other fields. In 1987–1988 the average salaries of assistant professors and full professors in education departments were ranked seventeenth and twentieth, respectively, out of twenty-one fields (American Association of University Professors, 1988). Also cited in Ginsburg and Clift (1990).

21. See Apple (1987) and Zeichner (1988a) for an analysis of some of the equity issues that are involved in moving teacher education beyond the four-year undergraduate context. Although substantial scholarship offerings for those who would be most likely excluded from participation in more lengthy teacher education programs might be able to offset their negative consequences, it is not clear that this financial commitment is forthcoming on the scale that would be needed or for the long run.

22. Taylor (1983) confirms this as a problem in England as well as in the U.S. and argues that "people from schools of education need to be seen and heard in and about every corner of their parent university" (p. 48).

23. As was pointed out in chapter 1, the cultivation of these relationships has been a major goal in teacher education reform projects for many years. Examples include the federally funded TTT programs (Provus 1975) and the current Carnegie-funded "Project 30" (Givens 1988). See Johnston et al. (1989) for many examples of strategies for enhancing the importance of teacher education among liberal arts faculty.

24. There is another dimension to these problems that is related to the limited kinds of experiences that many education faculty bring with them to their teacher education programs. Haberman (1988) estimates, for example, that fewer than 5 percent of the 45,000 or so education faculty in the U.S. have taught for even one year in the classrooms of the 120 largest urban school districts.

25. For examples of plans to recruit minority students into teacher education see Middleton & Mason (1988).

26. One of the major benefits of certain aspects of the National Teacher Corps, for example, was the multiracial environment that existed for both students and faculty. See, for example, Tabachnick and Lemes (1975).

27. See Zeichner (1986a; 1990c) for discussion of problems in the structure of clinical teacher education in the U.S..

28. For example, see the Holmes Group (1990).

29. It should be noted that one reason for the increased use of school advisory committees and other collaborative mechanisms with schools with regard to teacher education is that collaborative activity with schools is mandated by many states in the standards used to accredit teacher education programs, and by National Council for the Accreditation of Teacher Education (NCATE) standards. It should also be pointed out that the increased involvement of rank-and-file teachers in college and university teacher education programs has not necessarily included the unions that represent those teachers. This failure to cultivate relationships with the organized teaching profession, in addition to those efforts made with individual teachers, has had serious consequences in some cases. For example, in a recent controversy in Wisconsin where the state education department sought to dictate more precisely the curriculum of teacher education programs in the state, the largest teachers' union in the state, the Wisconsin Education Association Council, actively supported these state department efforts in part because they felt shut out of university teacher education in the state. (See Prestine 1989.)

30. The dominant teacher presence on the Carnegie-sponsored National Board for Professional Teaching Standards (Carnegie 1989), is another example of how the organized teaching profession has gained in its ability to influence the conduct of teacher education programs. Those associated with this project expect that the new national teacher certification standards, although voluntary and not even requiring the completion of a teacher education program, will have a major impact on the curriculum of preservice teacher education in the U.S. because of the eventual articulation of a statement about the specific knowledge and skills thought to be needed by exemplary teachers at different levels of schooling and in different subject areas. (Personal correspondence, David Mandel, January 1990).

31. Although as Darling-Hammond and Berry (1988) point out, these policies deregulating teaching came along with greater regulation of teachers themselves through more rigorous standards for teacher education programs and teacher certification.

32. This is also not to deny the influence of concentrations of power and authority in "invisible centers of private power" (such as textbook publishers and testing agencies) whose personnel are neither elected nor accountable to anyone who is elected (Cohen 1978).

33. Carnegie (1986), National Governors' Association (1986).

34. We should especially support those efforts that in their advocacy for more democratic schools attend to the legitimate interests of all parties in school policy issues: administrators, teachers, parents and students. See Zeichner (1990a) for a discussion of this issue.

35. The Institute for Democratic Education is coordinated by George Wood of Ohio University and publishes the journal *Democratic Education*. The Rethinking Schools group is coordinated by a group of classroom teachers in Milwaukee, Wisconsin, and publishes a newspaper with the same name.

36. In giving our support to such responsive teaching practices as whole language instruction and a process-oriented approach to writing, we must not lose sight of the need to see that students acquire the technical skills they will have to have to make it in the mainstream. This tension between the acquisition of technical skills and the development of the capability to think critically and creatively about school curriculum is particularly salient in our urban schools (Delpit 1986).

37. These shadowing activities became part of the curriculum in some university courses and were followed up by class discussions which focused on various aspects of teachers' work using the case studies as data. The undergraduate students were aware that the data they gathered would be used to support the teachers and could choose not to participate.

38. One might say that teachers have been working throughout this century through their unions to better their professional situation. Although this is true, in some respects, it is also the case that many of these efforts have been focused on wages and benefits and have ignored teachers' daily working conditions. In the particular case described here the teachers' union was initially reluctant to pursue the issue of planning time brought to them by a group of teachers and had to be persuaded to incorporate the issue into the bargaining process.

39. See Canter and Canter (1983), Performance Learning Systems (1986), and Gentile (1988).

40. The elementary teachers in Madison were told by their superintendent, for example, that there might not be enough money available to support the additional released time. While we are not saying that school districts should abandon the use of external consultants, we do feel that their use should be severely curtailed.

41. A good example of a desire to produce simple solutions to complex problems can be found in the recent U.S. Department of Education publication *What Works* (1986).

42. See Slavin (1989) for a discussion of the cycle that many recent fads have followed.

43. Render et al. (1989) provide similar data about the lack of research support (despite claims to the contrary) for Assertive Discipline.

44. See Render, Padilla, and Krank (1989) and Slavin (1989).

45. The elevation of the education of elementary teachers to the collegiate level has been one of the major developments in twentieth-century American teacher education stimulated by state requirements (Monroe 1952). Since 1970, all states have required the bachelor's degree for the elementary certificate. Currently, state mandates are responsible in many cases for the extension of preservice preparation beyond four years of undergraduate education. In Wisconsin for example, the implementation of new teacher certification and program accreditation standards in 1986 has resulted in a five-year minimum completion time in Wisconsin teacher education programs.

46. Clark and McNergney (1990) argue that this increased role of states in teacher education is in part a response to the decreased federal role in education in the 1980s under President Reagan. It is also consistent with efforts to more closely regulate higher education in general in the U.S. (Nickerson and Stampen 1978) and with recent efforts in other countries to exert tighter governmental controls over the tertiary sector in general and teacher education in particular. For example, see Aspin (1988) and Whitty, Barton, and Pollard (1987) for a discussion of recent events in the U.K. that have involved closer governmental regulation of teacher education programs. Sykes (1986) argues that the history of state regulation in teacher education reflects teacher education's uneasy regard among the public and a lack of public confidence in teachers.

47. As was pointed out earlier, Darling-Hammond and Berry (1988) argue that this increased regulation of teacher education programs and teachers by states has come in exchange for the increased deregulation of teaching itself.

48. Senate Bill 994 in Texas, which was signed into law in 1987, abolishes the undergraduate degree in education and limits pedagogical requirements for teacher certification to eighteen credit hours, including student teaching.

49. One flaw in the logic of these state mandates (even when the specific requirements are supportive of social justice and equity) is that the prescriptions lack any sense of teacher learning as a career-long process. If the decision is made that teachers need to be given certain kinds of information or exposed to certain kinds of issues, states have automatically assumed that they need these experiences, knowledge, etc., prior to entry to teaching. In our view, a decision that teachers need something does not automatically mean that they need it during their preservice education. A more reasonable strategy would be to spread some of these requirements over at least the beginning years of teachers' careers as part of district staff development programs. This would lighten the burden on an already overcrowded preservice teacher education curriculum and would be more congruent with what we know about how teachers learn to teach.

50. See Dilworth (1984), Smith (1987), and Witty (1982) for discussions of some of the discriminatory effects of state policies in teacher education.

51. For example, the common practice of admitting students to teacher education programs on the basis of test scores and grade point averages alone does not address the moral commitment of teacher candidates to social justice (e.g., to provide an equitable education to all students, their knowledge of and sensitivity to diverse cultural traditions, etc.). (See Haberman 1987).

52. In Wisconsin for example, the Department of Public Instruction has recently given public backing and financial support to a program developed by Linda Post and Martin Haberman of the University of Wisconsin-Milwaukee to provide structured inner-city school experiences for students from around the state of Wisconsin.

53. These are the Council of Chief State School Officers and the National
     Council of State Directors of Teacher Education (see Cruickshank and
     Armaline 1986).
54. The one professional association in which social-reconstructionist perspec-
     tives have always been very visible is the American Educational Studies
     Association, an organization composed of faculty who are involved in
     teaching the educational foundations courses in teacher education pro-
     grams. As was pointed out in chapter 1, social foundations courses in
     teacher education programs emerged out of the social reconstructionism
     of the 1930. (See Borman 1990 for further discussion of the links between
     the field of educational foundations and social reconstructionism.)
55. Our position is that social-reconstructionist teacher educators need to
     become involved in one or both of the two organizations devoted exclu-
     sively to teacher education (AACTE or ATE) in addition to their involve-
     ment in the various subject matter and or specialty associations. This is
     particularly important for members of the American Educational Studies
     Association where social-reconstructionist perspectives are well repre-
     sented.
56. In 1987, according to the Washington-based Center on Budget and Policy
     Priorities, the poorest fifth of American families received only 4.6 percent
     of the national family income, while the top fifth's share was 43.7 percent.
     This gap was the largest in forty years, as was the number of Americans
     who are ill housed, poorly educated, and without health care (Caplan
     1990). It has been estimated, for example, that only one-fifth of the
     children eligible for the federal Head Start program are now being served
     (Fiske 1990), and that 35 million Americans are without any medical
     insurance.
57. It is estimated, for example, that to bring spending on precollegiate educa-
     tion in the U.S. up to the average level of the other fifteen countries in the
     study reported above by Mishel and Rasell (1989), we would have to raise
     spending by more than $20 billion a year, an amount roughly equal to the
     entire budget of the U.S. Department of Education (Miller 1989).
58. This has certainly been true of every major report that has focused on
     teacher education in the United States through the end of 1989 (e.g., the
     National Commission for Excellence in Teacher Education 1985, Holmes
     Group 1986, Carnegie Forum on Education and the Economy 1986). While
     the more recent reports of the Holmes Group Consortium, "Tomorrow's
     Schools" (1990), and the report of the national curriculum committee of
     the Holmes Group (1990) give more explicit attention to issues of social
     justice and equity in schooling than the initial report, neither of these
     reports deals in an extended manner with the social prerequisites (i.e.,
     changes in economic, political, and social structures) that are necessary
     for realizing the kinds of school reforms they advocate (Zeichner 1990a).
59. While we have not focused here on the kinds of specific changes in
     the economic, political, and social structures of society that we would

personally support, one example of the kinds of programs that we have in mind can be found in Raskin's (1986) proposals for promoting the "common good" in our society. While we do not agree with everything that Raskin proposes, especially with regard to education, we find his ideas as a whole to be very close to our own.

60. See Zeichner (1990a) for a discussion of some of the contradictions and tensions in the movements to empower teachers and to restructure schools.

61. We also think that there is a price to pay in remaining silent on the need for societal transformation and then accepting money from corporate interests to finance particular reforms in teaching and teacher education. For example, while it is commendable that teacher educators in the state of Michigan have recently been able to secure $48 million from various sources to finance the development of professional development schools throughout the state (Michigan 1990), charity from corporate magnates, even $48 million of it, is not going to enable us to address the kinds of educational and social problems that we have discussed in this book. One thing that we need to do is to change the conditions that enable this one entrepreneur (but certainly many others as well) to amass such huge individual fortunes in the first place while so many have so little.

62. This includes a reluctance (even among institutions located in urban areas) today to place student teachers in culturally diverse urban classrooms (Goodlad 1990).

63. We agree with the Holmes Group's (1990) recent criticisms of the narrowness of the educational reform movement of the 1980s, which they say has focused largely on making the U.S. more economically competitive in world markets. They raise an important question for those who have exclusively stressed enhanced economic competitiveness as the justification for school reform: "What purposes are served by a nation that is more competitive in economic terms if its citizens are divided against one another by the harsh realities of racism and poverty?" (p. 2).

64. This is not to deny the need for continuing research. Clayton (1989) implies, though—and we agree—that all the research in the world will not make a dent in the crisis of inequality in schools and society unless we have the political will to initiate the kinds of societal transformations and redistributive polices that will enable all student to benefit from the research.

References

Adler, S., and Goodman, J. 1986. Critical Theory as a foundation for methods courses. *Journal of Teacher Education* 37(4): 2–8.

Allen, D., and Ryan, K. 1969. *Micro teaching.* Reading, Mass.: Addison-Wesley.

Althusser, L. 1971. *Lenin and philosophy.* New York: Monthly Review Press.

Amarel, M. 1988. Developmental teacher education. In *Dialogues in teacher education* (Issue Paper 88–4). East Lansing, Mich.: National Center for Research on Teacher Education.

American Association of Colleges for Teacher Education. 1988. *Teacher education pipeline: Schools, colleges, and departments of education enrollments by race and ethnicity.* Washington, D.C.: AACTE.

American Association of University Professors. 1988. Mastering the academic marketplace: The annual report of the economic status of the profession. *Academe* 74(2): 3–16.

American Federation of Teachers. 1986. *The revolution that is overdue: Looking toward the future of teaching and learning.* Washington, D.C.: American Foundation of Teachers.

Ammon, P., and Black, A. 1988. A response to M. Amarel. In *Dialogues in teacher education* (Issue Paper 88–4). East Lansing, Mich.: National Center for Research on Teacher Education.

Anyon, J. 1979. Ideology and U.S. history textbooks. *Harvard Educational Review* 49(3): 361–86.

Anyon, J. 1980. Social class and the hidden curriculum of work. *Journal of Education* 162: 67–92.

Apple, M. 1972. Behaviorism and conservatism: The educational views in four of the "systems" models of teacher education. In *Perspectives for reform in teacher education,* edited by B. Joyce & M. Weil, pp. 237–62. Englewood Cliffs, N.J.: Prentice-Hall.

Apple, M. 1979. *Ideology and education.* Boston: Routledge and Kegan Paul.

Apple, M. 1982. *Education and power.* Boston: Routledge and Kegan Paul.

Apple, M. 1986. *Teachers and texts: A political economy of class and gender relations in education.* Boston and London: Routledge and Kegan Paul.

Apple, M. 1987. Will the social context allow a tomorrow for tomorrow's teachers? In *Reforming teacher education,* edited by J. Soltis, pp. 20–27. New York: Teachers College Press.

Apple, M., Cornbleth, C. Weis, L., Wexler, P., and Zeichner, K. 1989. *Toward tomorrow's schools.* Buffalo, N.Y.: State University of New York at Buffalo, School of Education.

Arfedson, G. 1979. Teachers' work. In *Code, context and curriculum processes,* edited by U. Lundgren and S. Patterson. Lund, Sweden: Gleerup.

Armaline, W., and Hoover, R. 1989. Field experience as a vehicle for transformation: Ideology, education and reflective practice. *Journal of Teacher Education* 40(2): 42–48.

Ashcroft, K., and Griffiths, M. 1989. Reflective teachers and reflective tutors: School experience in an initial teacher education course. *Journal of Education for Teaching* 15(1): 35–52.

Aspin, D. 1988. *Teacher education: Reforms and strategies. Some U.K. perspectives.* Paper presented at the First Asia-Pacific Conference on Teacher Education, Bangkok, Thailand.

ASPIRA. 1983. *Racial and ethnic high school dropout rates in New York City.* New York: Author.

Association of Teacher Educators. 1986. *Visions of reform: Implications for the education profession.* Reston, Va.: Association of Teacher Educators.

Atkin, J. M. 1973. "Practice Oriented Inquiry: A third approach to research in education." *Educational Researcher* (July).

Atkin, J. M., and Raths, J. 1974. *Changing patterns of teacher education in the U.S.* Paris: Organization for Economic Co-operation and development.

Ayer, A. 1931. Freedom for the student teacher. *Progressive Education* 8(3): 256–60.

Ayers, W. 1989. Headaches: On teaching and teacher education. *Action in Teacher Education* 11(2): 1–7.

Ayers, W. 1989. Reforming schools and rethinking classrooms: A Chicago chronicle. *Rethinking Schools* 4(1): 6–10.

Ball, D. L., and McDiarmid, G. W. 1990. The subject-matter preparation of teachers. In *Handbook of research on teacher education,* edited by W. R. Houston, pp. 437–49. New York: Macmillan.

Baptiste, H. P., Baptiste, M., and Gollnick, D. 1980. *Multicultural teacher education: Preparing educators to provide educational equity.* Vol. 1. Washington, D.C.: American Association of Colleges of Teacher Education.

Bartholomew, J. 1976. Schooling teachers: The myth of the liberal college. In *Explanations in the politics of school knowledge,* edited by G. Whitty and M. Young, pp. 114–24. Driffield, England: Nafferton.

Bastian, A., Fruchter, N., Gottell, M., Greer, C., and Haskins, K. 1985. *Choosing equality: The case for democratic schooling.* Philadelphia: Temple University Press.

Beatty, W. 1933. Training the teacher for the new school. *Progressive Education* 10(5): 248–53.

Belenky, M. F., Clinchy, B. M., Goldberger, N. R., and Tarule, J. M. 1986. *Women's ways of knowing: The development of self, voice, and mind.* New York: Basic Books.

Ben-Peretz, M. 1984. Curriculum theory and practice in teacher education. In *Advances in teacher education,* edited by L. Katz and J. Raths. Vol. 1., pp. 9–27. Norwood, N.J.: Ablex.

Berger, J. 1990. New York city fails to train many of its novice teachers. *New York Times,* February 22, A21.

Berlak, A., and Berlak, H. 1981. *Dilemmas of schooling.* New York: Methuen.

Berliner, D. 1984. The half-full glass: A review of research on teaching. In *Using what we know about teaching,* edited by P. Hosford, pp. 51–77. Alexandria, Va.: Association of Supervision and Curriculum Development.

Berliner, D. 1985. "Laboratory settings for the study of teacher education." *Journal of Teacher Education* 36(6): 2–8.

Bernstein, R. 1978. *The reconstruction of social and political theory.* Philadelphia: University of Pennsylvania Press.

Bestor, A. 1953. *Educational wastelands.* Urbana, Ill.: University of Illinois Press.

Bestor, A. 1955. *The restoration of learning.* New York: Knopf.

Beyer, L. 1984. Field experience, ideology, and the development of critical reflectivity. *Journal of Teacher Education* 35(3): 36–41.

Beyer, L. 1988. *Knowing and acting: Inquiry, Ideology, and Educational Studies.* London: Falmer Press.

Biddle, B. 1989. Implications of government funding policies for research on teaching and teacher education. *Teaching and Teacher Education* 5(4): 275–82.

References

Bigelow, D., ed. 1971. *The liberal arts and teacher education*. Lincoln, Nebr.: University of Nebraska Press.

Bloom, A. 1987. *The closing of the American mind*. New York: Simon and Schuster.

Bode, B. 1935. Dr. Bode replies. *The Social Frontier* 2(2): 42.

Bode, B. 1938. *Progressive education at the crossroads*. New York: Newson and Company.

Bolster, A., Jr. 1983. Toward a more effective model of research on teaching. *Harvard Educational Review* 53(3): 294–308.

Bonser, G. 1929. The training of teachers for the new education. *Progressive Education* 6: 111–21.

Book, C. 1983. Alternative programs for prospective teachers. *Action in Teacher Education* 5: 57–62.

Book, C., Byers, J., and Freeman, D. 1983. Student expectations and teacher education traditions with which we can and cannot live. *Journal of Teacher Education* 34(1): 9–13.

Borg, W. 1970. *The minicourse*. Beverly Hills, Calif.: Macmillan Educational Services.

Borman, K. 1990. Foundations of education in teacher education. In *Handbook of research on teacher education*, edited by W. R. Houston, pp. 393–402. New York: Macmillan.

Borrowman, M. 1956. *The liberal and technical in teacher education*. New York: Teachers College Press.

Borrowman, M. 1965. Liberal education and the professional preparation of teachers. In *Teacher education in the U.S.: A documentary history*, edited by M. L. Borrowman, pp. 1–53. New York: Teachers College Press.

Bowers, C. A. 1969. *The progressive educator and the depression: The radical years*. New York: Random House.

Bowles, S., and Gintis, H. 1974. *Schooling in capitalist America*. New York: Basic Books.

Boyer, E. 1987. *College: The undergraduate experience in America*. New York: Harper & Row.

Brameld, T. 1947, June 21. Philosophy of education in an age of crisis. *School and Society* LXV(1695): 452.

Brameld, T. 1955. *Philosophies of education in cultural perspective*. New York: The Dryden Press.

Brameld, T. 1962. *Toward a reconstructed philosophy of education*. New York: Holt, Rinehart and Winston.

Brenton, M. 1970. *What's happened to teacher?* New York: Avon Books.

Brosio, R. 1990. Teaching and learning for democratic empowerment: A Critical Evaluation. *Educational Theory* 90(1): 69–82.

Broudy, H. 1973. *A critique of PBTE.* Washington, D.C.: American Association of Colleges of Teacher Education.

Broudy, H. 1990. Case studies: Why and how. *Teachers College Record* 91(3): 449–459.

Brown, H. 1938. A challenge to teachers' colleges. *Social Frontier* 4(37): 327–29.

Buchmann, M. 1984. The use of research knowledge in teacher education and teaching. *American Journal of Education* 92(4): 421–34.

Buchmann, M. 1986. Role over person: Morality and authenticity in teaching. *Teachers College Record* 87(4): 529–43.

Buchmann, M. 1987a. Impractical philosophizing about teachers' arguments. *Educational Theory* 37(4): 409–12.

Buchmann, M. 1987b. Teaching knowledge: The lights that teachers live by. *Oxford Review of Education* 13(2): 151–64.

Bullough, R. 1990. *Personal history and teaching metaphors in preservice teacher education.* Paper presented at the Annual Meeting of the American Educational Research Association, Boston.

Bush, R. 1987. Teacher education reform: Lessons from the past half century. *Journal of Teacher Education* 38(3): 13–19.

Butt, R., Raymond, D., and Yamagishi, L. 1988. Autobiographic praxis: Studying the formation of teachers' knowledge. *Journal of Curriculum Theorizing* 1(4): 87–164.

Cabello, B., and Dash, R. 1988. *Programs for the recruitment, preparation and retention of teachers to work with diverse student populations.* San Francisco: Far West Laboratory for Educational Research and Development.

Calderhead, J. 1989. Reflective teaching and teacher education. *Teaching and Teacher Education,* 5(1): 43–51.

California Commission on the Teaching Profession. 1985. *Who will teach our children?* California: Author.

Canter, L., and Canter, M. 1983. *Assertive discipline.* Santa Monica, Calif.: Canter and Associates, Inc.

Caplan, A. 1990. Health care for poor shames America. *Wisconsin State Journal* February 25: 19A.

Carnegie Foundation for the Advancement of Teaching. 1988. *An imperiled generation: Saving urban schools.* Lawrenceville, N.J.: Princeton University Press.

Carnegie National Board for Professional Teaching Standards. 1989. *Toward high and rigorous standards for the teaching profession.* Washington, D.C.

Carnegie Task Force on Teaching as a Profession. 1986. *A nation prepared: Teachers for the 21st Century.* New York: Carnegie Corporation.

Carnoy, M., and Levin, H. 1985. *Schooling and work in the democratic state.* Stanford, Calif.: Stanford University Press.

Carr, W., and Kemmis, S. 1986. *Becoming critical: Education, knowledge, and action research.* London: Falmer Press.

Charters, W. W., and Waples, D. 1929. *Commonwealth teacher-training study.* Chicago: University of Chicago Press.

Childs, J. 1956. *American pragmatism and education.* New York: Henry Holt and Company.

Clandinin, D. J. 1986. *Classroom practice.* London: Falmer Press.

Clark, C. 1988. Asking the right questions about teacher preparation: Contributions of research on teacher thinking. *Educational Researcher,* 17(2): 5–12.

Clark, D., and Guba, E. 1976. *Institutional self-reports on knowledge production and utilization* (RITE Occasional Paper Series). Bloomington, Ind.: Indiana University School of Education.

Clark, D., and Marker, G. 1975. The institutionalization of teacher education. In *Teacher education,* edited by K. Ryan, pp. 53–86. Chicago: University of Chicago Press.

Clark, D., and McNergney, R. 1990. Governance of teacher education. In *Handbook of research on teacher education,* edited by W. R. Houston, pp. 101–18. New York: Macmillan.

Clarke, S. C. T. 1969. The story of elementary teacher education models. *Journal of Teacher Education* 20(3): 283–93.

Clayton, C. 1989. We can educate all our children. *The Nation,* July 24, 31, 132–35.

Clegg, S. R. 1989. *Frameworks of power.* Newbury Park, Calif.: Sage.

Clifford, G. J. 1987. Gender expectation and American teachers. *Teacher Education Quarterly,* 14(2, Spring): 6–16.

Clifford, G. J., and Guthrie, J. W. 1988. *ED school.* Chicago: University of Chicago Press.

Cochran-Smith, M., and Lytle, S. 1990. Research on teaching and teacher research: The issues that divide. *Educational Researcher* 19(2): 2–11.

Cohen, D. 1978. Reforming school politics. *Harvard Educational Review* 48: 429–447.

Cohen, S. 1976. The history of the history of American education. *Harvard Educational Review* 46(3): 298–330.

Cohn, M. 1979. *The interrelationship of theory and practice in teacher education: A description and analyses of the LITE program.* Ph.D. diss., Washington University, Graduate Institute of Education.

Cohn, M. 1981. A new supervision model for linking theory to practice. *Journal of Teacher Education* 32(3): 26–31.

Cohn, M., and Gellman, V. C. 1988. Supervision: A developmental approach for fostering inquiry in preservice teacher education. *Journal of Teacher Education* 39(2): 2–8.

Cole, A. 1989. Researcher and teacher: Partners in theory building. *Journal of Education for Teaching* 15(3): 225–37.

Coley, R. 1985. *State policies affecting teacher education and certification: Status, variations, and changes.* Paper presented at the annual meeting of the American Educational Research Association, Chicago.

Coley, R., and Thorpe, M. 1986. *A look at the M.A.T. model of teacher education and its graduates: Lessons for today.* Princeton, N.J.: Educational Testing Service.

Combs, A. 1972. Some basic concepts for teacher education. *Journal of Teacher Education* 22: 286–90.

Combs, A., Blume, R., Newman, A., and Wass, H. 1974. *The professional education of teachers: A humanistic approach to teacher education.* Boston: Allyn & Bacon.

Comeaux, M. 1991. But is it teaching? The use of collaborative learning in teacher education. In *Issues and practices in inquiry-oriented teacher education,* edited by B. R. Tabachnick and K. Zeichner, pp. 151–65. London: Falmer Press.

Comer, J. 1988. Educating poor minority children. *Scientific American* 259(5): 42–48.

Committee for Economic Development. 1987. *Children in need: Investment strategies for the educationally disadvantaged.* Washington, D.C.: Author.

Committee on Policy for Racial Justice. 1989. *Visions of a better way: A black appraisal of public schooling.* Washington, D.C.: Joint Center for Political Studies Press.

Conant, J. 1963. *The education of American teachers.* New York: McGraw-Hill.

Confrey, J. 1987. Bridging research and practice. *Educational Theory* 37(4): 383–94.

Connell, R. W. 1985. *Teacher's work.* Boston: George, Allen and Unwin.

References

Connelly, F. M., and Clandinin, D. J. 1988. *Teachers as curriculum planners.* New York: Teachers College Press.

Corcoran, T., Walker, L., and White, J. L. 1988. *Working in urban schools.* Washington, D.C.: Institute for Educational Leadership.

Corwin, R. 1973. *Reform and organizational survival: The Teacher Corps as an instrument of educational change.* New York: Wiley-Interscience.

Counts, G. 1932. *Dare the schools build a new social order?* New York: The John Day Co.

Cowley, M. 1934. *Exile's return.* New York: Viking Press.

Cremin, L. 1953. The heritage of American teacher education. *Journal of Teacher Education* 4(2): 163–70.

Cremin, L. 1961. *The transformation of the school: Progressivism in American Education, 1876–1957.* New York: Vintage Books.

Cremin, L. 1988. *American education: The metropolitan experience 1876–1980.* New York: Harper and Row.

Cremin, L., Shannon, D., and Townsend, M. E. 1954. *A history of Teachers College, Columbia University.* New York: Columbia University Press.

Crittenden, B. 1973. Some prior questions in the reform of teacher education. *Interchange* 4(2–3): 1–11.

Cronbach, L. J. 1982. Prudent aspirations for social inquiry. In *The social sciences,* edited by W. Kruskal, pp. 61–82. Chicago: The University of Chicago Press.

Cronin, J. 1983. State regulation of teacher preparation. In *Handbook of teaching and policy,* edited by L. Shulman and G. Sykes, pp. 171–91. New York: Longman.

Crook, P. 1974. A study of selected teacher training programs in the U.S. committed to a philosophy of "open education." Ph.D. diss., Syracuse University.

Cruickshank, D. R. 1974. The protocol materials movement: An exemplar of efforts to wed theory and practice in teacher education. *Journal of Teacher Education* 25(4): 300–311.

Cruickshank, D. 1984. *Models for the preparation of America's teachers.* Bloomington, In.: Phi Delta Kappa Educational Foundation.

Cruickshank, D., and Armaline, W. 1986. Field experiences in teacher education: Considerations and recommendations. *Journal of Teacher Education* 37(3): 34–40.

Cruickshank, D. 1987. *Reflective teaching.* Reston, Va.: Association of Teacher Educators.

Cuban, L. 1984. *How teachers taught: Constancy and change in American classrooms, 1890–1980*. New York: Longman.

Cuban, L. 1989. The "at risk" label and the problem of urban school reform. *Phi Delta Kappan* 70(10): 780–84, 799–801.

Current, L., and Hirabayashi, J., eds. 1989. *Teachers as researchers: Papers and commentary from the 10th annual northern California conference of Division G of the American Educational Research Association*. Oakland, Calif.: Mills College.

Cushman, M. 1975. Influences on teacher education by funding agencies. In *The governance of teacher education*, edited by M. Cushman, pp. 113–35. Berkeley, Calif.: McCutchan.

Dale, R. 1977. Implications of the rediscovery of the hidden curriculum for the sociology of teaching. In *Identity and structure: Issues in the sociology of education*, edited by D. Gleason. Driffield, England: Naferton.

Damerell, R. 1985. *Education's smoking gun: How teachers colleges have destroyed education in America*. New York: Freundlich Books.

Darling-Hammond, L., and Berry, B. 1988. *The evolution of teacher policy*. Washington, D.C.: Rand.

DeCharms, R. 1968. *Personal causation*. New York: Academic Press.

Delpit, L. 1986. Skills and other dilemmas of a progressive black educator. *Harvard Educational Review* 56(4): 379–85.

Densmore, K. 1987. Professionalism, proletarianization, and teacher work. In *Critical studies in teacher education*, edited by T. Popkewitz, pp. 130–60. London: Falmer Press.

Devaney, K. 1989. Liberal arts curricula and pedagogy pondered at third annual meeting. *Holmes Group Forum* 3(3): 9.

Dewey, J. [1902] 1956. *The child and the curriculum/the school and society*. Chicago: The University of Chicago Press.

Dewey, J. 1916. *Democracy and education*. New York: The Free Press.

Dewey, J. 1938. *Experience and education*. New York: Collier Books.

DiChiro, G., Robottom, I., and Tinning, R. 1988. An account of action research in a tertiary context. In *The action research planner*, 3d ed. edited by S. Kammis and R. McTaggart. Geelong: Deakin University Press.

Dilworth, M. 1984. *Teachers' totter: A report on teacher certification issues*. Washington, D.C.: Harvard University Institute for the Study of Educational Policy.

Drummond, W., and Andrews, T. 1980. The influence of federal and state governments on teacher education. *Phi Delta Kappan* 62(2): 97–99.

Ducharme, E., and Agne, R. 1989. Professors of education: Uneasy residents of academe. In *The professors of teaching,* edited by R. Wisniewski & E. Ducharme, pp. 67–86. Albany: State University of New York Press.

Duckworth, E. 1987. *The having of wonderful ideas.* New York: Teachers College Press.

Eaton, W. 1975. *The American Federation of Teachers 1916–1961.* Carbondale, Ill.: Southern Illinois University Press.

Edelman, M. W. 1989. Children at risk. In *Caring for America's children,* edited by F. Macchiarola and A. Gartner, pp. 20–30. New York: Academy of Political Science.

Edmundson, P. 1990. A normative look at the curriculum in teacher education. *Phi Delta Kappan* 71(9): 717–23.

Elbaz, F. 1983. *Teacher thinking: A study of practical knowledge.* London: Croom Helm.

Elisberg, J. 1981. "A study of selected master of arts in teaching programs in the U.S." Ph.D. diss., Northwestern University.

Elliott, J. 1985. Educational action research. In *Research, policy and practice: World yearbook of education,* edited by J. Nisbet and S. Nisbet, pp. 231–50. London: Kegan Page, Nichols Publishing.

Elliott, J. 1990. Teachers as researchers: Implications for supervision and for teacher education. *Teaching and Teacher Education* 6(1): 1–26.

Ellner, C., and Barnes, B. J. 1977. *Schoolmaking: An alternative in teacher education.* Lexington, Mass.: Lexington Books.

Ellsworth, E. 1989. Why doesn't this feel empowering? Working through the repressive myths of critical pedagogy. *Harvard Educational Review* 59(3): 297–324.

Emmer, E., Evertson, C., Sanford, J., Clements, B., and Worsham, M. 1984. *Classroom management for secondary teachers.* Englewood Cliffs, N.J.: Prentice-Hall.

Ervay, S. 1985. Campus-field compatibility in student teaching. *Action in Teacher Education* 7(3): 37–42.

Eubanks, E. 1988, December. *Socio-economic trends and education in the 21st century: A mission in search of a culture.* Paper presented to the University of Wisconsin System Steering Committee on Strategic Planning in Teacher Education. Madison: University of Wisconsin System.

Fay, B. 1987. *Critical social science: Liberation and its limits.* Ithaca, N.Y.: Cornell University Press.

Feiman-Nemser, S. 1990. Teacher preparation: Structural and conceptual alternatives. In *Handbook of research on teacher education,* edited by W. R. Houston, pp. 212–33. New York: Macmillan.

Feiman-Nemser, S., and Buchmann, M. 1985. Pitfalls of experience in teacher education. *Teachers College Record* 87: 49–65.

Feiman-Nemser, S., and Buchmann, M. 1986. The first year of teacher preparation: Transition to pedagogical thinking. *Journal of Curriculum Studies* 18(3): 239–56.

Feiman-Nemser, S., and Floden, R. 1980. *A consumer's guide to teacher development*. East Lansing, Mich.: Institute for Research on Teaching, Michigan State University.

Feiman-Nemser, S., and Floden, R. 1986. The cultures of teaching. In *Handbook of research on teaching*, edited by M. C. Wittrock, pp 505–26. New York: Macmillan.

Feinberg, W. 1983. *Understanding education*. New York: Cambridge University Press.

Feistritzer, C. E. 1985. *The condition of teaching: A state by state analysis*. Princeton, N.J.: Carnegie Foundation for the Advancement of Teaching.

Fennema, E., Carpenter, T., and Peterson, P. 1989. Teachers' decision making and cognitively guided instruction: A new paradigm for curriculum development. In *Facilitating change in mathematics education*, edited by K. Clements and N. F. Ellerton, pp. 174–187. Geelong, Australia: Deakin University Press.

Fenstermacher, G. 1980. On learning to teach from research on teacher effectiveness. In *Time to learn*, edited by C. Denham and A. Lieberman. Washington, D.C.: National Institute of Education.

Fenstermacher, G. D. 1986. Philosophy of research on teaching: Three aspects. In *Handbook of research on teaching*, edited by M. C. Wittrock, pp. 37–49. New York: Macmillan.

Fenstermacher, G. D. 1987. A reply to my critics. *Educational theory* 37(4): 413–21.

Fenstermacher, G. D. 1988. The place of science and epistemology in Schon's conception of reflective practice. In *Reflection in teacher education*, edited by P. Grimmett and G. Erickson, pp. 39–46. New York: Teachers College Press.

Fine, M. 1987. Contexts that constrict and construct the lives and minds of public-school adolescents. In Council of Chief State School Officers, *School success for students at risk*, pp. 89–119. Orlando, Fla.: Harcourt Brace Jovanovich.

Fiske, E. 1990. Finding a way to define the new buzzword of American education: How about perestroika? *New York Times*, February 14, B8.

Flexner, A. 1930. *Universities: American, English, German*. Oxford: Oxford University Press.

References

Florio-Ruane, S. 1989. Social organization of classes and schools. In *Knowledge base for the beginning teacher,* edited by M. Reynolds, pp. 163–72. New York: Pergamon.

Freedman, S., Jackson, J., and Boles, K. 1983. Teaching: An imperiled profession. In *Handbook of teaching and policy,* edited by L. Shulman and G. Sykes, pp. 261–99. New York: Longman.

Freedman, S., Jackson, J., and Boles, K. 1986. *The effect of teaching on teachers.* Grand Forks, N.D.: University of North Dakota Press.

Freire, P. 1973. *Education for critical consciousness.* New York: Seabury Press.

Freire, P. 1974. *Pedagogy of the oppressed.* New York: Seabury Press.

Fuller, F. 1972. *Personalizing teacher education.* Austin, Tex.: Research and Development Center for Teacher Education.

Fuller, F. 1974. A conceptual framework for a personalized teacher education program. *Theory into Practice* 13(2): 112–22.

Fuller, F., and Bown, O. 1975. Becoming a teacher. In *Teacher Education,* edited by K. Ryan, pp. 25–52. Chicago: University of Chicago Press.

Gage, N. 1970. *Teacher effectiveness and teacher education.* Palo Alto, Calif.: Pacific Books.

Gage, N. 1989. The paradigm wars and their aftermath: *Teachers College Record* 91(2): 135–50.

Gage, N., and Winne, P. 1975. Performance-based teacher education. In *Teacher education,* edited by K. Ryan, pp. 146–72. Chicago: University of Chicago Press.

Galluzzo, G. R., and Arends, R. I. 1989. The RATE Project: A profile of teacher education institutions. *Journal of Teacher Education* 40(4): 56–58.

Garfinkel, I., and McLanahan, S. 1985, April. *The feminization of poverty: Nature, causes and a partial cure.* Madison: University of Wisconsin Institute for Research on Poverty.

Gay, G. 1986. Multicultural teacher education. In *Multicultural education in western societies,* edited by J. Banks and J. Lynch, pp. 154–77. New York: Praeger.

Gentile, J. R. 1988. *Instructional improvement: Summary and analysis of Madeline Hunter's essential elements of instruction and supervision.* Oxford, Ohio: National Staff Development Council.

Giddens, A. 1979. *Central problems in social theory.* Berkeley, Calif.: University of California Press.

Gideonse, H. D. 1982. The necessary revolution in teacher education. *Phi Delta Kappan* 64(1): 15–18.

260

Gifford, B. 1986. Excellence and equity in teacher competency testing: A policy perspective. *Journal of Negro Education* 55(3): 251–71.

Ginsburg, M. 1988. *Contradictions in teacher education and society: A Critical Analysis.* London: Falmer Press.

Ginsburg, M., and Clift, R. 1990. The hidden curriculum of preservice teacher education. In *Handbook of research on teacher education,* edited by W. R. Houston, pp. 450–68. New York: Macmillan.

Giroux, H., and McLaren, P. 1987. Teacher education and the politics of engagement: The case for democratic schooling. In *Teaching, teachers, and teacher education,* edited by M. Okazawa-Ray, J. Anderson, and R. Traver, pp. 157–82. Cambridge, Mass.: Harvard Educational Review Reprint.

Giroux, H. 1988. *Teachers as intellectuals.* Granby, Mass.: Bergin & Garvey.

Gitlin, A., and Teitelbaum, K. 1983. Linking theory and practice: The use of ethnographic methodology by prospective teachers. *Journal of Education for Teaching* 9: 225–34.

Givens, S. 1988. Thirty institutions chosen for project to redesign teacher education. *AACTE Briefs* 9(5–6): 4, 12.

Glassberg, S., and Sprinthall, N. 1980. Student teaching: A developmental approach. *Journal of Teacher Education* 31: 31–38.

Golby, M. 1989. Teachers and their research. In *Quality in Teaching: Arguments for a reflective profession,* edited by W. Carr, pp. 163–72. London: Falmer Press.

Gold, A. 1988. Boston schools set to overhaul busing policies. *New York Times,* December 28, A18.

Goldberg, M. 1990. Portrait of Madeline Hunter. *Educational Leadership* 47(5): 41–43.

Goldberger, P. 1990. Taj Mahal: Part Vegas, Part Disney, All Trump. *New York Times,* April 6, B1.

Goldhammer, R. 1969. *Clinical supervision.* New York: Holt, Rinehart and Winston.

Gollnick, D. 1978. *Multicultural education in teacher education: The state of the scene.* Washington, D.C.: American Association of Colleges of Teacher Education.

Gollnick, D., Osayande, K., and Levy, J. 1980. *Multicultural teacher education: Case studies of thirteen programs,* Vol. 2. Washington, D.C.: American Association of Colleges of Teacher Education.

Gomez, M. L. 1990. Reflections on research for teaching: Collaborative inquiry with a novice teacher. *Journal of Education for Teaching* 16(1): 45–56.

261

References

Good, T. 1987. Two decades of research on teacher expectations. *Journal of Teacher Education* 38(4): 32–48.

Goodlad, J. 1990. *Teachers for our nation's schools*. San Francisco: Jossey-Bass.

Goodlad, J., Soder, R., and Sirotnik, K., eds. 1990. *Places where teachers are taught*. San Francisco: Jossey-Bass.

Goodman, J. 1986a. Making early field experiences meaningful: A critical approach. *Journal of Education for Teaching* 12(2): 109–25.

Goodman, J. 1986b. Teaching prospective teachers a critical approach to curriculum design. *Curriculum Inquiry* 16(2): 179–201.

Goodman, J. 1988. Masculinity, feminism and the male elementary school teacher: A case study of preservice teachers' perspectives. *Journal of Curriculum Theorizing* 7(2): 30–60.

Goodman, J. (1991). Using a methods course to promote reflection and inquiry among preservice teachers. In *Issues and practices in inquiry-oriented teacher education*, edited by B. R. Tabachnick and K. Zeichner, pp. 56–76. London: Falmer Press.

Gore, J. 1990. The struggle for pedagogies: Critical and feminist discourses as "regimes of truth". Ph.D. diss., University of Wisconsin-Madison.

Gore, J., and Zeichner, K. 1990. *Action research and reflective teaching in preservice teacher education*. Paper presented at the annual meeting of the American Educational Research Association, Boston.

Goswami, D., and Stillman, P. 1987. *Reclaiming the classroom: Teacher research as an agency for change*. Montclair, N.J.: Boynton Cook.

Graham, P. 1988. *Revolution in pedagogy*. Paper presented at the University of Wisconsin System Conference on Future Societal Trends: Implications for Teacher Education in the 21st Century, Madison, University of Wisconsin System.

Grant, C., and Koskella, R. 1986. Education that is multicultural and the relationship between preservice campus learning and field experiences. *Journal of Educational Research* 79: 197–203.

Grant, C., and Secada, W. 1990. Preparing teachers for diversity. In *Handbook of research on teacher education*, edited by W. R. Houston, pp. 403–22. New York: Macmillan.

Green, T. 1971. *The activities of teaching*. New York: McGraw-Hill.

Green, T. 1976. Teacher competence as practical rationality. *Educational Theory* 26: 249–58.

Greene, M. 1979. The matter of mystification: Teacher education in unquiet times. In *Landscapes of learning*, pp. 53–73. New York: Teachers College Press.

Greene, M. 1989. Social and political contexts. In *Knowledge base for the beginning teacher*, edited by M. Reynolds, pp. 143–54. New York: Pergamon Press.

Griffin, G., et al. 1983. *Clinical preservice teacher education: Final report of a descriptive study*. Austin, Tex.: University of Texas Research and Development Center for Teacher Education.

Grundy, S. 1982. Three modes of action research. *Curriculum Perspectives* 2(3): 23–34.

Gutmann, A. 1987. *Democratic Education*. Princeton, N.J.: Princeton University Press.

Guyton, E., and McIntyre, D. J. 1990. Student teaching and school experiences. In *Handbook of research on teacher education*, edited by W. R. Houston, pp. 514–34. New York: Macmillan.

Haberman, M. 1983. Research on preservice laboratory and clinical experiences. In *The education of teachers: A look ahead*, edited by K. Howey and W. Gardner, pp. 98–117. New York: Longman.

Haberman, M. 1987. *Recruiting and selecting teachers for urban schools*. New York: ERIC Clearinghouse on Urban Education, Institute for Urban and Minority Education.

Hahn, A., Danzerger, J., and Lefkowitz, B. 1987. *Dropouts in America*. Washington, D.C.: Institute for Educational Leadership.

Hallinan, M. 1984. Summary and implications. In *The social context of instruction*, edited by P. Peterson, L. Wilkinson, and M. Hallinan. New York: Academic Press.

Handal, G., and Lauvas, P. 1987. *Promoting reflective teaching: Supervision in action*. Milton Keynes, UK: Open University Press.

Heath, R. W., and Nielson, M. 1974. The research basis for performance-based teacher education. *Review of Educational Research* 44(4): 463–84.

Heath, S. B. 1982. Questioning at home and at school. A comparative study. In *Doing the ethnography of schooling*, edited by G. Spindler, pp. 102–31. New York: Holt, Rinehart & Winston.

Heath, S. B. 1983. *Ways with words*. New York: Cambridge University Press.

Hedges, W. 1989. We must remove elementary teacher training from the state universities. *Phi Delta Kappan* 70(8): 623–25.

Henderson, J. 1989. Positioned reflective practice: A curriculum decision. *Journal of Teacher Education* 40(2): 10–14.

References

Hendrick, I. 1967. Academic revolution in California. *Southern California Quarterly* 49(2, 3, 4): 127–66, 253–95, 359–406.

Herbst, J. 1989. *And sadly teach: Teacher education and professionalization in American culture.* Madison, Wis.: University of Wisconsin Press.

Hirsch, E. D., Jr. 1988. *Cultural literacy.* New York: Vintage Books.

Hirst, P. 1965. Liberal education and the nature of knowledge. In *Philosophical analysis of education,* edited by R. D. Archambault, pp. 113–38. New York: Humanities Press.

Hitchcock, G., and Hughes, D. 1989. *Research and the teacher: A qualitative introduction to school-based research.* London: Routledge.

Hochschild, A., and Machung, A. 1989. *Second shift: Inside the two-job marriage.* New York: Penguin.

Hodgkinson, H. 1985. *All one system: Demographics of education.* Washington, D.C.: Institute for Educational Leadership.

Holmes, H. 1932. The teacher in politics. *Progressive Education* 4: 414–18.

The Holmes Group. 1986. *Tomorrow's teachers.* East Lansing, Mich.: The Holmes Group, Inc., Michigan State University, School of Education.

The Holmes Group. 1990. *The preparation and continuing education of tomorrow's teachers: Toward a community of learning.* East Lansing, Mich: Author.

The Holmes Group. 1990. *Tomorrow's Schools: Principles for the design of professional development schools.* East Lansing, Mich.: The Holmes Group, Inc., Michigan State University, School of Education.

Hook, S. 1989. Civilization and its malcontents. *National Review* 41(19): 30–33.

Hopkins, D. 1985. *A teacher's guide to action research.* Milton Keynes, U.K.: Open University Press.

Houston, W. R., ed. 1990. *Handbook of research on teacher education.* New York: Macmillan.

Houston, W. R., and Howsam, R. 1972. *Competency-based teacher education.* Chicago: Science Research Associates.

Howey, K. 1989. Research about teacher education: Programs of teacher preparation. *Journal of Teacher Education* 40(6): 23–25.

Howey, K., and Zimpher, N. 1989. *Profiles of preservice teacher education.* Albany: State University of New York Press.

Howey, K., and Zimpher, N. 1990. Professors and deans of education. In *Handbook of research on teacher education,* edited by W. R. Houston, pp. 349–72. New York: Macmillan.

Hustler, D., Cassidy, T., and Cuff, T., eds. 1986. *Action research in classrooms and schools*. London: Allen & Unwin.

Hutchins, R. M. 1947. *Education for freedom*. Baton Rouge, La.: Louisiana State University Press.

Imig, D. 1988. Texas revisited. *AACTE Briefs* 9(7): 2.

Issac, J., and Ashcroft, K. 1988. A leap into the practical: A BEd (Hons) programme. In *The enquiring teacher: Supporting and sustaining teachers' research*, edited by J. Nias and S. Groundwater-Smith, pp. 85–92. London: Falmer Press.

Jackson, P. 1968. *Life in classrooms*. New York: Holt, Rinehart & Winston.

James, S. 1984. *The content of social explanation*. New York: Cambridge University Press.

Johnson, D. 1990. Milwaukee plans college guarantee. *New York Times*, February 7, B7.

Johnston, J., Spalding, J., Paden, R., and Ziffren, A. 1989. *Those who can: Undergraduate programs to prepare arts and science majors for teaching*. Washington, D.C.: Association of American Colleges.

Joyce, B. 1975. Conceptions of man and their implications for teacher education. In *Teacher education*, edited by K. Ryan, pp. 111–45. Chicago: University of Chicago Press.

Joyce, B., Yarger, S., and Howey, K. 1977. *Preservice teacher education*. Palo Alto, Calif.: Booksend Laboratory.

Joyce, B., Hersh, R., and McKibbin, M. 1983. *The structure of school improvement*. New York: Longman.

Joyce, B., and Showers, B. 1984. *Power for staff development through research on training*. Washington, D.C.: Association for Supervision and Curriculum Development.

Joyce, B., and Clift, R. 1984. The phoenix agenda: essential reform in teacher education. *Educational Researcher* 13(4):5–18.

Joyce, B., Weil, M., and Wald, R. 1974. Models of teaching in teacher education: An evaluation of instructional systems. *Interchange* 4: 47–73.

Judge, H. 1982. *American graduate schools of education: A view from abroad*. New York: Ford Foundation.

Kanter, R. M. 1979. *Men and women of the corporation*. New York: Basic Books.

Katznelson, I., and Weir, M. 1985. *Schooling for all: Class, race, and the decline of the democratic ideal*. Berkeley, Calif.: University of California Press.

Kelly, G., and Nihlen, A. 1982. Schooling and the reproduction of patriarchy.

In *Cultural and economic reproduction in education,* edited by M. Apple, pp. 162–80. Boston: Routledge & Kegan Paul.

Kemmis, S. 1985. Action research and the politics of reflection. In *Reflection: Turning experience into learning,* edited by D. Boud, R. Keogh, and D. Walker, pp. 139–64. London: Croom Helm.

Kemmis, S., and McTaggart, R. 1988. *The action research planner,* 3d ed. Geelong: Deakin University Press.

Kennedy, M., and Zeichner, K. 1989. Ken Zeichner reflecting on reflection. *Colloquy* 2(2): 15–21.

Keppel, F. 1986. A field guide to the land of teachers. *Phi Delta Kappan* 67: 18–23.

Kerr, D. 1983. Teaching competence and teacher education in the U.S. In *Handbook of teaching and policy,* edited by L. Shulman and G. Sykes, pp. 126–49. New York: Longman.

Kilpatrick, W., ed. 1933. *The educational frontier.* New York: The Century Co.

King, J. E., and Ladson-Billings, G. 1990. The teacher education challenge in elite university settings: Developing critical perspectives for teaching in a democratic and multicultural society. *European Journal of Intercultural Studies.* 1(2):15–30.

Kirk, D. 1986. Beyond the limits of theoretical discourse in teacher education: Towards a critical pedagogy. *Teaching and Teacher Education* 2: 155–67.

Kliebard, H. 1975. The rise of scientific curriculum making and its aftermath. *Curriculum Theory Network* 5(1): 27–38.

Kliebard, H. 1986. *The struggle for the American curriculum, 1893–1958.* Boston: Routledge & Kegan Paul.

Kneller, G. F. 1964. *Introduction to the philosophy of education.* New York: John Wiley and Sons.

Kniesner, T., McElroy, M., and Wilcox, S. 1986, September. *Family structure, race, and the feminization of poverty.* Madison: University of Wisconsin Institute for Research on Poverty.

Koehler, V. 1985. Research on preservice teacher education. *Journal of Teacher Education* 36(1): 23–30.

Koerner, J. 1963. *The miseducation of American teachers.* Boston: Houghton Mifflin.

Koff, R. 1985. *The politics of reform in teacher education.* Albany, N.Y.: State University of New York at Albany, School of Education.

Kolbert, E. 1988. Albany report says schools are split into rich and poor. *New York Times,* November 22, A9.

Kozol, J. 1980. *The night is dark and I am far from home.* New York: Continuum.

LaFontaine, H. 1988. Educational challenges and opportunities in serving limited-English-proficient students. In Council of Chief State School Officers, *School success for students at risk,* pp. 120–53. Orlando, Fla.: Harcourt Brace Jovanovich.

Laird, S. 1988. Reforming "woman's true profession": A case for feminist pedagogy in teacher education. *Harvard Educational Review* 58(4): 450–63.

Lanier, J. 1986. Research on teacher education. In *Third handbook of research on teaching,* edited by M. Wittrock, pp. 527–68. New York: Macmillan.

Lather, P. 1989. Postmodernism and the politics of enlightenment. *Educational Foundations* 3(3): 7–28.

Lawn, M. 1989. Being caught in school work: The possibilities of research in teachers-work. In *Quality in teaching: Arguments for a reflective profession,* edited by W. Carr, pp. 147–62. London: Falmer Press.

Layder, D. 1981. *Structure, interaction and social theory.* Boston: Routledge and Kegan Paul.

Layder, D. 1985. Power, structure and agency. *Journal of the theory of social behavior* 15(2): 131–49.

Lazerson, M. 1989. Research and teacher education in the American University. In *Fit to teach: Teacher education in international perspective,* edited by E. Gumbert, pp. 65–86. Atlanta: Center for Cross-Cultural Education, Georgia State University.

Leach, M. 1988. Teacher education and reform: "What's sex got to do with it?". *Educational Foundations* 2(2):4–14.

Leatherman, C. 1988. Reforms in education of school teachers face tough new challenges. *The Chronicle of Higher Education,* April 20, 34(32): A1, A30–A36.

Leinhardt, G., and Smith D. 1985. Expertise in mathematics instruction: Subject matter knowledge. *Journal of Educational Psychology* 77: 247–271.

Levin, R. 1990. "Recurring themes and variations." In *Places where teachers are taught,* edited by J. Goodlad, R. Soder, and K. Sirotnik. San Francisco: Jossey-Bass.

Lickona, T. 1976. Project change: A person-centered approach to CBTE. *Journal of Teacher Education* 27(2): 122–28.

Lightfoot, S. L. 1978. *Worlds apart.* New York: Basic Books, Inc.

Lightfoot, S. L. 1983. *The good high school.* New York: Basic Books.

Limbert, P. 1934. Political education at New College. *Progressive Education* 11(2): 118–24.

References

Lindblom, C., and Cohen, D. K. 1979. *Usable knowledge*. New Haven: Yale University Press.

Lindsey, M. 1961. *New horizons for the teaching profession*. Washington, D.C.: National Commission on Teacher Education and Professional Standards of the National Education Association.

Liston, D., and Zeichner, K. 1987a. Critical pedagogy and teacher education. *Journal of Education* 169(3): 117–37.

Liston, D., and Zeichner, K. 1987b. Reflective teacher education and moral deliberation. *Journal of Teacher Education* 38(6): 2–8.

Liston, D. P. 1988a. Faith and evidence. Examining Marxist explanations of schools. *American Journal of Education* 96(3): 323–50.

Liston, D. P. 1988b. *Capitalist schools*. New York: Routledge.

Liston, D., and Zeichner, K. 1989. *Action research and reflective teaching in preservice teacher education*. Paper presented at the Annual Meeting of the American Educational Research Association, San Francisco.

Lortie, D. 1975. *School teacher: A sociological study*. Chicago: University of Chicago Press.

Lovin, R. 1988. The school and the articulation of values. *American Journal of Education* 96: 143–61.

Lucas, P. 1988. An approach to research-based teacher education through collaboration inquiry. *Journal of Education for Teaching* 14(1): 55–73.

Lukes, S. 1978. The underdetermination of theory by data. *Proceedings of Aristotelian Society* 3 (supplement): 98.

Lynd, A. 1953. *Quackery in the public schools*. Boston: Little Brown.

Maas, J. (1991). Writing and reflection in teacher education. In *Issues and practices in inquiry-oriented teacher education*, edited by B. R. Tabachnick and K. Zeichner, pp. 211–225. London: Falmer Press.

MacIntyre, A. 1984. *After virtue*. South Bend, Ind.: University of Notre Dame Press.

MacIntyre, A. 1988. *Whose justice? Which rationality?* South Bend, Ind.: University of Notre Dame Press.

Macmillan, C. J. B. 1987. Defining teaching: Role versus activity. In *Philosophy of education 1987*, edited by B. Arnstine and D. Arnstine, pp. 363–72. Normal, Ill.: Philosophy of Education Society.

Madison Metropolitan School District. 1989. *Elementary minority student achievement committee report*. Madison, Wis.: MMSD.

Maher, F. (1991). Gender, reflexivity, and teacher education. In *Issues and practices in inquiry-oriented teacher education*, edited by B. R. Tabachnick and K. Zeichner, pp. 22–34. London: Falmer Press.

Maher, F., and Rathbone, C. 1986. Teacher education and feminist theory: Some implications for practice. *American Journal of Education* 94(2): 214–35.

Martin, J. R. 1981. The Ideal of the Educated Person. *Educational Theory* 31(3): 97–109.

Martin, J. R. 1985. *Reclaiming a conversation: The ideal of the educated woman.* New Haven: Yale University Press.

Martin, J. R. 1987. Reforming teacher education: Rethinking liberal education. *Teachers College Record* 88(3): 406–410.

McCarthy, C. 1986. Teacher training contradictions. *Education and Society* 4(2): 3–15.

McDonald, F. 1973. Behavior modification and teacher education. In *Behavior modification in education,* edited by C. Thoresen, pp. 41–76. Seventy-second Yearbook of the National Society for the Study of Education. Chicago: University of Chicago Press.

McLaughlin, M. W., Pfeifer, R. S., Swanson-Owens, D., and Yu, S. 1986. Why teachers won't teach. *Phi Delta Kappan* 67(6): 420–26.

McPherson, G. 1972. *Small town teacher.* Cambridge, Mass.: Harvard University Press.

Metz, M. 1989. How Social Class Differences Shape the Context of Teachers' Work, Unpublished manuscript.

The Michigan partnership for new education. 1990. East Lansing, Mich.: Michigan State University, School of Education.

Middleton, E., and Mason, E., eds. 1988. *Recruitment and retention of minority students in teacher education.* Dubuque, Iowa: Kendall/Hunt.

Miller, M. 1989. Peer supervision in a prestudent teaching practicum. Ph.D. diss., University of Wisconsin-Madison.

Mishel, L., and Rasell, E. 1989. *Shortchanging education: How U.S. spending on grades K–12 lags behind other industrialized nations.* Washington, D.C.: Economic Policy Institute.

Mitchell, L. S. 1931. Cooperative schools for student teachers. *Progressive Education* 8: 251–55.

Mohr, M., and MacLean, M. 1987. *Working together: A guide for teacher-researchers.* Urbana, Ill.: National Council of Teachers of English.

Monroe, W. 1952. *Teaching-learning theory and teacher education 1890 to 1950.* Urbana, Ill.: University of Illinois Press.

Moore-Johnson, S. 1990. *Teachers at work: Achieving success in our schools.* New York: Basic Books.

Murray, F., and Fallon, D. 1989. *The reform of teacher education for the 21st century: Project 30 year one report.* Newark, Del.: University of Delaware College of Education.

Nash, R., and Agne, R. 1971. Competency in teacher education: A prop for the status quo. *Journal of Teacher Education* 22(2): 147–56.

National Center for Education Statistics. 1977. *The state of teacher education.* Washington, D.C.: NCES.

National Center for Research on Teacher Education. 1988. Teacher education and learning to teach: A research agenda. *Journal of Teacher Education* 39(6): 27–32.

National Coalition of Advocates for Students. 1985. *Barriers to Excellence: Our Children at Risk.* Boston: National Coalition of Advocates for Students.

National Commission on Excellence in Education. 1983. *A nation at risk.* Washington, D.C.: U.S. Government Printing Office.

National Commission for Excellence in Teacher Education. 1985. *A call for change in teacher education.* Washington, D.C.: American Association of Colleges for Teacher Education.

National Educational Association. 1982. *Excellence in our schools: Teacher education.* Washington, D.C.: Author.

National Governors' Association. 1986. *Time for results.* Washington, D.C.: National Governors' Association.

National Institute of Education. 1984. *Involvement in learning: Realizing the potential of American higher education.* Washington, D.C.: U.S. Department of Education.

National Survey of the Education of Teachers. 1933. E. S. Evenden, Director. *Bulletin No. 10, Vol. 6: Summary and Interpretation.* Washington, D.C.: U.S. Office of Education.

Neckerman, K. M., and Wilson, J. 1988. Schools and poor communities. In Council of Chief State School Officers, *School success for students at risk,* pp. 25–44. Orlando, Fla.: Harcourt Brace Jovanovich.

New College. 1936. *Teachers College Record* 38(1): 1–73.

Nickerson, J., and Stampen, J. 1978. Political and programmatic impacts of state-wide governance of higher education. In *The changing politics of education,* edited by E. Mosher and J. Wagoner, Jr., pp. 274–81. Berkeley, Calif.: McCutchan.

Nixon, J., ed. 1981. *A teacher's guide to action research.* London: Grant McIntyre.

Noddings, N. 1987. Fidelity in teaching, teacher education and research for teaching. In *Teachers, teaching, and teacher education,* edited by M. Okazawa-Rey, J. Anderson, and R. Traver, pp. 384–400. Cambridge, Mass.: Harvard Educational Review (Reprint Series No. 19).

Noffke, S. 1990. *Action research: A multidimensional analysis.* Ph.D. diss., University of Wisconsin-Madison.

Noffke, S., and Brennan, M. (1991). Action research and reflective student teaching at the University of Wisconsin-Madison: Issues and examples. In *Issues and practices in inquiry-oriented teacher education,* edited by B. R. Tabachnick and K. Zeichner, pp. 186–201. London: Falmer Press.

Noffke, S., and Zeichner, K. 1987. *Action research and teacher thinking.* Paper presented at the annual meeting of the American Educational Research Association, Washington, D.C.

Oakes, J. 1985. *Keeping track: How schools structure inequality.* New Haven: Yale University Press.

O'Brien, M. 1982. Feminist theory and dialectical logic. *Signs* 1: 144–157.

Ogbu, J. 1987. Variability in minority school performance: A problem in search of an explanation. *Anthropology and Education Quarterly* 18: 312–34.

Oja, S. N., and Smulyan, L. 1989. *Collaborative action research: A developmental approach.* London: Falmer Press.

Olson, L. 1988. Work conditions in some schools said "intolerable." *Education Week* 8(4): 1, 21.

Orfield, G. 1988. Race, income, and educational inequality. In Council of Chief State School Offices, *School success for students at risk,* pp. 45–71. Orlando, Fla.: Harcourt Brace Jovanovich.

Ornstein, A., and Levine, D. 1989. Social class, race, and school achievement: Problems and prospects. *Journal of Teacher Education* 40(5): 17–23.

Paley, V. G. 1981. *Wally's stories.* Cambridge, Mass.: Harvard University Press.

Paley, V. G. 1989. *White teacher.* Cambridge, Mass.: Harvard University Press.

Pallas, A., Natriello, G., and McDill, E. 1989. The changing nature of the disadvantaged population: Current dimensions and future trends. *Educational Researcher* 18(5): 16–22.

Palmer, J. 1985. Teacher education: A perspective from a major public university. In *Colleges of education: Perspectives on their future,* edited by C. Case and W. Matthes, pp. 51–70. Berkeley, Calif.: McCutchan.

Performance Learning Systems. 1986. *We can show you the secrets of creating a championship teaching staff.* Emerson, N.J.: Author.

Perrone, V. 1989. *Working papers: Reflections on teachers, schools, and communities.* New York: Teachers College Press.

Persell, C. H. 1977. *Education and inequality.* New York: The Free Press.

References

Peseau, B. 1982. Developing an adequate resource base for teacher education. *Journal of Teacher Education* 33(4): 13–15.

Peseau, B., and Orr, P. 1979. *An academic and financial study of teacher education programs through the doctoral level in public state universities and land-grant colleges.* Montgomery: University of Alabama, College of Education.

Peseau, B., and Orr, P. 1980. The outrageous underfunding of teacher education. *Phi Delta Kappan* 62(2): 100–102.

Peseau, B., and Orr, P. 1981. *Second annual academic and financial study of teacher education programs in senior state universities and land-grant colleges.* Montgomery: University of Alabama College of Education.

Philadelphia Teachers Learning Cooperative. 1984. On becoming teacher experts: Buying time. *Language Arts* 6(1): 731–35.

Phillips, D. C. 1978. A skeptical consumers' guide to educational research. *The Andover Review* 5(2): 39–53.

Phillips, D. C. 1980. What do the researcher and the practitioner have to offer each other? *Educational Researcher* 9(11): 17–20, 24.

Pollard, A. 1982. A model of classroom coping strategies. *British Journal of the Sociology of Education* 3: 19–37.

Pollard, A. 1988. Reflective teaching: The sociological contribution. In *Sociology and teaching: A new challenge for the sociology of education,* edited by P. Woods and A. Pollard, pp. 54–75. London: Croom Helm.

Pollitzer, M. 1931. Growing teachers for our schools. *Progressive Education* 8(3): 247–50.

Popkewitz, T. 1987a. Improving teaching and teacher education. *Social Education* 51(7): 493–495.

Popkewitz, T. 1987b. Ideology and social formation in teacher education. In *Critical studies in teacher education,* edited by T. Popkewitz, pp. 2–34. London: Falmer Press.

Powell, A. G. 1976. University schools of education in the twentieth century. *Peabody Journal of Education* 54(1): 3–20.

Powell, A. G. 1980. *The uncertain profession.* Cambridge, Mass.: Harvard University Press.

Prestine, N. 1989. The struggle for control of teacher education: A case study. *Educational Evaluation and Policy Analysis* 11(3): 285–300.

Progressive Education. 1931. Editorial. *Progressive Education* 8: 280–81.

Provus, M. 1975. *The grand experiment: The life and death of the TTT program as seen through the eyes of its evaluators.* Berkeley, Calif.: McCutchan.

Ptak, D. 1988. *Report on the achievement of black high school students in the*

Madison Metropolitan School District, 1987–1988. Madison, Wisc.: Urban League.

Raskin, M. 1986. *The common good: Its politics, policies, and philosophy.* New York: Routledge.

Rauth, M., Biles, B., Billies, L., and Veitch, S. 1983. *Executive summary, training and research manual.* American Federation of Teachers Educational Research and Dissemination Program (NIE 6–81–0021). Washington, D.C.: American Federation of Teachers.

Rawls, J. 1971. *A theory of justice.* Cambridge, Mass.: Harvard University Press.

Reilly, D. 1989. A knowledge base for education. Cognitive science. *Journal of Teacher Education* 40(3): 9–13.

Render, G. F., Padilla, J. M., and Krank, H. M. 1989. Assertive discipline: A critical review and analysis. *Teachers College Record* 90(4): 607–30.

Reynolds, M., ed. 1989. *Knowledge base for the beginning teacher.* New York: Pergamon Press.

Rhoades, G. 1985. *The costs of academic excellence in teacher education* (Working Paper #5). Los Angeles: Comparative Higher Education Research Group, UCLA, Graduate School of Education.

Richert, A. 1991. Case methods and teacher education: Using cases to teach teacher reflection. In *Issues and practices in inquiry-oriented teacher education,* edited by B. R. Tabachnick and K. M. Zeichner. London: Falmer Press.

Rist, R. 1970. Student social class and teacher expectations. *Harvard Educational Review* 40: 411–51.

Robottom, I. 1988. A research-based course in science education. In *The enquiring teacher: Supporting and sustaining teacher research,* edited by J. Nias and S. Groundwater-Smith, pp. 106–20. London: Falmer Press.

Rosen, H. 1987. The Voices of Communities and Language in Classrooms. In *Teachers Teaching and Teacher Education,* edited by M. Okazawa-Rey, J. Anderson, and R. Traver, pp. 443–52. Cambridge, Mass.: Harvard Educational Review.

Rosewater, A. 1989. Child and family trends: Beyond the numbers. In *Caring for America's children,* edited by F. Macchiarola and A. Gartner, pp. 4–19. New York: Academy of Political Science.

Ross, D. 1987. Action research for preservice teachers: A description of why and how. *Peabody Journal of Education* 64(3): 131–50.

Ross, D., and Kyle, D. 1987. Helping preservice teachers learn to use teacher effectiveness research. *Journal of Teacher Education* 38: 40–44.

References

Ruddick, J. 1985. Teacher research and research-based teacher education. *Journal of Education for Teaching* 11(3): 281–89.

Ruddick, S. 1989. *Maternal thinking*. Boston: Beacon Press.

Rugg, H. 1931. *Culture and education in America*. New York: Harcourt, Brace & Co.

Rugg, H. 1952. *The teacher of teachers*. New York: Harper and Brothers Publishers.

Sadker, D., and Sadker, M. 1985. The treatment of sex equity in teacher education. In *Handbook for achieving sex equity through education*, edited by S. Klein, pp. 145–61. Baltimore: Johns Hopkins University Press.

Sandefur, J. T. 1986. State assessment trends. *AACTE Briefs* 7: 12–14.

Sandefur, W. S., and Nicklas, W. L. 1981. Competency-based teacher education in AACTE institutions: An update. *Phi Delta Kappan* 62: 747–48.

Sarason, S. 1971. *The culture of the school and the problem of change*. Boston: Allyn and Bacon.

Sarason, S., Davidson, K., and Blatt, B. 1986. *The preparation of teachers: An unstudied problem*, 2d ed. New York: Wiley.

Saxe, R. 1965. Evaluating the breakthrough programs. *Journal of Teacher Education* 16: 202–9.

Schaefer, R. 1967. *The school as a center of inquiry*. New York: Harper and Row.

Schneider, B. 1987. Tracing the provenance of teacher education. In *Critical studies in teacher education*, edited by T. Popkewitz. London: Falmer Press.

Schon, D. 1983. *The reflective practitioner*. New York: Basic Books.

Schon, D. 1987. *Educating the reflective practitioner*. San Francisco: Jossey-Bass, Inc.

Schorr, L. 1988. *Within our reach: Breaking the cycle of disadvantage*. New York: Anchor Books.

Schram, P., Wilcox, S., Lanier, P., and Lappan, G. 1988. *Changing mathematical conceptions of preservice teachers* (Research Report No. 88–4). East Lansing, Mich.: National Center for Research on Teacher Education.

Schwab, J. J., Westbury, I., and Wilkof, N., eds. 1978. *Science, curriculum and liberal education*. Chicago: University of Chicago Press.

Schwebel, M. 1982. Research productivity of education faculty: A comparative study. *Educational Studies* 13: 224–39.

Schwebel, M. 1989. The new priorities and the education faculty. In *The professors of teaching*, edited by R. Wisniewski and E. Ducharme, pp. 52–66. Albany: State University of New York Press.

Sears, J. 1985. Rethinking teacher education: Dare we work toward a new social order? *Journal of Curriculum Theorizing* 6(2): 24–79.

Shannon, P. 1977. Reading instruction and social class. *Language Arts* 62(6): 604–13.

Shor, I. 1987. Equality is excellence: Transforming teacher education and the labor process. In *Teaching, teachers, and teacher education,* edited by M. Okazawa-Rey, J. Anderson, and R. Traver, pp. 183–203. Cambridge, Mass.: Harvard Educational Review.

Shulman, L. 1986. Paradigms and research programs in the study of teaching. In *Third Handbook of Research on Teaching,* edited by M. Wittrock, pp. 3–36. New York: Macmillan.

Shulman, L. 1987. Knowledge and teaching: Foundations of the new reform. *Harvard Educational Review,* 57: 1–22.

Sikes, P., and Troyna, B. 1990. *Life history and critical reflection for beginning teachers.* Paper presented at the Annual Meeting of the American Educational Research Association, Boston.

Simms, R., and Miller, J. 1988. Assault on teacher education in Texas. *Journal of Teacher Education* 39(6): 17–20.

Simon, A., and Boyer, G. 1967. *Mirrors for behavior.* Philadelphia: Research for Better Schools.

Sirotnik, K. 1990. Society, schooling, teaching and preparing to teach. In *The moral dimensions of teaching,* edited by J. Goodlad, R. Soder, and K. Sirotnik, pp. 296–328. San Francisco: Jossey Bass.

Sirotnik, K., and Goodlad, J. 1988. *School-university partnerships in action.* New York: Teachers College Press.

Slavin, R. 1989. PET and the pendulum: Faddism in education and how to stop it. *Phi Delta Kappan* 70(10): 752–58.

Smith, B. O. 1969. *Teachers for the real world.* Washington, D.C.: American Association of Colleges of Teacher Education.

Smith, B. O. 1980. *A design for a school of pedagogy.* Washington, D.C.: U.S. Department of Education.

Smith, G. P. 1987. The impact of competency tests on teacher education: Ethical and legal issues in selecting and certifying teachers. In *Advances in teacher education,* edited by M. Haberman and J. Backus, Vol. 3, pp. 218–47. Norwood, N.J.: Ablex.

Smith, G. P., Chang Miller, M., and Joy, J. 1988. A case study of the impact of performance-based testing on the supply of minority teachers. *Journal of Teacher Education* 34(4): 45–53.

275

References

Smith, L., and Geoffrey, W. 1968. *The complexities of an urban classroom.* New York: Holt, Rinehart and Winston, Inc.

Smith, L., Klein, P., Prunty, J., and Dwyer, D. 1986. *Educational innovators: Then and now.* London: Falmer Press.

Smith, L., Klein, P., Prunty, J., and Dwyer, D. 1987. *The fate of an innovative school.* London: Falmer Press.

Smith, L., Klein, P., Prunty, J., and Dwyer, D. 1988. *Innovation and change in schooling.* London: Falmer Press.

Smith, R., and Sachs, J. 1988. It really made me stop and think: Ethnography in preservice teacher education. In *The enquiring teacher: Supporting and sustaining teacher research,* edited by J. Nias and S. Groundwater-Smith, pp. 71–84. London: Falmer Press.

Smith, W. 1980. The American Teacher Corps Programme. In *Professional development of teachers,* edited by E. Hoyle and J. Megarry, pp. 204–18. London: Nichols.

Smyth, J. 1984. *Case studies in clinical supervision.* Geelong, Australia: Deakin University Press.

Smyth, J., and Gitlin, A. 1989. *Teacher evaluation: Educative alternatives.* London: Falmer Press.

Soltis, J., ed. 1987. *Reforming teacher education.* N.Y.: Teachers College Press.

Somersan, A. 1988, November. *The rural development challenge: Agriculture's place in strategies to strengthen the rural economy.* Paper presented at the Council on Agricultural Research, Extension, and Teaching Annual Meeting, Dallas, Texas.

Sprinthall, N., and Thies-Sprinthall, L. 1983. The teacher as an adult learner: A cognitive developmental view. In *Staff development,* edited by G. Griffin, pp. 13–35. Chicago: University of Chicago Press.

Stallings, J. 1985. A study of the implementation of Madeline Hunter's model and its effects on students. *Journal of Educational Research* 78: 325–37.

Stanley, W. B. 1985. Social reconstructionism for today's social education. *Social Education* 49(5): 384–89.

Stinchcombe, A. 1986. Milieu and structure updated. *Theory and Society* 15: 901–13.

Stone, J. C. 1968. *Breakthrough in teacher education.* San Francisco: Jossey Bass.

Stones, E. 1984. *Supervision in teacher education.* London: Methuen.

Stover, D. 1988. Those in-service hotshots: Are they worth what they charge? *The Executive Educator* 10(1): 15–18, 29.

Strang, H. R., Badt, K., and Kauffman, J. 1987. Micro-computer-based simulations for training fundamental teaching skills. *Journal of Teacher Education* 38(1): 20–26.

Stroh, M. 1931. No title. *Progressive Education* 8(3): 260.

Study Commission on Undergraduate Education and the Education of Teachers. 1976. *Teacher education in the U.S.: The responsibility gap.* Lincoln, Neb.: University of Nebraska Press.

Sykes, G. 1984. Teacher education and the predicament of reform. In *Against mediocrity,* edited by C. E. Finn, D. Ravitch, and R. Fancher, pp. 172–94. New York: Holmans and Meier.

Tabachnick, B. R. 1980. Intern-teacher roles: Illusion, disillusion and reality. *Journal of Education* 162: 122–37.

Tabachnick, B. R. 1981. Teacher education as a set of dynamic social events. In *Studying teaching and learning: Trends in Soviet and American research,* edited by B. R. Tabachnick, T. Popkewitz, and B. Szekely, pp. 76–86. New York: Praeger.

Tabachnick, B. R., Popkewitz, T., and Zeichner, K. 1979. Teacher education and the professional perspectives of student teachers. *Interchange* 10: 12–29.

Tabachnick, B. R., and Zeichner, K., eds. (1991). *Issues and practices in inquiry-oriented education.* London: Falmer Press.

Tabachnick, J., and Ma-Luk Lemes, B. 1975. *Together: A photographic essay of the Corps Member Training Institute.* Madison: University of Wisconsin-Madison School of Education.

Tate, P. 1988. Whale or shark? A description of state policy domains for teacher education. *Journal of Teacher Education* 39(6): 21–26.

Taylor, C. 1983. Political theory and practice. In *Social theory and political practice,* edited by C. Lloyd, pp. 61–85. Oxford: Clarendon Press.

Taylor, W. 1983. The crisis of confidence in teacher education: An international perspective. *Oxford Review of Education* 9(1): 39–49.

Teitelbaum, K., and Britzman, D. 1991. Reading and doing ethnography: Teacher education and reflective practice. In *Issues and practices in inquiry-oriented teacher education,* edited by B. R. Tabachnick and K. M. Zeichner, pp. 166–185. London: Falmer Press.

Tetreault, M. K. 1985. Feminist phase theory: An experience-derived evaluation model. *Journal of Higher Education* 56: 363–84.

Tetreault, M. K. 1987. The scholarship on women and teacher education. *Teacher Education Quarterly* 14(2): 77–83.

Tetreault, M. K., and Braunger, J. 1989. Improving mentor teacher seminars: Feminist theory and practice at Lewis and Clark College. In *Building bridges for educational reform: New approaches to teacher education,* edited by J. DeVitis and P. Sola, pp. 63–86. Ames, Iowa: Iowa State University Press.

Tom, A. 1980. The reform of teacher education through research: A futile quest. *Teachers College Record* 82(1): 15–30.

Tom, A. 1984. *Teaching as a moral craft.* New York: Longman.

Tom, A. 1988. The practical art of redesigning teacher education: Teacher education reform at Washington University, 1970–1975. *Peabody Journal of Education* 65(2): 158–179.

Travers, E., and Sacks, S. 1987. *Teacher education and the liberal arts: The position of the Consortium for Excellence in Teacher Education.* Swarthmore, Pa.: Swarthmore College.

Travers, R. 1973. *The second handbook of research on teaching.* Chicago: Rand McNally.

Turney, C. 1977. *Innovation in teacher education.* Sydney, Australia: Sydney University Press.

Turney, C., et al. 1982. *The practicum in teacher education.* Sydney, Australia: Sydney University Press.

Uhler, S. 1987. *Alternative paths to entry: New Jersey and elsewhere.* Paper presented at the Annual Meeting of the American Educational Research Association, Washington, D.C.

University of Wisconsin System. 1990. *Strategic planning in teacher education.* Madison, Wis.: University of Wisconsin.

Urban, W. 1982. *Why teachers organized.* Detroit: Wayne State University Press.

Urban, W. 1989. Essay review: Old and new problems in teacher unionism. *Educational Studies* 20(4): 355–64.

U.S. Department of Education. 1986. *What works: Research about teaching and learning.* Washington, D.C.: Author.

U.S. Department of Education. 1988. *The condition of education.* Washington, D.C.: Office of Educational Research and Improvement.

U.S. House of Representatives. 1987. *U.S. children and their families: Current conditions and recent trends.* A Report of the Select Committee on Children, Youth and Families, Washington, D.C., U.S. Government Printing Office.

Van Mannen, M. 1977. Linking ways of knowing with ways of being practical. *Curriculum Inquiry* 6205–28.

Walker, R. 1985. *Doing research: A handbook for teachers.* London: Methuen.

Warnock, M. 1975. The neutral teacher. In *Philosophers discuss education,* edited by S. Brown, pp. 159–71. Totowa, N.J.: Rowman and Littlefield.

Wass, H., Blume, R., Combs, A., and Hedges, W. 1974. *Humanistic teacher education*. Fort Collins, Colo.: Shields.

Weiler, K. 1988. *Women teaching for change: Gender, class and power*. Massachusetts: Bergin and Garvey.

Weinshank, A., Trumbull, E., and Daly, P. 1983. The role of the teacher in school change. In *Handbook of teaching and policy*, edited by L. Shulman and G. Sykes, pp. 300–14. New York: Longman.

White, W. T., Jr. 1982. The decline of the classroom and the Chicago Study of Education, 1909–1929. *American Journal of Education*, 90(2): 144–74.

Whitty, G., Barton, L., and Pollard, A. 1987. Ideology and control in teacher education: A review of recent experiences in England. In *Critical studies in teacher education*, edited by T. Popkewitz, pp. 161–184. London: Falmer Press.

Williams, M. W. 1989. *Neighborhood organizing for urban school reform*. New York: Teachers College Press.

Wilson, S., Shulman, L., and Richert, A. 1987. 150 different ways of knowing: Representations of knowledge in teaching. In *Exploring teachers thinking*, edited by J. Calderhead, pp. 104–24. London: Cassell.

Winter, R. 1987. *Action research and the nature of social inquiry*. Aldershot, England: Avebury Press.

Wirth, A. (n.d.). *An inquiry-personal commitment model of teacher education: The Hawthorne Teacher Education Project*. St. Louis: Washington University, Graduate Institute of Education.

Wise, A. 1979. *Legislated learning*. Berkeley: University of California Press.

Wittrock, M. 1986. *Third handbook of research on teaching*. New York: Macmillan.

Witty, E. 1982. *Prospects for black teachers: Preparation, certification, employment*. Washington, D.C.: ERIC Clearinghouse on Teacher Education (No. SP 019 491).

Wood, P. 1988. Action research: A field perspective. *Journal of Education for Teaching*, 14(2): 135–50.

Woodring, P. 1957. *New directions in teacher education*. New York: Ford Foundation Fund for the Advancement of Education.

Woodring, P. 1975. The development of teacher education. In *Teacher education*, edited by K. Ryan, pp. 1–24. Chicago: University of Chicago Press.

Woods, P. ed. 1980. *Teacher strategies: Explorations in the sociology of the school*. London: Croom Helm.

Woods, P. 1986. *Inside schools: Ethnography in educational research*. London: Routledge.

References

Zeichner, K. 1983. Alternative paradigms of teacher education. *Journal of Teacher Education* 34: 3–9.

Zeichner, K. 1986a. The practicum as an occasion for learning to teach. *South Pacific Journal of Teacher Education* 14(2): 11–27.

Zeichner, K. 1986b. Social and ethical dimensions of reform in teacher education. In *Clinical teacher education,* edited by J. Hoffman and S. Edwards, pp. 87–108. New York: Random House.

Zeichner, K. 1987. Preparing reflective teachers. *International Journal of Educational Research* 11(5): 565–76.

Zeichner, K. 1988a. *Understanding the character and quality of the academic and professional components of teacher education.* East Lansing, Mich.: National Center for Research on Teacher Education.

Zeichner, K. 1988b. Learning from experience in graduate teacher preparation. In *Research perspectives on the graduate preparation of teachers,* edited by A. Woolfolk, pp. 12–29. Englewood Cliffs, N.J.: Prentice-Hall.

Zeichner, K. 1989. *Learning to teach writing in the elementary school.* Paper presented at the Annual Meeting of the American Educational Research Association, San Francisco.

Zeichner, K. 1990a. *Contradictions and tensions in the professionalization of teaching and the democratization of schools.* Paper presented at the Annual Meeting of the American Educational Research Association, Boston.

Zeichner, K. 1990b. When you've said reflection, you haven't said it all. In *Guided practice in teacher education,* edited by T. Stoddard. East Lansing, Mich.: National Center for Research on Teacher Education.

Zeichner, K. 1990c. Changing directions in the practicum: Looking to the 1990's. *Journal of Education for Teaching* 16(2): 105–132.

Zeichner, K., and Gore, J. 1990. Teacher socialization. In *Handbook of research on teacher education,* edited by W. R. Houston, pp. 329–48. New York: Macmillan.

Zeichner, K., and Liston, D. 1985. Varieties of discourse in supervisory conferences. *Teaching and Teacher Education* 1(2): 155–74.

Zeichner, K., and Liston, D. 1987. Teaching student teachers to reflect. *Harvard Educational Review* 57(1): 1–22.

Zeichner, K., Liston, D., Mahlias, M., and Gomez, M. 1988. The structure and goals of a student teaching program and the character and quality of supervisory discourse. *Teaching and Teacher Education* 4: 349–62.

Zeichner, K. and Liston, D. 1990. *Traditions of reform and reflective teaching in U.S. teacher education* (Issue Paper 90–1). East Lansing, Mich.: National Center for Research on Teacher Education.

Zeichner, K., and Tabachnick, B. R. 1981. Are the effects of university teacher education washed out by school experience? *Journal of Teacher Education* 32: 7–11.

Zeichner, K., and Tabachnick, B. R. 1991. Reflections on reflective teaching. In *Issues and practices in inquiry-oriented teacher education,* edited by B. R. Tabachnick and K. Zeichner, pp. 1–21. London: Falmer Press.

Zeichner, K., and Teitelbaum, K. 1982. Personalized and inquiry-oriented teacher education. *Journal of Education for Teaching* 8(2): 95–117.

Zimpher, N. 1989. The RATE project: A profile of teacher education students. *Journal of Teacher Education* 40(6): 27–30.

Zumwalt, K. 1982. Research on teaching: Policy implications for teacher education. In *Policymaking in education,* edited by A. Lieberman and M. McLaughlin, pp. 215–48. Chicago: University of Chicago Press.

Name Index

Adler, S., 33, 159, 160, 161, 168, 180, 193
Agne, R., 18, 200, 201, 243n
Allen, D., 16
Althusser, L., 121
Amarel, M., 25
Ammon, P., 26
Anderson, A., 31
Andrews, T., 13, 210
Anyon, J., 181
Apple, M., 18, 49, 114, 121, 160, 187, 189, 190, 204, 212, 217, 221n, 231n, 241n, 243n
Arends, R. I., 231n
Arfedson, G., 124
Armaline, W., 232n, 247n
Ashcroft, K., 163
Aspin, D., 246n
Atkin, J. M., 15, 156, 210, 233n
Ayer, A., 24
Ayers, W., 222n, 232n

Badt, K., 20
Baker, F., 31
Ball, D. L., 11, 221n
Baptiste, H. P., 13
Baptiste, M., 13
Barnes, B. J., 222n, 240n
Bartholomew, J., 239n
Barton, L., 246n

Bastian, A., 182
Beatty, W., 24, 225n
Belenky, M. F., 228n, 235n
Benne, K., 31
Ben-Peretz, M., 168
Berger, J., 222n
Berlak, A., 228n
Berlak, H., 228n
Berliner, D., 18, 19, 20, 209, 236n, 238n
Bernstein, R., 230n
Berry, B., 204, 244n, 246n
Bestor, A., 6, 7, 9, 31, 47
Beyer, L., 32, 156, 157, 179, 180, 184, 200, 233n, 234n, 235n, 236n
Biddle, B., 215
Bigelow, D., 4
Black, A., 26
Blatt, B., 3
Bloom, A., 47
Bode, B., 27, 48
Boles, K., 91, 150
Bolster, A., 122, 123, 124, 128
Bonser, G., 23
Book, C., 192, 233n
Borg, W., 17
Borman, K., 89, 247n
Borrowman, M., 5, 9, 13, 31, 200, 223n
Bowers, C. A., 156, 225n, 226n

Guthrie, J. W., 3, 9, 129, 130, 156, 194, 195, 196, 198, 199, 226n
Gutmann, A., 54, 55, 95, 96
Guyton, E., 203, 242n

Haberman, M., 169, 240n, 243n, 246n
Hahn, A., 222n
Hall, G. S., 20
Hallinan, M., 86, 87, 88, 230n
Handal, G., 235n
Heath, R. W., 16
Heath, S. B., 101, 105, 106, 107, 109, 119, 124, 127, 139, 140, 141, 142, 143
Hedges, W., 199
Henderson, J., 232n
Hendrick, I., 10
Herbst, J., 3, 194, 241n
Hersh, R., 109
Hirabayashi, J., 148
Hirsch, E. D., 47, 48, 165
Hirst, P., 47, 165
Hitchcock, G., 231n
Hochschild, A., 229n
Hodgkinson, H., 201
Holmes, H., 27, 129
Hook, S., 165
Hoover, R., 232n
Hopkins, D., 148
Houston, W. R., 15, 16
Howey, K., 16, 202
Howsam, R., 15, 16
Hughes, D., 231n
Hunter, M., 20, 172, 208, 209
Hustler, D., 148
Hutchins, R. M., 47

Imig, D., 13, 214
Isaac, J., 163

Jackson, J., 91, 150
Jackson, P., 62

James, S., 90, 120, 121, 230n
Johnson, D., 4
Johnston, J., 2, 200, 239n
Joy, J., 202
Joyce, B., 2, 4, 5, 12, 16, 17, 19, 109, 224n
Judge, H., 194

Kanter, R. M., 158
Kaufmann, J., 20
Kemmis, S., 148, 170, 178, 234n, 235n
Kennedy, M., 234n
Keppel, F., 12, 218
Kerr, D., 2, 194, 196, 198, 239n
Kilpatrick, W., 27, 28, 29, 31, 38
King, J. E., 179, 232n
Kirk, D., 4
Kliebard, H., 4, 9, 14, 20, 26, 34, 227n
Koehler, V., 197
Koerner, J., 6, 7, 8, 31, 197, 210
Koskella, R., 13
Kozol, J., 49, 165
Krank, H. M., 245n
Kyle, D., 20

Ladson-Billings, G., 179, 232n
LaFontaine, H., 239n
Laird, S., 11, 49, 111, 112, 114, 115, 119, 130, 139, 143, 144
Lanier, J., 9, 155, 156, 187, 192, 196, 198, 210, 214, 239n
Lather, P., 189
Lauvus, P., 235n
Lawn, M., 149, 152
Lawrence, S., 228n
Layder, D., 122, 230n
Lazerson, M., 197
Leatherman, C., 210
Lefkowitz, B., 222n
Leinhardt, G., 11
Lemes, B., 243n

Subject Index